Congress and air pollution

MANCHESTER
UNIVERSITY PRESS

Issues in Environmental Politics

Series editors Tim O'Riordan, Arild Underdal *and* Albert Weale

As the millennium approaches, the environment has come to stay as a central concern of global politics. This series takes key problems for environmental policy and examines the politics behind their cause and possible resolution. Accessible and eloquent, the books make available for a non-specialist readership some of the best research and most provocative thinking on humanity's relationship with the planet.

already published in the series

Animals, politics and morality *Robert Garner*

Sustaining Amazonia: grassroots action for productive conservation
Anthony Hall

The protest business? Mobilizing campaign groups
Grant Jordan and William Maloney

Environment and the nation state: the Netherlands, the European
Union and acid rain *Duncan Liefferink*

Valuing the environment *Raino Malnes*

Life on a modern planet: a manifesto for progress *Richard North*

The politics of global atmospheric change *Ian H. Rowlands*

Governance by green taxes *Mikael Skou Andersen*

European environmental policy: the pioneers
Mikael Skou Andersen and Duncan Liefferink (eds)

The new politics of pollution *Albert Weale*

Congress and air pollution

Environmental policies in the USA

WITHDRAWN

Christopher J. Bailey

Manchester University Press

Manchester and New York

Distributed exclusively in the USA by St. Martin's Press

Published by Manchester University Press
Oxford Road, Manchester M13 9NR, UK
and Room 400, 175 Fifth Avenue, New York, NY 10010, USA

Distributed exclusively in the USA by
St. Martin's Press, Inc., 175 Fifth Avenue, New York, NY 10010, USA

Distributed exclusively in Canada by
UBC Press, University of British Columbia, 6344 Memorial Road, Vancouver, BC, Canada V6T 1Z2

British Library Cataloguing-in-Publication Data
A catalogue record for this book is available from the British Library.

Library of Congress Cataloging-in-Publication Data applied for

ISBN 0 7190 3661 5 *hardback*

First published in 1998

05 04 03 02 01 00 99 98   10 9 8 7 6 5 4 3 2 1

Typeset in Sabon
by Northern Phototypesetting Co. Ltd, Bolton
Printed in Great Britain
by Bookcraft (Bath) Ltd, Midsomer Norton

Contents

Figures and tables

Figures

Tables

For Lauren and Imogen

Preface

The origins of this book date back to 1989 when I was fortunate enough to be selected as a Congressional Fellow by the American Political Science Association. The fellowship enabled me to work from December 1989 to July 1990 for Senator Harry Reid (Democrat, Nevada). In what was either a brave or foolhardy move – given my complete lack of knowledge about science, the environment or American law – Senator Reid gave me responsibility for dealing with environmental issues within his office. Fortunately, I was able to draw upon the considerable expertise of the staff of the Senate Environment and Public Works Committee, and somehow managed to avoid making too many blunders.

The majority of my work was connected to issues associated with Senator Reid's chairmanship of the Subcommittee on Toxic Substances, Environmental Oversight, Research and Development. I worked with the Subcommittee staff to organize committee hearings on subjects such as asbestos in schools, lawn-care chemicals and lead poisoning. I even helped to draft legislation – the Lead Exposure Reduction Act 1990 (S 2637) – which I later discovered had been enacted in a much revised form as Chapter 4 of the Toxic Substances Control Act 1976. The amount of interest group activity that was generated by what I thought would be a fairly non-controversial bill took me completely by surprise. I still recall fielding phone calls from the National Rifle Association who wondered whether guns and ammunition would be defined as 'toys' under the terms of the legislation; from artists who believed that banning the use of lead in paint would mean the disappearance of brilliant whites and yellows from their palettes; and from the electronics industry who argued that banning lead solder would lead to the destruction of their entire industry.

At the time that I was embroiled in such matters, Congress was considering the Clean Air Act Amendments 1990. Although I had only a bit part in the drama that surrounded this legislation – I helped to draft a successful amendment (S Amdt 1415) that mandated use of a liquefied gaseous fuels spills test facility in Nevada – I was well positioned to observe events, usually with complete bewilderment. I found the length and complexity of the legislation to be startling. It authorized the Environmental Protection Agency to set emissions standards for some pollutants, but provided for legislative standards for others; it employed a variety of means of setting levels of control – sometimes using health-based standards, sometimes using technological standards; it employed a variety of regulatory means for achieving required levels of control – from traditional command-and-control techniques to innovative market mechanisms; and it shared responsibility for implementation between the federal government, state governments and specially created air quality districts.

Once my bewilderment started to fade, I began to wonder how the production of this legislation could be explained. Two questions, in particular, began to puzzle me: why did Congress pass this law? and why did Congress seek to address the problem of air pollution in this way? The more I thought about these questions, the more important arriving at some answers appeared to be. Not only is air pollution a major public issue in the United States, and efforts to control the problem very expensive, but air pollution has a number of characteristics as an issue that are of general conceptual interest: it is a public good; it is multidimensional; it contains a large technical core; and its control, like all forms of social regulation, brings competing value systems into conflict.

As I began to investigate the subject in more depth, it soon became obvious that I needed to broaden my horizons. I realized that an adequate explanation of the 1990 Amendments could not be provided without cognition of its antecedents – the 1990 Amendments were *amendments* to an earlier law after all. What had been envisaged as a study of a specific piece of law-making evolved, as a result, into a study of law-making in a particular policy area. My two questions became: how can the production of air pollution control laws be explained? and how can the changing shape of these laws be explained? Efforts to provide answers to these questions led me to adopt a conceptual framework that viewed the production of laws as analogous to the production of goods. Borrowing unashamedly from economics I started to investigate the possibility of employing concepts such as benefits, costs and 'profit' in a legislative setting. The results are laid out in this book.

Numerous debts have been incurred in the struggle to complete this project. I must thank the American Political Science Association for awarding me a Congressional Fellowship. The experience was invaluable. Keele University and the British Academy provided vital funding that enabled me to collect needed data. I must also thank Senator Reid and his staff for making me feel welcome and employing me gainfully. Thanks are especially due to Sheila Humke for allowing me to help organize subcommittee hearings and guiding me through the intricacies of toxic substances policy.

A number of colleagues have helped me collect data and my thoughts. Paul Herrnson has provided a needed resting place and valuable advice on numerous occasions. Andy Dobson, Peter John, John Dumbrell, Jonathan Parker and Jonathan Herbert have given important critiques at important moments. Early versions of my ideas were given at Colorado State University, Oklahoma State University, the University of New Orleans and the annual conferences of the American Politics Group of the Political Science Association. Thanks to all the participants for their comments. Keele's Department of American Studies has been a wonderful base from which to operate.

I should also like to thank everyone at Manchester University Press. Their forbearance has been extraordinary.

Finally, I should like to thank my daughters, Lauren and Imogen, for helping me through a particularly difficult time. Their love has sustained me when much seemed bleak. I dedicate this book to them.

Abbreviations

BACT	best available control technology
CAA70	Clean Air Amendments, 1970
CAA77	Clean Air Act Amendments, 1977
CAA90	Clean Air Act Amendments, 1990
CAFE	Corporate Average Fuel Economy
CEQ	Council on Environmental Quality
CERCLA	Comprehensive Environmental Response, Compensation and Liability Act
CFC	chloroflurocarbon
CIS	Congressional Information Service
CQ	Congressional Quarterly
CRS	Congressional Research Service
D.	Democrat
EDF	Environmental Defense Fund
EOP	Executive Office of the President
EPA	Environmental Protection Agency
FEO	Federal Energy Office
GAO	General Accounting Office
GATT	General Agreement on Trade and Tariffs
GSA	General Service Administration
HEW	Department of Health, Education, and Welfare
LAER	lowest achievable emissions rate
LCV	League of Conservation Voters
MACT	Maximum Achievable Control Technology
NAAQS	National Ambient Air Quality Standards
NEPA	National Environmental Policy Act
NESHAPS	National Emission Standards for Hazardous Air Pollutants

NRDC	Natural Resources Defense Council
NSPS	New Source Performance Standards
OMB	Office of Management and Budget
OPEC	Organization of Petroleum Exporting Countries
OSHA	Occupational Safety and Health Administration
PAC	Political Action Committee
PHS	Public Health Service
PSD	prevention of significant deterioration
R.	Republican
RACT	reasonably available control technology
SIP	State Implementation Plan
SST	Supersonic Stratospheric-Flying Aircraft
TSCA	Toxic Substances Control Act
UAW	United Automobile Workers
VA-HUD	Veterans Affairs – Housing and Urban Development

1

Introduction

Congress has constructed an impressive framework of laws designed to control air pollution since the 1950s.[1] The Air Pollution Control (Clean Air) Act 1955 was the first federal statute to address the problem of air pollution, and has remained the main authorizing vehicle for federal efforts to control air pollution ever since.[2] Regarded as one of the most important environmental statutes ever passed in the United States, the Act is America's primary legislative vehicle for controlling air pollution.[3] Its most recent incarnation, the Clean Air Act Amendments 1990 (CAA90), was over 300 pages long.[4] In the same way that a nuclear-powered aircraft carrier is surrounded by a flotilla of picket and support vessels, however, the Clean Air Act is simply the most powerful of a number of statutes that are designed to battle air pollution. Not only do general environmental laws such as the National Environmental Policy Act 1969 (NEPA) and the Pollution Prevention Act 1990 impact upon air pollution, but particular pollutants are also addressed under other statutes.[5] Important amendments to the Toxic Substances Control Act 1976 (TSCA), for example, have sought to reduce exposure to asbestos, radon and lead.[6] Many statutes dealing with energy, transport, defence, education, science and agriculture also have an air pollution control dimension.

The regulatory regime established by such laws is extraordinarily complex. Not only have the goals and means of air pollution control varied across time, but considerable variation also exists across statutes. Different statutes have employed different methods of determining how much control of air pollution is needed and how the required levels of control are to be achieved. Most statutes use health-based standards to determine levels of control; others use technology-based standards.[7] Most statutes use command-and-control regulatory means to achieve levels of control; but some use economic incentives, direct government expenditure or moral suasion.[8] Complexity even appears to reign within individual statutes. The CAA90 refers to primary and secondary goals, requires both health-based and technology-based standards to be set, employs both command-and-control and market mechanisms as means of control, delegates authority to the Environmental Protection Agency (EPA) but also contains congressional standards, and divides responsibility for implementation and enforcement between various levels of government.

Few attempts have been made to explain the creation and shape of this impressive and extraordinarily complex framework of laws. Case studies of individual statutes have tended to dominate the literature on congressional efforts to control air pollution.[9] Only Charles O. Jones, James E. Krier and Edmund Ursin, Bruce A. Ackerman and William T. Hassler, and Lennart J. Lundqvist have attempted to produce explanations that move beyond a single case study.[10] Providing reasons for such a sparse literature is not easy. Perhaps congressional efforts to control air pollution have struck some scholars as uninteresting or unimportant; perhaps others have been put off by real or perceived methodological difficulties. This book is written in the belief that neither of these reasons for inaction is justified: that an examination of the way in which Congress has sought to control air pollution over the last four decades is an important subject; and that the undoubted methodological problems that hinder all studies of law-making may be muted even if they cannot be fully overcome. The intention is to explain why the air pollution control statutes that Congress has enacted since the 1950s have the specific form they do: why such laws have been produced at all, and why they have dealt with the problem in particular ways rather than others.

Why study air pollution control?

In his 1994 Presidential Address to the American Political Science Association, Charles O. Jones bemoaned the lack of direct attention afforded to law-making by congressional scholars.[11] He suggested that fears of having work which was 'bound to be issue-specific' patronized as 'just a *case study*', or of being condemned for failing to follow the latest 'methodological fashions', have left an important field of enquiry largely untilled. Congressional norms, procedures and structures have been extensively and properly studied, but few attempts have been made to show how such features affect the substance of the laws that Congress produces.[12] To instil confidence and reduce the threat of having their work dismissed as a case study, Jones counselled those wishing to study law-making to select an issue that has 'public importance and conceptual interest'.[13] Air pollution control has both of these attributes. Efforts to control air pollution are not only matters of significant public concern, but the problem has certain characteristics that congressional scholars, students of regulatory regimes and political scientists in general should find of interest.

The public importance of air pollution control
The public importance of air pollution control stems from both the damage caused by air pollution and the costs that result from its control. On the one hand, Americans have demanded that action be taken to mitigate the effects of air pollution. Opinion polls conducted since the 1960s have revealed general public support for efforts to control air pollution.[14] On the other hand, concern about the costs of control have also been apparent. Not all Americans have been willing to bear the economic and social costs that result from efforts to reduce air pollution. This conflict between a desire for what Samuel P. Hays termed 'beauty, health, and permanence', and a dominant social paradigm that stresses individualism, limited government and economic growth has spawned considerable public debate about the need, methods, and efficacy of the complex statutory framework that Congress has constructed to control air pollution since the 1950s.[15]

The health and environmental effects of air pollution are well known even if not easily quantifiable. Air pollution damages buildings, ruins vistas of great natural beauty, kills flora and fauna, causes acidification of lakes and adversely affects the health of millions of Americans.[16] Air pollution has also been indicted as a cause of long-term global climate change. The release of chloroflurocarbons (CFCs) has depleted the stratospheric ozone layer and allowed more ultraviolet radiation to reach the Earth's surface. Gases released when fossil fuels are burned have accumulated in the upper atmosphere and generated talk of 'a greenhouse effect' and 'global

warming'. Scientific opinion is divided as to the possible consequences of global warming, but suggested scenarios envisage
Florida and Louisiana disappearing under water if the polar ice caps
melt, climatic change which will bring persistent drought in the
midwestern farm-belt of the United States, and increased plagues of
insects and other pests.[17]

Some air pollution is the result of natural phenomena.[18] Volcanic
eruptions and forest fires release a variety of substances into the
atmosphere; radon, methane and asbestos occur naturally. The
damage caused by natural forms of air pollution can be massive.
Major volcanic eruptions, in particular, may both devastate the local
environment and change weather patterns on a global scale for several years. The 1980 eruption of Mount St Helens in Washington
State, for example, killed more than sixty people, laid waste to 154
square miles, blanketed most of the state with a layer of volcanic ash
and had an impact upon the world's climate. Much of the damage
caused by air pollution in the United States, however, is the result of
human activity. Industrial production, power generation, waste
incineration and transportation – particularly automobiles – are the
main sources of air pollution.[19] Carbon monoxide, ozone, particulate matter, sulphur oxides, and nitrogen oxides are the most
common of an estimated 7,000 air pollutants produced as a result
of human activity.[20] Carbon monoxide alone constitutes approximately half the measurable air pollution in the United States.

Natural forms of air pollution are practically impossible to control. Efforts have been made to solve the problem of indoor radon
by removing contaminated soil or sealing floors, but the value and
efficacy of such efforts is debatable.[21] Removal of the endangered
population to a place of greater safety is the only real response that
governments possess when forced to confront the threat posed by
most forms of natural air pollution. In the weeks leading up to the
Mount St Helens eruption all that state and local governments
could do was evacuate the population living in the immediate vicin-
ity of the volcano. The range of options available to government
when confronted with air pollution caused by human activity is
obviously much broader. Not only may governments move populations or seek to remedy effects, they may also take action to reduce
the amount of pollution that is produced. As with most forms of
social regulation, however, the amount and nature of the action that
is needed is hotly contested. In the words of John G. Francis:

Recurring controversies center on which values are to be protected, how serious is the risk that is the subject of regulation, who is responsible for the risk and for dealing with it, and what specific regulatory strategies are likely to be effective.[22]

Four fundamental questions, in particular, need to be answered before government action to control air pollution can take place: what precisely should be controlled? how much control is needed? what means should be employed to achieve that level of control? and who should have responsibility for implementing and enforcing that level of control?[23]

Patterns are discernible in the answers that have been found since the 1950s to some of these questions but not in others. Perhaps the clearest pattern is apparent in the compass of what should be controlled. The scope of air pollution control efforts has broadened considerably over the years as improved understanding of the problem has gradually brought a wide range of pollutants to the attention of government. The subject-matter of early efforts to control air pollution was simply 'smoke' or unspecified 'air pollution'; CAA90 in contrast specifies 6 'criteria' pollutants and no fewer than 189 hazardous air pollutants for the EPA to regulate. No clear answer has been found to the question of how much control is needed. Air pollution control statutes employ both health-based approaches which seek to establish a level of control that removes the threat posed by a specific air pollutant, and technology-based approaches which seek to control air pollution by requiring all emission sources to install pollution control equipment.[24] A slightly clearer pattern is discernible in the choice of means to achieve required levels of control. Although moral suasion, economic incentives and direct government expenditure have all been used, command-and-control regulatory strategies have been employed as the main means of control in almost all the federal air pollution control statutes of the last forty years.[25] Answers to the question of who should have responsibility for implementing and enforcing the required level of control are less clear. Most air pollution control statutes share responsibility between federal, state and local governments.[26]

Despite the various controversies that have clearly surrounded the wherewithal of regulation at different times, the framework of air pollution control laws that Congress has erected has undoubtedly contributed to an overall improvement in air quality.[27] Estimates of nation-wide emissions of the most common air pollutants reveal a decline in emissions of particulate matter and carbon monoxide since 1940, and a decline in emissions of sulphur oxides and ozone since 1970.[28] Only emissions of nitrogen oxides have not fallen – largely as a result of a failure to reduce total automobile emissions in urban areas sufficiently. National ambient concentrations of all these pollutants have fallen, but not as much as emission levels, and not evenly across the country.[29] Standards for ozone are exceeded in almost all the major urban areas of the United States, and standards for carbon monoxide and sulphur dioxide are exceeded in a significant number of the country's air quality regions.[30] Air pollution in the Los Angeles basin,in particular, has remained high. The 12 million people living and working in the four counties of Los Angeles, Orange, San Bernadino and Riverside have continued to be exposed to ambient concentrations of ozone, particulates, carbon monoxide and nitrogen dioxide far in excess of levels considered safe.

Calculations of the health and environmental benefits that have accrued from this improvement in air quality are beset by methodological difficulties. Part of the problem lies in isolating the benefits that result from cleaner air. Observed improvements in the health of a population may be due to better air quality, for example, but may also be the result of other factors such as better medical care or nutrition. Putting a monetary value on such benefits is also extraordinarily problematic.[31] Not only is it necessary to place a value on improved health, but a full audit must also value such items as cleaner buildings, greater biological diversity and better landscape aesthetics. The most comprehensive attempt to evaluate the benefits that have resulted from federal air pollution control efforts was made by A. Myrick Freeman in the early 1980s.[32] He estimated that total air pollution control benefits in 1978 ranged from approximately $12.6 billion to $132.5 billion (all figures are in 1990 US dollars) depending upon what assumptions were made about the health and other improvements that flowed from better air quality.[33] Freeman suggested that the best estimate of benefits was approximately $53.5 billion. Estimates of the annual benefits associated with CAA90 range from $6 billion to $25 billion.[34]

Although much uncertainty clearly surrounds calculations of the benefits that result from air pollution control, few would dispute the existence of at least some benefits. Efforts to control air pollution, however, do not only bring benefits, but also entail public and private costs. Government expenditure may be required to remove and compensate endangered populations; costs of production may rise if industry is forced to stop using the environment as a free dumping ground for unwanted by-products; and consumer choice may be reduced if particular industries are forced to stop production altogether.[35] The EPA has estimated that the total annual expenditure required by federal air pollution control statutes rose from approximately $9.5 billion in 1972 to $18.9 billion in 1978 to $33.16 billion in 1990 (all figures are in 1990 dollars).[36] Enactment of CAA90 will further increase annual costs by $25–35 billion in the long term.[37] Total costs of efforts to control air pollution control in the United States, including estimates of social costs, were believed to be in the region of $39.6 billion in 1985 – some $11.6 billion more than EPA estimates of expenditure on air pollution control.[38]

Estimates of the benefits and costs of air pollution control must obviously be treated with extreme caution because of the uncertainties that surround their calculation. Two important observations may be made, however, with relative confidence. First, the overall benefits of air pollution control have exceeded the costs of such control. Judged simply in terms of aggregate benefits and costs, the pollution control efforts of the United States should be regarded as successful. Some improvement in the quality of lives of Americans appears to have resulted from the quest for 'beauty, health, and permanence'. Second, the costs of air pollution control have probably risen faster than the benefits. Early control efforts appear to have resulted in sizeable benefits at relatively low cost, but the gains from later efforts appear to have been smaller and cost more to achieve. '[T]he marginal cost of air pollution control increases sharply as the level of control increases', Paul R. Portney has noted, 'while marginal benefits are likely to remain constant or even decline.'[39]

The incidence of benefits and costs, and the possibility that the costs of air pollution control have increased at a faster rate than the corresponding benefits, have provided ammunition for those concerned about the way that the problem of air pollution has been addressed in the United States. Considerable debate has arisen, in particular, about the methods that Congress has chosen to determine the level and means of control. Both health-based and technology-based approaches to establish how much control of air pollution is necessary have been criticized on practical and economic grounds. Uncertain scientific evidence and the possibility of sensitive populations mean that the EPA has found it very difficult to establish thresholds at which all adverse health effects caused by exposure to a particular air pollutant are eliminated.[40] Critics of technology-based approaches not only point to the difficulties of defining precisely what is required when the law calls for the use of 'best available control technology' (BACT) or 'reasonably available control technology' (RACT), but also argue that the imposition of a particular control technology inhibits the development of new and better means of control.[41] A problem common to both approaches is that costs are ignored when determining levels of control. Decisions about how much control is necessary are made according to criteria that make no explicit reference to costs.[42] Bruce A. Ackerman and William T. Hassler have argued that the technology-based approach to air pollution control contained in the Clean Air Act Amendments 1977 (CAA77) amounted to making policy 'in an ecological vacuum – without a sober effort to define the costs and benefits of designing one or another technology into the plants of the future'.[43] Debate has also raged about the means that have been employed to achieve levels of control. Most neo-classical economists, for example, argue that greater use of economic instruments such as taxes, subsidies, tradable permits, refundable deposits and environmental property rights to control air pollution would produce more cost-effective results than command-and-control regulatory strategies.[44] Economic instruments have been criticized, in turn, on the grounds that they may not lead to an improvement in local air quality even if a reduction in the aggregate level of air pollution is obtained.

A number of questions about the design of the laws that Congress has enacted to improve air quality are raised by the controversy surrounding the various methods that have been used to determine the level and means of control. Why has Congress enacted the laws that it has? What imperatives drive further efforts at control? Why have certain methods of determining how much control is needed been used in some circumstances but not in others? Why have command-and-control regulatory strategies been used so frequently to achieve required levels of control? Could the same benefits have been achieved at lower cost? Such questions have considerable political currency in the contemporary United States where politicians of all ilks have embraced the language of regulatory reform. Efforts to 'reinvent government' or 'roll back government' have focused attention as never before on the purpose, need and efficacy of government action to control things like air pollution.

The conceptual interest of air pollution control
Matters of considerable conceptual interest are raised by questions about the design of the laws that Congress has enacted to improve air quality. Explaining the supply and shape of air pollution control laws provides an opportunity to understand further the dynamics and limits of congressional policy-making. The circumstances that cause legislators to enact measures which support the general interest over particularistic interests, for example, are not well understood. Insights into the stability of congressional preferences and institutions may also be possible given the multi-dimensional nature of air pollution control. An issue that may be defined along different policy dimensions should interest congressional scholars whose concerns are agenda control, committee jurisdictions, interest group activity and roll-call voting. Further matters of conceptual interest are generated by the large technical core of air pollution control. These matters may be divided into concerns about process and outcomes: how does Congress process scientific information, and to what extent does the large technical core determine the choice of regulatory regime?

The supply of air pollution control legislation is not easily explained by existing theories of congressional action. The electoral incentive paradigm that has dominated congressional scholarship since the 1970s can easily explain why legislators will produce legislation laden with group or geographic benefits.[45] Pursuit of re-election generates a powerful incentive to support proposals that benefit particular constituencies immediately but pass costs on to the general population – preferably sometime in the future. Calculations of electoral interest can also explain the supply of legislation, perhaps a measure to promote medical research, that provides general benefits but imposes no direct group or geographic costs.[46] Less easily explained is the supply of air pollution control legislation which provides long-term general benefits but imposes short-term particularistic costs.

An attempt to show how the electoral incentive paradigm may explain the supply of such legislation has been advanced by R. Douglas Arnold in *The Logic of Congressional Action*. Arnold argues that legislators will supply legislation that serves the general interest and imposes costs on particularized interests if they can be persuaded that the legislation is consonant with either the 'expressed' preferences of an 'attentive public', or the 'potential' preferences of an 'inattentive public', and suitable legislative procedures can be developed which highlight those decisions that provide the benefits but obscure those that generate the particularized costs.[47] This suggestion that the 'potential' preferences of those who are not active in politics may influence legislative outcomes is an important theoretical innovation, but no appropriate empirical evidence is provided to support the claim that electoral calculations can explain the supply of legislation which provides general benefits and imposes particularistic costs.[48]

Part of the difficulty that electoral incentive models face when seeking to explain the supply of air pollution control legislation results from the opportunity costs associated with policy leadership on such an issue. Although electoral incentives may exist for legislators to engage in 'position-taking' and to support legislative proposals when public concern about air pollution is high, little incentive exists for a legislator to devote resources to developing legislation even during periods when the issue is salient. The time and effort that are involved in working to secure the passage of legislation could almost certainly be better employed if the goal is to enhance re-election prospects.[49] Casework, pork-barrelling, and the like, all offer a more cost-effective means of pursuing re-election than playing a leading role in developing air pollution control policy.[50] The opportunity costs associated with policy leadership become less of an obstacle to explanations of the supply of such legislation if an assumption is made that some legislators have a strong interest in the issue, wish to make a personal mark on policy or simply want to exercise power.[51] Some reduction in the relentless pursuit of re-election may be tolerated either to make good public policy, to make a difference in a particular policy area or to gain power and prestige within the legislature.

The suggestion that legislators are motivated by a range of goals probably offers a more promising means of explaining the supply of air pollution control legislation than can be provided by electoral incentive models. The circumstances under which a legislator is willing and able to accept the opportunity cost associated with a leading role in making air pollution control policy, however, are not fully understood. A large number of questions, in particular, beg answers. How can the interest of a legislator in air pollution be explained? Do demographic or constituency characteristics account for the variance that is evident in the interests of legislators? Is a willingness to accept the opportunity cost associated with policy leadership on air pollution control dependent upon electoral security? How do institutional arrangements affect policy leadership? Possible answers to these questions may obviously be sought in the wider literature on Congress. The seminal study on participation in Congress produced by Richard L. Hall, for example, offers a number of general observations that should have specific relevance.[52] Other studies by Richard F. Fenno and John R. Hibbing make a number of observations about the way that a legislator's priorities change over time, that may help explain the circumstances under which policy leaders emerge.[53] Possible answers may also be sought in the literature that addresses the response of Congress to other issues. Unfortunately, few studies offer immediate answers to the specific questions posed.

Similar difficulties and lacunae are encountered when an explanation of the shape or content of air pollution control legislation is sought among existing theories of congressional action. The electoral incentive paradigm can easily explain those aspects of air pollution control legislation which seek to promote research, authorize grants-in-aid to states and local government, and provide a range of subsidies and tax incentives. Less easily explained are the answers that have been found to two of the questions that lie at the heart of regulatory efforts: how much control is needed, and what means should be employed to achieve the required level of control? David R. Mayhew offers a basis for a possible explanation with the claim that: 'Attentive publics judge positions on means as well as on ends.'[54] Legislators need to craft legislation, in short, that not only addresses the desire of 'attentive publics' for cleaner air, but does so in a way which accords with their views about the way that the air should be cleaned. Arnold suggests that reasoning of this sort makes legislators reluctant to support policy options which deal with a problem in a way that is not fully understood by the public.[55] '[I]t is the causal logic of citizens that is important, not that of experts', he argues, when it comes to explaining the predilection for command-and-control regulatory techniques found in air pollution control legislation. Simple commands to reduce or stop polluting have a logic that is better understood by the public, and indeed most legislators, than that advanced in support of economic incentives.[56]

An important aspect of congressional policy-making is undoubtedly captured by such arguments. Few would contest the notion that legislators are more likely to support regulatory strategies that they understand and feel capable of selling to constituents than those which defy easy comprehension and marketing. How such considerations explain the variation in regulatory strategy that is found both within and across air pollution control statutes, however, is not immediately clear. The wide variety of strategies contained within CAA90, for example, do not appear easily amenable to the sort of explanations advanced by electoral incentive theorists. How do considerations of comprehension and marketing explain the use of health-based standards to establish National Ambient Air Quality Standards (NAAQS), and the use of technology-based standards to establish New Source Performance Standards (NSPSs) and to determine levels of control for 'hazardous air pollutants'?[57] Why is the logic of market incentives understood and capable of being sold as a means to control sulphur dioxide, but not for the other 'criteria pollutants'?[58] Changes in regulatory strategy over time are also difficult to explain. What changes in comprehension and marketability prompted Congress to depart from the health-based approach to controlling hazardous air pollutants that had been adopted in the CAA70 to the technology-based approach adopted in CAA90?[59]

The simplest way to explain variation in regulatory strategy is to assume that policy leaders attempt to match appropriate solutions to each problem they need to address. Health-based approaches are perceived as the best way to determine levels of control for 'criteria pollutants' whereas technology-based approaches are perceived as the best way to deal with 'hazardous air pollutants'. Similarly, change in regulatory strategy may be a consequence of policy-learning. Old solutions that do not appear to work are rejected in favour of those that appear to offer a better chance of achieving desired ends. The possibility that legislators may alter their views on the appropriateness of particular strategies as a result of changes in information about the efficacy of solutions to problems, however, is difficult to reconcile with a strong emphasis on comprehension and marketability. A model of congressional action that views policy leaders as wishing to make good public policy overcomes this difficulty: obtaining information about the suitability and effectiveness of different regulatory strategies is a *sine qua non* of making good policy.

Although the suggestion that policy leaders are motivated by a desire to make good public policy offers a promising means of explaining the variation and change in regulatory strategies that is evident in air pollution control legislation, a number of questions still demand answers. How do policy leaders obtain the information they need about a subject? Is the process for gathering information biased? Do asymmetries of information empower policy leaders? To what extent is the goal of making good policy compromised by the desire to enact legislation? A burgeoning literature on the role of information in Congress addresses many of these questions at a general level.[60] Keith Krehbiel, for example, has developed an 'informational model' of Congress that emphasizes institutional needs and individual incentives for acquiring information.[61] General assertions about the importance and problems of obtaining reliable information also permeates most of the literature on environmental policy-making, but little specific attention has been paid to the way that Congress acquires and uses information about air pollution.[62]

An opportunity to address numerous questions of interest to congressional scholars is clearly afforded by a study of the supply and shape of air pollution control laws. Observations gleaned from such a study should prove useful both to those looking at Congress in general and to those focusing upon specific policy areas. Scholars of interest groups, public policy and the origins of regulation should also find much of interest.

How to study air pollution control

The case that congressional efforts to control air pollution is an important subject would appear to be compelling. Few can doubt that the subject has the 'public importance and conceptual interest' that Charles O. Jones counselled were necessary in a study of lawmaking. Jones's admonition to 'do it right', however, also encompassed method.[63] A study of law-making should ideally achieve two goals. First, and most obviously, the study should improve understanding of the way that the law on a particular subject is fashioned. A study of the production and shape of air pollution control legislation in the United States should advance knowledge of the subject through improved conceptualization and the marshalling of better empirical evidence. Second, the study should contribute to the broader understanding of law-making. The findings of a study into law-making on a particular subject should help illuminate law-making on another subject, and perhaps even law-making in a different political system. Providing a conceptual framework and employing an appropriate methodology are essential if both of these goals are to be achieved. Simple description would allow neither improved conceptualization nor the integration of findings into the wider literature.

Understanding law-making

A conceptual framework which provides 'a broad language and a form of reference in which reality can be examined' is essential if law-making is to be understood. Without such a framework it is impossible to make sense of a complex and chaotic law-making universe composed of large numbers of political actors, institutions, ideas and events. Constructing an adequate framework within which to operate, however, is fraught with difficulties. Decisions have to be made not only about the appropriate level and unit of analysis that the framework needs to capture, but also about the best way of depicting the dynamics that drive the law-making process once a level and unit of analysis have been determined.

The first stage in constructing a conceptual framework to understand law-making is to establish the appropriate level and unit of analysis. Potential explanations of the origins and shape of air pollution control legislation in the United States could take a number of different forms. First, a Marxist/historical-cultural framework could be developed which emphasizes the explanatory value of socio-economic variables. The supply of air pollution control legislation could be viewed as a consequence of what Theda Skocpol, albeit in a different context, has termed 'the logic of industrialization'.[64] A simple version of such a theory might posit that increased industrial production will generate more pollution which government will be forced to control. Another possibility is a pluralist/interest group framework which stresses the importance of interest groups. Legislation might be the result of the pressure that interest groups are able to exert on government to deal with a particular problem. A study of the origins and shape of air pollution control legislation that employed such a conceptual framework would focus on the nature of interest representation that surrounds the issue. A further possibility is an institutional rational choice framework which places government institutions at centre stage. Politicians and bureaucrats might be viewed as the key actors in determining the supply of legislation. Political preferences and institutional structures would form the main focus of such a framework.

Although no specific explanation of the origins and shape of air pollution control legislation based on socio-economic variables has been developed, an inkling of the form that a sophisticated version of such an explanation might take can be gleaned from the work of Samuel P. Hays. In *Beauty, Health, and Permanence* Hays argues that the increased concern for the environment that has been evident in the United States since the end of the Second World War is a product of fundamental changes in the American economy.[65] The thesis proffered by Hays is that economic development has allowed a new mass middle-class to emerge that places a premium on 'quality of life' issues. As economic growth has provided a higher disposable income and more leisure time, the 'production' orientation of a previous generation has gradually been replaced by a 'recreational consumerism' with a strong emphasis on health and outdoor pursuits.[66] The result has been an increase in demands for environmental protection.

Hays's fundamental insight is that changes in American attitudes towards the environment in the post-war period are not simply a reaction to the devastation caused by economic growth but a product of that very growth.[67] His arguments help to explain why the smoke-filled skies of Pittsburgh could be regarded as a sign of economic progress in the 1930s, and as a harbinger of death and illness a generation later. Whether such arguments could form the basis of a conceptual framework that can explain environmental lawmaking, however, is a matter of considerable doubt. Important and provocative as an insight into the origins of environmental concern, the thesis advanced by Hays fails to explain both the precise timing of legislative enactments or their content. Changes in the American economy may have been necessary for air pollution control legislation to be supplied, but these changes are not sufficient to explain why particular laws have been passed at particular times, or why some regulatory strategies have been favoured and others rejected. What is needed is a framework that is sensitive to the factors that determine the timing and content of legislation.

Marxist/historical-cultural explanations of law-making face enormous difficulties in accounting for the precise timing of legislative enactments. The variables identified as important in such explana-

tions are too general and insensitive to pick up the political factors
that determine the timing of legislation. A conceptual framework
that is more acutely attuned to the pulse of politics is needed to
explain why a law is passed at a particular time. Similar problems
afflict Marxist/historical-cultural explanations of the content of legislation. Explanations of this sort usually focus on the social part of
socio-economic, and posit that the content of legislation is shaped
by cultural values. In a general discussion of the different styles of
environmental regulation found in the United States and Britain, for
example, David Vogel suggests that the political culture of each
country determines the choice of regulatory method. 'The relative
formalism of the American regulatory system (its reliance upon
clearly defined rules and standards)', he concludes, 'reflects the
inadequacy of informal mechanisms of social control within a
highly individualistic culture.'[68] Others have also stressed a connection between political culture and the way that environmental problems are addressed in the United States.[69]

Explanations of legislative content based on cultural values
undoubtedly help to account for the parameters of policy choice.
The fact that direct government control of the means of production
has not been employed as a method of air pollution control in the
United States may be largely attributed to the individualistic political culture that Vogel describes. Cultural explanations become less
helpful when the spectre of regulatory variation is raised. As
Christopher J. Bosso has pointed out: 'culture is not destiny,
because that same American public also at times accepts the need to
cede (what they define as individual freedom) for the common
good'.[70] The problem is that cultural explanations are too insensitive to political factors to account properly for the content of laws:
they are 'too holistic and essentialist' to provide the 'explanatory
leverage' that is necessary to account for variation in policy choice.[71]
Explanations of legislative content need more precise analytical
tools than such approaches can provide. General statements about
cultural values are valuable up to a point, but should not be worked
too hard. The pertinent question that explanations of law-making
need to answer is whose values are important when laws are
crafted?[72] It is a question that cultural explanations do not have the
capacity to answer.

Some sensitivity to variables below general socio-economic factors
clearly needs to be apparent if the timing and content of legislation

is to be explained. One way in which this might be achieved is to develop a pluralist/interest group framework which focuses on the actions of interest groups. Laws could be explained as a consequence of the resources that different interests are able to mobilize to secure their particular goals. The vision conjured by such an approach is very familiar.[73] Competing interest groups make demands upon government with victory going to the best resourced, is its central dictum. 'What may be called public policy is actually the equilibrium reached in the group struggle at any given moment', noted one early proponent of this approach.[74] The more recent efforts of economists such as George Stigler, Richard A. Posner, Sam Peltzman and Gary Becker, to explain the origins and nature of regulation take a similar line.[75] In one essay, for example, Posner asserts that: 'legislation is a good demanded and supplied much as other goods, so that legislative protection flows to those groups that derive the greatest value from it, regardless of overall social welfare'.[76] The language may be different but the message is much the same: legislation is regarded as the product of bargaining between different interest groups.

An explanation of the origins and shape of air pollution control legislation that emphasizes the role of interest groups in determining legislative outcomes is certainly a possibility. Interest groups of different ilks have undoubtedly played an important role in structuring the way that government has responded to the problem of air pollution. Environmental groups have sought to persuade politicians that the problem warrants government attention; business groups have often, though not always, sought to dissuade government from taking action.[77] Most environmental groups have favoured command-and-control regulatory strategies to control air pollution; business groups have often sought to promote the efficacy of economic incentives.[78] No doubt evidence of this sort could be used to develop an explanation of the supply of air pollution control legislation – at least from the late 1960s. Whether a pluralist/interest group framework could explain the supply of air pollution control legislation during the 1950s and early 1960s is altogether more problematic as few groups appear to have been active in this policy arena at that time. To account for the supply of these early statutes, an explanation is needed that acknowledges that political actors other than interest groups may have an have impact on legislative outcomes.

A major flaw in pluralist/interest group explanations of law-making is that the role played by government officials in determining legislative outcomes is played down. In the words of one major study: 'Much of the literature virtually ignores the officials and appears to assume that, like billiard balls, they will go wherever the interest groups send them'.[79] This failure to recognize that government officials may have interests of their own makes it very difficult to account for the origins of air pollution control legislation in the 1950s – a period when no cue appears to have been available to set the billiard balls moving. Pluralist/interest group explanations may even have difficulty explaining the supply of air pollution control legislation in the late 1960s when numerous groups were actively seeking to influence policy. As E. Donald Elliot and colleagues have pointed out:

> A theory that explains the early federal environmental statutes in terms of conventional interest group politics is untrue in the sense that one can detect no striking imbalance between the organizational presence of environmentalists and industry in 1970 which might account for the stringent provisions of the Clean Air Act.[80]

Attention needs to be given to the role of government officials if a plausible explanation of the timing and content of CAA70 is to be produced. The idea that government officials simply do the bidding of interest groups has little explanatory power. Even the most perfectly struck billiard ball may miss the pocket if the table has a bias.

A simple way to incorporate government officials into a pluralist/interest group framework is to expand the range of political actors that are recognized as having an impact on legislative outcomes. The supply of air pollution control legislation could be explained in terms of the interaction of a range of public and private groups operating within a policy subsystem or network.[81] Such an approach would acknowledge the part that members of Congress, presidents, federal bureaucrats, state and local government officials, environmental groups, business organizations and others have played in shaping legislative outcomes. Paul A. Sabatier has argued, for example, that air pollution control in the 1970s was shaped by the actions of two competing 'advocacy coalitions': a dominant 'clean air coalition' and an opposing 'economic feasibility coalition'. The 'clean air coalition' was composed of environmental/public health groups, their allies in Congress (for example, Senator Muskie), most pollution control officials in EPA (the Environmental Protection Agency), a few labor unions, many state and local pollution control officials (particularly in large cities with serious problems), and some researchers.

The 'economic feasibility coalition' was composed of

industrial emission sources, energy companies, their allies in Congress (for example, Congressman Broyhill), several labor unions (particularly after the Arab oil boycott, some state and local pollution control official, and a few economists.[82]

According to Sabatier each coalition was bound together by a system of shared values and beliefs.

The advantage that subsystem or network explanations of legislation have over simple interest group theories is an improved specification of the political actors involved in shaping legislative outcomes. Although Sabatier's grouping of these political actors into two 'advocacy coalitions' is a matter for debate and empirical verification, his account of the policy arena is descriptively richer than that found in the pluralist/interest group explanations of legislation propounded by many economists. Simply identifying more participants, however, does not necessarily mean that the timing and content of legislation is properly explained. What is needed is a better account of the dynamics that shape the interactions between the various political actors within the subsystem. Sabatier fails to explain, for example, why the 'clean air coalition' rather than the 'economic feasibility coalition' should dominate the policy process. The danger is that unless such a fundamental question can be answered the utility of subsystem explanations may be limited to little more than 'metaphorical heuristics'.[83]

A failure to recognize fully that government institutions endow government officials with properties that differentiate them from other political actors is a significant flaw in many subsystem explanations of law-making. Institutions provide specific political actors in the policy process with the power to make authoritative decisions.[84] Not only does this place government officials in a privileged position when decisions about the supply of legislation are made, but also means that they are able to influence the shape and operation of the subsystem. The 'identities, goals, and capacities' of other political actors within a subsystem will be influenced by the actions of government officials.[85] Some may be helped, even encouraged, by government action; others may be hindered or obstructed. New interests may be mobilized as a result of government action; others may be made redundant. Such consequences may either stem from the deliberate actions of government officials or simply flow from the bias that is inherent in all institutional arrangements.[86]

Recognition that government institutions are crucial to law-making is essential if a plausible explanation of the supply of air pollution control legislation is to be produced. An explanation of the timing and content of laws that is centred on institutions is able to provide the sensitivity to the pulse of politics that is lacking in other explanations. Proper account may be taken of the preferences of a privileged set of political actors, and due attention paid to structural arrangements that determine who is empowered to define alternatives and who is able to make authoritative decisions at particular points in time. An important element of dynamism can be introduced into the explanation if government institutions are not viewed in isolation from the wider context in which they operate. A conceptual framework that treats institutions as closed systems would be static and incomplete. Institutions are shaped by the external forces to which they are subject. Preferences and structures may change as new problems and priorities become apparent and require resolution. Acknowledgement that institutions may shape these external forces also provides an opportunity to take account of 'feedback' and 'policy learning'.

A number of government institutions can be identified as having a role in the supply of air pollution control legislation. Congress, the President, staff of the Executive Office of the President (EOP), federal bureaucrats and the courts may all contribute to law-making. As Daniel J. Fiorino has observed: 'if this were a baseball game, it would be a very crowded playing field'.[87] To explain the timing and content of legislation, however, the focus needs to be on Congress. Not only is Congress the place where the law is actually made, but contrary to much conventional wisdom also plays a prominent role in initiating policy.[88] Almost all studies of environmental policy-making have emphasized the prime role that Congress has played. Michael E. Kraft notes that: 'its [Congress's] historical role in the formation of environmental policy has been both highly influential and unquestionably responsive to the American public's concern over environmental degradation'.[89] From the first stirrings of interest in air pollution control in the late 1940s to efforts to engineer regulatory reform in the late 1990s, senators and representatives have been important in setting the agenda, defining the issue, proffering solutions and legitimizing action.

An institutional explanation of law-making that is centred on Congress would obviously give considerable attention to preferences and rules. The knowledge that members have of a problem, their commitment to addressing it, their political skills in crafting acceptable solutions and the opportunities for action provided by institutional structures and rules are central to understanding how and why particular laws are supplied. To treat Congress as a closed system and focus simply on endogenous variables, however, would produce an incomplete and static explanation of law-making. Without some reference to variations in public opinion, changes in elite and general knowledge about the problem, and shifts in interest group activity, important questions about how members acquire knowledge about the problem, why their commitment should vary over time, and why some solutions should be preferred at particular times and not at others, would be difficult to answer. 'We need always to plant our study of [Congress] firmly in its surroundings, its social, political, and economic milieu, and, particularly, its issue agenda', is advice proffered by Christopher J. Bosso that should be heeded.[90] Congress does not exist in a vacuum.

Acknowledgement that Congress is not a closed system would also allow the political outcomes of air pollution control legislation to be taken into account. Evan J. Ringquist has shown that the environmental protection laws of the United States have had: 'effects on political participation, effects on the political power of various groups, and effects on interagency and intergovernmental dynamics'.[91] Laws such as the Clean Air Act have fostered a sense of civic involvement, promoted interest group formation and activity, and altered the balance of power between federal and state governments. To ignore such consequences would seriously flaw an explanation of the development of air pollution control legislation in the United States. The actions of Congress have influenced the shape and operation of the air pollution control subsystem in ways that have had an impact on future legislative outcomes.

One way to capture the interaction between Congress and its surroundings is to develop a conceptual framework similar to that employed by economists to explain the production of commodities such as automobiles, Coca-Cola and computers. Conceptualizing law-making as a form of production forces consideration of both the causes and consequences of congressional action. Attention must be paid not only to the circumstances that lead to production of a law, but also to the way that production changes those circumstances. Law-making will initially occur when a legislative entrepreneur perceives the possibility of making a 'profit' from the production of legislation and possesses the necessary resources to meet the 'costs' of production. 'Benefits', 'costs' and the 'market' will all be transformed, however, once a law is produced. 'Profit' will attract rivals into the market, 'barriers to entry' will be erected, a scramble for resources will occur, and incentives to change the 'product' will emerge. Dynamism is an essential feature of a theory of legislative production.

A conceptual framework that treats law-making as a form of production offers the best basis for explaining the supply and shape of air pollution control legislation. Purposive behaviour, institutional context and the broader 'social, political and economic milieu' can all be incorporated within such a theory as the costs and benefits that determine legislative entrepreneurship are derived from both endogenous and exogenous sources. The benefits of fashioning legislation may flow from the high public saliency of an issue or the expectations of colleagues. The magnitude of the costs associated with legislative entrepreneurship will depend upon the complexity of the issue and levels of opposition both within and outside the institution. A conceptual framework of this sort also allows comparison with law-making on other issues. The production of air pollution control laws can be compared to the production of agricultural laws. It may even be possible to adapt the theory to explain law-making in different countries.

Conceptual difficulties and methodological problems
Although the basic outline of a conceptual framework that treats law-making as a form of production is relatively easy to sketch, a number of conceptual difficulties and methodological problems must be addressed to translate the theory into something useable. Key terms such as 'profit', 'benefits' and 'costs' need to be defined. What is the profit that may result from legislative entrepreneurship? Can it be measured? What costs are involved in the production of legislation? Can they be measured? Appropriate data about the production of air pollution control legislation needs to be collected.

How is the subject to be defined? How are legislative entrepreneurs to be identified? Can information about benefits and costs be obtained? Not all of these questions can be answered in ways that will allow a predictive theory of law-making to be developed. Answers can be found, however, to validate the interpretative power of a theory of legislative production.

To define 'profit' in a legislative setting it is necessary to specify the benefits and costs of fashioning a law. The definition of both terms is problematic. Examples of corruption suggest that it is not inconceivable for a legislative entrepreneur to be motivated by the promise of personal financial reward, but such a narrow definition of benefit will almost certainly fail to explain the actions of most legislators. What is needed is a definition which accords with current thinking about the goals of legislators. Benefit in this context may mean enhanced re-election prospects, greater prestige among one's peers, or even the personal satisfaction gained from addressing a major public issue. 'Profit' will be made when these benefits outweigh the costs of legislative production. Information costs and transaction costs will need to be met to enact a law. Time and resources must be devoted to developing policy expertise and persuading colleagues to support the proposed solution. Not all legislators are equally endowed with the resources to meet such costs.[92]

The disadvantage of employing such nebulous definitions of benefits and costs is obvious. They lack the precision that is necessary for measurement. What such definitions do allow is the generation of hypotheses about the circumstances under which legislative entrepreneurship is likely to take place. High levels of public or elite concern about a problem are likely to promote interest in fashioning legislation because the benefits of action will probably be high. Discovery that the problem is complex or that no simple solutions are available will discourage legislative activity because information and transaction costs are likely to be high. The need for resources to meet costs also means that legislative entrepreneurs are most likely to be party leaders or chairs of committees and subcommittees. Few other legislators have the ability to overcome the 'barriers to entry' that restrict entrepreneurship.

The qualified nature of these hypotheses results from the observation that legislative entrepreneurship is dependent upon a legislator's perception of the 'profit' that can be made from law-making activity. This makes firm predictions about legislative behaviour impossible. Some legislative entrepreneurs may fail to see an opportunity. Not everyone has an 'eye for the market'. Others may see an opportunity that proves illusory. Failed entrepreneurs are commonplace. The subjective nature of the decision to engage in legislative entrepreneurship limits the utility of aggregate data in studies of law-making. Aggregate data provides important evidence about trends in legislative activity, but fails to capture the individual-level calculations that influence the timing and content of laws. Detailed case studies provide the only means of determining the importance of specific individuals, rules and events at particular times.[93]

Obtaining sufficient evidence to explain legislative entrepreneurship is difficult. Richard F. Fenno has argued persuasively that the best way to understand what goes on in Congress is to interview and observe those involved.[94] An important 'research mode' for those wishing to explain some contemporary action, the use of such qualitative data becomes virtually impossible if the purpose is to explain the development of legislation over four decades or more. The legislators of the early 1950s clearly cannot be observed in the manner pioneered by Fenno, and although surviving politicians from an earlier generation may certainly be interviewed, the representativeness and accuracy of their recollections may be questioned. The difficulty of obtaining reliable qualitative data means that an explanation of the development of legislation must rely heavily upon the written record and whatever quantitative data is available. Obtaining even this type of data may be difficult, however, given the passage of time. Apart from gaps in data, an obvious difficulty is posed by the fact that understanding of the nature of a problem like air pollution has changed over time. This means that the problem that Congress addressed in 1990 was not the same problem that it addressed in 1955. Employing contemporaneous definitions is probably the only way to deal with this difficulty.

The data sets of air pollution control bills and committee hearings employed in this study have been generated by searching the indices of the *Congressional Record* and the Congressional Information Service (CIS) reports of congressional activity using the term 'air pollution' as a key word. The *Congressional Record* was searched manually for the years 1930 to 1996. The CIS reports were searched for all congresses using a CD-ROM. Reliance upon these methods of creating data sets has some pitfalls, of course. It is possible that some air pollution bills are not indexed under the term 'air pollution', and that the classification used by the CIS indexers is not quite the same as that used in the *Congressional Record*. But the advantages of employing contemporaneous definitions of air pollution outweigh both a possible loss of absolute comprehensiveness and any marginal inconsistencies in classification.

These solutions to the conceptual and methodological difficulties that plague studies of law-making will not find favour with everyone. No pretence is entertained that they allow rigorous testing of hypotheses. The hope is that such solutions will enable sufficient evidence to be gathered to illustrate the explanatory value of a conceptual framework that treat laws as goods.

Overview of the study

A conceptual framework that treats laws as analogous to goods is developed in Chapter 2. Aggregate data on bill introductions, committee hearings and roll-call votes is used in Chapter 3 to produce an overview of congressional efforts to control air pollution, and test a set of expectations about the supply and shape of air pollution control legislation in the United States. The inadequacies of aggregate data, however, means that the bulk of the study is made up of detailed accounts of discrete stages in the development of air pollution control law.

The awakening of congressional interest in air pollution between 1945 and 1963 is examined in Chapter 4. Evidence is produced to show that the spark that ignited this interest was an air pollution episode in Donora, Pennsylvania in 1948, but that the fuel that fed the fires of congressional activity was the growing problem of smog in California. This period is shown to be important in shaping the future development of air pollution control legislation for three reasons. First, it legitimized federal involvement in controlling air pollution. Second, it established legislative structures that institutionalized concern about air pollution. Finally, it launched a process of 'problem identification and definition' that would create a momentum for future action.

The rapid development of congressional involvement in controlling air pollution which culminated in the enactment of CAA70 is examined in Chapter 5. Evidence is produced to show that growing elite and public awareness of the problem, activity by the states and competition for the presidency produced circumstances that generated considerable legislative activity. The result of this activity was enactment of a law which dramatically expanded the scope of conflict associated with the issue.

The consequences of this expanded scope of conflict are examined in Chapter 6 which covers the period from 1970 to 1977. Problems with the 1970 law, conflict between environmental groups and industrial groups, and the exigencies of the energy crisis served to change the structure of benefits and costs associated with air pollution control. Efforts to rein in the ambition of CAA70 culminated in enactment of CAA77 which postponed many of the emission deadlines specified in the earlier law.

The problems left unresolved by CAA77 generated a struggle over policy that would last until enactment of CAA90. Evidence is produced in Chapter 7 to show that the structure of benefits and costs associated with the issue changed dramatically over this period. The early 1980s were characterized by low benefits and high costs. President Reagan wanted to emasculate the law, prominent congressional leaders came from constituencies whose interests were harmed by the law, and the issue had a low saliency among the public. The late 1980s were characterized by high benefits and reduced costs. President Bush proved slightly more sympathetic to environmental concerns than his predecessor, new congressional leaders emerged and the public concern about the problem escalated.

The period of regulatory reform that has been evident since 1990 is examined in Chapter 8. Particular attention is paid to Republican efforts to undermine air pollution control legislation. The chapter shows that continued public support for high levels of environmental protection have blunted much of these efforts.

The study concludes with an evaluation of the framework of laws that Congress has produced to control air pollution. A case is made that contrary to much received wisdom, Congress does have the ability to legislate on a complex issue and in the collective interest.

Notes.

1 See Arthur C. Stern 'History of Air Pollution Legislation in the United States', *Journal of the Air Pollution Control Association* (1982) 32:44–61; Congressional Research Service 'Environmental Protection Laws and Treaties: Reference Guide', CRS, 89–356 ENR, 18 September 1989.

2 Air Pollution Control Act 1955, 69 stat. 3221.
3 Gary C. Bryner *Blue Skies, Green Politics* (Washington, DC: Congressional Quarterly Press, 1993), p.1.
4 The Clean Air Act Amendments 1990, PL 101–549, 104 stat. 2399.
5 National Environmental Policy Act 1969, 42 USC 4321–70d; Pollution Prevention Act 1990, 42 USC 13101–9.
6 Toxic Substances Control Act 1976, as amended, 15 USC 2601–92. New subchapters pertaining to asbestos, radon and lead were added to the 1976 statute with the enactment of the Asbestos Hazard Emergency Response Act 1986, the Indoor Radon Abatement Act 1988 and the Lead Exposure Reduction Act 1992.
7 See Noel de Nevers 'Air Pollution Control Philosophies', *Journal of the Air Pollution Control Association* (1977), 27:198.
8 See William J. Baumol and Wallace E. Oates *Economics, Environmental Policy, and the Quality of Life* (Englewood Cliffs, NJ: Prentice-Hall, 1979), chapter 15.
9 Examples include Randall B. Ripley 'Congress and Clean Air: The Issue of Enforcement, 1963' in Frederick N. Cleaveland and associates (eds), *Congress and Urban Problems* (Washington, DC: Brookings, 1969); Helen Ingram 'The Political Rationality of Innovation: The Clean Air Act Amendments of 1970' in Ann F. Friedlaender (ed.), *Approaches to Controlling Air Pollution* (Cambridge, MA: MIT Press, 1978); Richard E. Cohen *Washington at Work: Back Rooms and Clean Air* (New York: Macmillan, 1992); Bryner, *Blue Skies, Green Politics*.
10 Charles O. Jones *Clean Air* (Pittsburgh, PA: University of Pittsburgh Press, 1975); James E. Krier and Edmund Ursin *Pollution and Policy* (Berkeley, CA: University of California Press, 1977); Lennart J. Lundqvist *The Hare and the Tortoise: Clean Air Policies in the United States and Sweden* (Ann Arbor, MI: University of Michigan Press, 1980); Bruce A. Ackerman and William T. Hassler *Clean Coal/Dirty Air* (New Haven, CN: Yale University Press, 1981). See also E. Donald Elliot, Bruce A. Ackerman, and John C. Millian 'Toward a Theory of Statutory Evolution: The Federalization of Environmental Law', *Journal of Law, Economics, and Organization* (1985), 1:313–40.
11 See Charles O. Jones, 'A Way of Life and Law', *American Political Science Review* (1995), 89:1–9.
12 Michael E. Kraft has also recently noted that 'the literature on Congress has been notably deficient in relating internal structures and decision-making processes to policy outputs'. See Michael E. Kraft 'Congress and Environmental Policy' in James P. Lester (ed.), *Environmental Politics and Policy* 2nd edition (Durham, NC: Duke University Press, 1995), p.170.
13 Jones 'A Way of Life and Law', p.2.

14 See Riley E. Dunlap 'Public Opinion and Environmental Policy' in James P. Lester (ed.), *Environmental Politics and Policy*, pp.63–114; Carl Everett Ladd 'Clearing the Air: Public Opinion and Public Policy on the Environment', *Public Opinion* (1982), 5:16–20.

15 Samuel P. Hays *Beauty, Health and Permanence: Environmental Politics in the United States, 1955–1985* (Cambridge: Cambridge University Press, 1987). See also Willett Kempton, James S. Boster and Jennifer A. Hartley *Environmental Values in American Culture* (Cambridge, MA: MIT Press, 1995).

16 A good exposition of the problems caused by air pollution is Derek M. Elsom *Atmospheric Pollution: A Global Problem*, 2nd edition (Oxford: Basil Blackwell, 1992).

17 See Kent E. Portney *Controversial Issues in Environmental Policy* (Newbury Park, CA: Sage, 1992), pp.9–10.

18 The definition of air pollution is a contested issue. Air pollution is defined in this study as 'the presence of substances in the ambient atmosphere, resulting from the activity of man or natural processes, causing adverse effects to man and the environment'. See E. Weber *Air Pollution: Assessment Methodology and Modelling* vol. 2 (New York: Plenum, 1982).

19 See US Environmental Protection Agency *National Air Pollutant Emissions Estimates 1940–1990* (Washington, DC: EPA, 1991) p.4.

20 Bryner *Blue Skies, Green Politics*, p.41.

21 See Leonard A. Cole *Element of Risk: The Politics of Radon* (Oxford: Oxford University Press, 1993).

22 John G. Francis *The Politics of Regulation* (Oxford: Blackwell, 1993), p.126; see also Peter H. Schuck 'The Politics of Regulation', *Yale Law Review* (1981), 90:702–25.

23 Lester B. Lave *The Strategy of Social Regulation* (Washington, DC: Brookings, 1981). See also de Nevers 'Air Pollution Control Philosophies', 27:198.

24 Robert W. Hahn and Robert N. Stavins 'Incentive-Based Environmental Regulation: A New Era from an Old Idea', *Ecology Law Quarterly* (1991), 18:5.

25 Organization of Economic Co-operation and Development *Economic Instruments for Environmental Protection* (Paris: OECD, 1989), p.109; Paul R. Portney 'EPA and the Evolution of Federal Regulation' in Paul R. Portney (ed.), *Public Policies for Environmental Protection* (Washington, DC: Resources for the Future, 1990), p.21.

26 'Conjoint Federalism' is a term that has been coined to characterize this relationship between federal and state governments. See David M. Welborn 'Conjoint Federalism and Environmental Regulation in the United States', *Publius* (1988), 18:27–43.

27 Not all emission reductions are the result of air pollution control policy. Energy prices, economic activity, technological change, and weather patterns can have an impact on emission levels. See Paul R. Portney 'Air Pollution Policy' in Paul R. Portney (ed.), *Public Policies for Environmental Protection* (Washington, DC: Resources for the Future, 1990), pp.49–50; and Paul MacAvoy *The Regulated Industries and the Economy* (New York: Norton, 1979). Crandall has argued that air pollution control policies are not only ineffective, but are also counterproductive. See Robert Crandall *Controlling Industrial Air Pollution* (Washington DC: Brookings, 1983).

28 US Environmental Protection Agency *National Air Pollutant Emissions Estimates, 1940–1987* (Washington, DC: EPA, 1989); US Environmental Protection Agency *Environmental Investments: The Cost of a Clean Environment* (Washington, DC: EPA, 1990).

29 Council on Environmental Quality *Environmental Quality 1990* (Washington, DC: CEQ, 1990).

30 Evan J. Ringquist 'Evaluating Environmental Policy Outcomes' in James P. Lester (ed.), *Environmental Politics and Policy* (Durham, NC: Dyke University Press, 1995), p.311.

31 See Organization of Economic Co-operation and Development *Environmental Policy Benefits: Monetary Valuation* (Paris: OECD, 1989).

32 A. Myrick Freeman *Air and Water Pollution Control: A Benefit-Cost Assessment* (New York: Wiley, 1982).

33 Freeman's original estimates have been transformed into 1990 dollars using the consumer price index.

34 Paul R. Portney 'Economics and the Clean Air Act', *Journal of Economic Perspectives* (1990), 4:173–81.

35 The literature on the economics of pollution control is vast. Good introductions include: Michael Common *Environmental and Resource Economics: An Introduction* (London: Longman, 1988); Robert Dorfman and Nancy S. Dorfman (eds) *Economics of the Environment* (New York: Norton, 1993).

36 US Environmental Protection Agency *Environmental Assessments: The Cost of a Clean Environment* tables 8.3 and 8.6.

37 Portney 'Economics and the Clean Air Act'; US Environmental Protection Agency *Environmental Investments*.

38 Portney, 'Air Pollution Policy', p.68.

39 Portney, 'Air Pollution Policy', pp.70–1.

40 See Marc K. Landy, Marc J. Roberts and Stephen R. Thomas *The Environmental Protection Agency* expanded edition (New York: Oxford University Press, 1994) for a discussion of these difficulties.

41 Organization of Economic Co-operation and Development *Environmental Policy and Technological Change* (Paris: OECD, 1985).

42 The EPA is expressly prohibited from taking costs into consideration when establishing NAAQS. Challenges to this requirement have been defeated in the courts. See *Lead Industries Association v. Environmental Protection Agency* 647 F.2d. 1130 (DC Cir, 1980); and *American Petroleum Institute v. Costle* 665 F.2d. 1176 (DC Cir, 1981). An argument could be made that cost considerations are implicit in the distinction between BACT and RACT.

43 Ackerman and Hassler *Clean Coal/Dirty Air*, p.12.

44 The literature on this subject is vast. A good introduction to the main arguments is Allen V. Kneese and Charles L. Schultze *Pollution, Prices, and Public Policy* (Washington, DC: Brookings, 1975).

45 David R. Mayhew *Congress: The Electoral Connection* (New Haven, CN: Yale University Press, 1974), pp.127–31.

46 R. Douglas Arnold *The Logic of Congressional Action* (New Haven, CN: Yale University Press, 1990), p.4.

47 *Ibid.*, pp.14–15; see also John W. Kingdon *Congressmen's Voting Decisions* 3rd edition (Ann Arbor, MI: University of Michigan Press, 1989), p.60.

48 See the review of *The Logic of Congressional Action* by Lawrence C. Dodd in the *American Political Science Review* (1992), 86:1052–3. See also Arthur T. Denzau and Michael C. Munger 'Legislators and Interest Groups: How Unorganized Groups Get Represented', *American Political Science Review* (1986), 80:89–106.

49 Kraft 'Congress and Environmental Policy', p.172.

50 See Arnold *The Logic of Congressional Action*, footnote 7, p.8.

51 See Richard F. Fenno *Congressmen in Committees* (Boston: Little, Brown, 1973); Lawrence C. Dodd 'Congress and the Quest for Power' in Lawrence C. Dodd and Bruce I. Oppenheimer (eds), *Congress Reconsidered* (New York: Praeger, 1977); Richard L. Hall 'Participation and Purpose in Committee Decision-Making', *American Political Science Review* (1987), 81:105–28; Glenn R. Parker *Institutional Change, Discretion, and the Making of the Modern Congress* (Ann Arbor, MI: University of Michigan Press, 1992).

52 Richard L. Hall *Participation in Congress* (New Haven, CN: Yale University Press, 1996).

53 Richard F. Fenno *Home Style* (Boston: Little, Brown, 1978); John R. Hibbing *Congressional Careers* (Chapel Hill, NC: University of North Carolina Press, 1991).

54 Mayhew *Congress*, p.138.

55 Arnold *The Logic of Congressional Action*, pp.79–80.

56 Some empirical support for this argument is provided in Steven J. Kelman *What Price Incentives? Economists and the Environment* (Boston: Auburn House, 1981).

57 The Clean Air Act Amendments 1970 (CAA70) directed the EPA to establish NSPSs to control air pollution from newly constructed sources based on the 'best technological system of continuous emission reduction' available. The 1977 Amendments (CAA77) expanded the use of technology-based approaches. New sources of pollution that wished to locate in areas that had not met a least one of the NAAQS were required to install technology that would ensure the 'lowest achievable emissions rate' (LAER), major new sources in other areas had to install 'reasonably available control technology' (RACT).

58 CAA90 created a market for tradable emissions allowances in sulphur dioxide. See Brennan Van Dyke 'Emissions Trading to Reduce Acid Deposition', *Yale Law Review* (1991), 100:2707–26. The first trades took place in May 1992 when the Wisconsin Power and Light Co. sold 10,000 permits to the Tennessee Valley Authority for $250–$300 per ton. See Alan Ingham 'The Market for Sulphur Dioxide Permits in the USA and UK', *Environmental Politics* (1993), 2:114.

59 CAA70 required the EPA to identify chemicals that 'might reasonable be anticipated to result in an increasing mortality or an increase in serious irreversible, or incapacitating reversible illness', and then to issue National Emission Standards for Hazardous Air Pollutants (NESHAPs) that would protect public health by an ample margin of safety.

60 See William H. Robinson and Clay H. Wellborn (eds), *Knowledge, Power and the Congress* (Washington, DC: Congressional Quarterly Press, 1991); Bruce Bimber 'Information As A Factor In Congressional Politics', *Legislative Studies Quarterly* (1991), 16:585–606; Paul Sabatier and David Whiteman 'Legislative Decisionmaking and Substantive Policy Formation: Models of Information Flow', *Legislative Studies Quarterly* (1985), 10:395–421; and Robert Zwier 'The Search for Information: Specialists and Non-Specialists in the US House of Representatives', *Legislative Studies Quarterly* (1979), 4:31–42.

61 Keith Krehbiel *Information and Legislative Organization* (Ann Arbor, MI: University of Michigan Press, 1991).

62 An important exception is Jones *Clean Air*.

63 Jones 'A Way of Life and Law', p.2.

64 Theda Skocpol *Protecting Mothers and Soldiers* (Cambridge, MA: Harvard University Press, 1992), p.12.

65 See also Samuel P. Hays 'Three Decades of Environmental Politics: The Historical Context' in Michael J. Lacey (ed.), *Government and Environmental Politics* (Washington, DC: Woodrow Wilson Center Press, 1989), pp.19–79.

66 For a more general discussion of these changes see Ronald Inglehart *Culture Shift in Advanced Industrial Society* (Princeton, NJ: Princeton University Press, 1990).

67 See Michael J. Lacey 'The Environmental Revolution and the Growth of the State: Overview and Introduction' in Michael J. Lacey (ed.), *Government and Environmental Politics* (Washington, DC: Woodrow Wilson Center Press, 1989), p.4.

68 David Vogel *National Styles of Regulation* (Ithaca, NY: Cornell University Press, 1987) p.250.

69 See Zachary A. Smith *The Environmental Policy Paradox* (Englewood Cliffs, NJ: Prentice-Hall, 1992), pp.7–8.

70 Christopher J. Bosso 'Environmental Values and Democratic Institutions' in John Martin Gilroy (ed.), *Environmental Risk, Environmental Values, and Political Choice* (Boulder, CO: Westview Press, 1993), p.74.

71 Skocpol, *Protecting Mother and Soldiers*, p.17.

72 *Ibid.*, p.22.

73 This approach to the study of policy-making dates back to Arthur Bentley *The Process of Government* (Chicago: University of Chicago Press, 1908). See also David Truman *The Governmental Process* (New York, Knopf, 1951).

74 Earl Latham 'The Group Basis of Politics: Notes for a Theory' *American Political Science Review* (1952), 46:390.

75 The economic literature on regulatory origins is vast. Seminal studies include: George Stigler 'The Theory of Economic Regulation', *Bell Journal of Economics and Management Science* (1971), 2:3–21; Richard A. Posner 'Theories of Economic Regulation', *Bell Journal of Economics and Management Science* (1974), 5:335–58; Sam Peltzman 'Toward a More General Theory of Regulation', *Journal of Law and Economics* (1976), 19:211–40; Gary Becker 'Competition Among Interest Groups for Political Influence', *Quarterly Journal of Economics* (1983), 98:371–98.

76 Richard Posner, 'Economics, Politics, and the Reading of Statutes and the Constitution', *University of Chicago Law Review* (1982), 59:265.

77 Business groups have been accused of promoting 'non-decisionmaking'. See Matthew Crenson *The Un-politics of Air Pollution: A Study of Non-decisionmaking in the Cities* (Baltimore: Johns Hopkins University Press, 1971). Conversely, the auto manufacturers promoted national emissions standards in the late 1960s in order to forestall the introduction of state emission standards. See Susan Rose-Ackerman 'Does Federalism Matter? Political Choice in a Federal Republic', *Journal of Political Economy* (1981), 89:152–65.

78 Christopher J. Bailey 'Explaining the Choice of Air-Pollution Control Strategies in the United States: Some Evidence of Institutional Bias', *Environmental Politics* (1996), 5:85–9.

79 John P. Heinz, Edward O. Laumann, Robert L. Nelson and Robert H.

Salisbury *The Hollow Core* (Cambridge, MA: Harvard University Press, 1993), p.12.

80 Elliot, Ackerman and Millian 'Toward a Theory of Statutory Evolution, p.321.

81 The literature on policy subsystems or networks is enormous. For a sample see Hugh Heclo 'Issue Networks and the Executive Establishment' in Anthony King (ed.), *The New American Political System* (Washington, DC: American Enterprise Institute, 1978); Brinton H. Milward and Gary Walmsley 'Policy Subsystems, Networks, and the Tools of Public Management' in Robert Eyestone (ed.), *Public Policy Formation and Implementation* (New York: JAI Press, 1984); Paul Sabatier 'Political Science and Public Policy', *PS: Political Science and Politics* (1991), 24:144–56; Heinz, Laumann, Nelson and Salisbury *The Hollow Core*; and Robert M. Stein and Kenneth N. Bickers *Perpetuating the Pork Barrel: Policy Subsystems and American Democracy* (Cambridge: Cambridge University Press, 1995).

82 Sabatier 'Political Science and Public Policy', pp.132–3, 140–1.

83 See Keith Dowding 'Model or Metaphor? A Critical Review of the Policy Network Approach', *Political Studies* (1995), 43:136–58.

84 Sabatier acknowledges that 'institutions bring critical resources – e.g. the authority to make certain types of authoritative decisions – to members of the [advocacy] coalition' ('Political Science and Public Policy', p.140), but does not develop this point further.

85 See Skocpol *Protecting Mothers and Soldiers*, p.47.

86 See E. E. Schattschneider *The Semi-Sovereign People* (Hinsdale, IL: Dryden Press, 1960), p.71.

87 Daniel J. Fiorino *Making Environmental Policy* (Berkeley, CA: University of California Press, 1995), p.23.

88 The importance of Congress to agenda-setting and policy innovation is examined in John W. Kingdon *Agendas, Alternatives, and Public Policies* (Boston: Little, Brown, 1984) and Nelson W. Polsby *Policy Innovation in America* (New Haven, CN: Yale University Press, 1984).

89 Kraft 'Congress and Environmental Policy', p.170.

90 Christopher J. Bosso *Pesticides and Politics* (Pittsburgh, PA: University of Pittsburgh Press, 1987), p.14.

91 Ringquist 'Evaluating Environmental Policy Customers', p.304.

92 Hall *Participation in Congress*, pp.86–7.

93 See H. Eckstein 'Case Study and Theory in Political Science' in Fred I. Greenstein and Nelson W. Polsby (eds), *Handbook of Political Science* vol. 7 (Reading, MA: Addison-Wesley, 1975), pp.79–137.

94 Richard F. Fenno 'Observation, Context, and Sequence in the Study of Politics', *American Political Science Review* (1986), 80:3–16.

2
Understanding legislative production

Why has Congress enacted air pollution control laws at particular times? Why was the first air pollution control law enacted in 1955? Why were significant amendments to the Clean Air Act passed in 1963, 1970, 1977 and 1990? Why are some forms of air pollution addressed in these statutes and others not? How can Congress's choice of solutions to these problems be explained? Why has Congress chosen health-based standards to control certain forms of air pollution and technology-based standards to control others? How can changes in the means of air pollution control be explained?

Providing satisfactory answers to these questions is not easy. The air pollution control laws of the United States have been shaped by a wide range of factors: problem definition, understanding and saliency; constitutional arrangements that divide power between different levels of government; the goals and skills of legislators; institutional arrangements that confer parliamentary authority and specify procedures for aggregating preferences; and the vagaries of 'lady luck'. To impose some initial order on this swirling tangle of people, rules, problems and events a conceptual framework is needed which can provide 'a broad language and a form of reference in which reality can be examined'.[1] The challenge is to make sufficient sense of a complex law-making universe to allow observations about the importance and relationship of the various variables to be made.

Treating the production of laws as analogous to the production of goods offers a conceptual framework that can provide necessary order. Some disquiet may be felt about treating laws as goods as they obviously do not share all the attributes of commodities like automobiles.[2] The idea of a market in good quality, previously owned, low-mileage air pollution control laws, for example, is patently absurd. Characterizing laws as goods, however, serves both mnemonic and analytical functions. It affords an important reminder that laws have to be fashioned. Law-making does not simply involve a choice between paired alternatives. A legislative entrepreneur is needed to identify a problem, craft a solution and obtain the support of colleagues.[3] Treating laws as goods also focuses attention on the resources needed to produce legislation. It invites consideration of the costs and benefits involved in law-making.[4]

A conceptual framework

Adopting a conceptual framework that treats laws as goods means that economic theories of enterprise and production may be used to impose some order on the complex law-making universe. Law-making will occur when a legislative entrepreneur believes that the 'profit' that can be obtained from crafting a law will be greater than could be achieved by alternative forms of action, and has both the skill and resources necessary to overcome obstacles to production. The shape of the law that is produced will be determined by both a legislative entrepreneur's purpose and the resources that are available for law-making. This simple appropriation of economic theory, however, is of little practical value without further clarification of key terms. Particular attention needs to be given to the notion of what constitutes 'profit' in a legislative setting. What 'benefits' will a legislative entrepreneur enjoy from crafting a law? How will these 'benefits' change over time? What 'costs' must be borne if a law is to be produced? Are these costs fixed or variable? Answers to these questions need to be given if the timing and shape of air pollution control laws is to be explained.

The benefits of legislative enterprise
Virtually all economic theories of enterprise posit that entrepreneurs are motivated by the prospect of personal financial reward. 'Alert' individuals 'discover' or 'create' market opportunities which can be exploited to make money.[5] Little explanatory power is gained, unfortunately, by suggesting that legislative entrepreneurs are motivated by the prospect of monetary gain.[6] Although examples of corruption in Congress suggest that it is not inconceivable

for a legislative entrepreneur to be motivated by the promise of personal financial reward, the prospect of making money from crafting laws is too limited to serve as the motivation for all legislative action.[7] The notion of 'profit' in a legislative setting requires a much broader appreciation of what might motivate a legislator to craft a law than simple monetary gain.

The rich literature on Congress suggests that legislators are motivated by a 'mix' of goals.[8] They may wish to promote their chances of gaining re-election, make good public policy, gain institutional prestige, help the President achieve his objectives or even become rich. A necessary condition of law-making, therefore, is that legislative entrepreneurship must offer the prospect of advancing these goals. This does not mean that legislators have a 'generally applicable motivational map that they introspectively consult' when deciding whether to take action.[9] It simply means that legislators will evaluate law-making opportunities to determine whether the benefits of activity are relevant to their interests at that time. No law-making will occur if appropriate benefits are absent or not identified.

Some of the benefits that can be derived from crafting a law depend upon the characteristics of the issue under consideration. Levels of constituency concern, the availability of 'legislative pork', and the prospect of securing campaign contributions from interest groups will help determine the level of electoral benefits that may be accrued from legislative entrepreneurship. Not only may re-election prospects be boosted from legislative entrepreneurship if an issue is salient to constituents and a solution can be fashioned with a strong distributive element, but interest groups may also make contributions to a legislator's campaign fund as a 'reward' for legislative activity.[10] Levels of public and elite concern will help determine the amount of satisfaction that a legislative entrepreneur may gain from addressing a major public problem. An opportunity to establish a reputation as a national rather than parochial politician may be available if legislation can be fashioned which deals with a national problem.

Other potential benefits from legislative entrepreneurship are largely independent of the characteristics of the issue under consideration. Whereas any electoral and policy benefits from law-making depend primarily upon the *product* that is crafted, it is more the *act* of legislative enterprise that will further a legislator's reputation with colleagues and the White House. Institutional prestige depends upon how other legislators evaluate performance. The act of legislative entrepreneurship is probably more important in influencing these evaluations than the product of that enterprise. Similarly, a legislator's reputation as a friend or lackey of the White House is determined by efforts to promote the presidential agenda. It is activity on behalf of the President that is important and not the product of that activity.

The various benefits (see Table 2.1) that may be derived from legislative entrepreneurship are neither uniform, mutually exclusive nor necessarily unidirectional. Associated with each law-making opportunity is a particular matrix of benefits. Some may offer a wide range of benefits. Crafting a law may boost legislators' chances of re-election, enhance their institutional prestige, make them feel good about addressing a major public problem, and secure them credit with the administration. Other opportunities may offer a more limited range of benefits. Law-making may boost legislators' re-election prospects but bring no other benefits. Yet other opportunities may offer benefits in some areas but incur costs in others. Making good public policy may bring a warm glow to legislators' hearts, but might harm their re-election prospects if it imposes particularistic costs on their constituencies or detracts too much from casework.

The individual and subjective nature of the evaluation of benefits means that it is impossible to predict with certainty which law-making opportunities will attract legislative entrepreneurs. Not all legislators are imbued with the same entrepreneurial nous or zest. Some may not perceive the benefits that may accrue from action. Not everyone, after all, has an eye for a market opportunity. The existence of benefits will become more obvious, of course, if a legislative entrepreneur has already exploited a market opportunity. Successful 'profit-making' will send a signal to other legislators that benefits are available and competition should follow as a result. Even such signals, however, may be insufficient to generate activity in all quarters. A legislator may perceive benefits but lack the energy to do anything about them. The world is filled with bar-room entrepreneurs with cast-iron plans to become millionaires.

Even when legislators have identified the benefits that may accrue from a law-making opportunity and also possesses sufficient energy to engage in entrepreneurial activity, they may be unable to assemble

Table 2.1 *The incidence of legislative benefits*

	Electoral	Good policy	Institutional prestige	Help president	Make money
High	Issue affects constituency Opportunities for pork-barrelling Opportunities for PAC contributions	Issue has national prominence Elite concern about issue	Opportunity to impress peers	Presidential interest in issue	Opportunity for corruption
Low	Issue does not affect constituency Few opportunities for pork-barrelling Limited PAC interest	Issue does not have national prominence Little elite concern about issue	No opportunity to impress colleagues	No presidential interest in issue	No opportunity for corruption

the resources that are needed to take action. Fashioning a law involves costs that need to be met. Not all legislators are equally endowed with adequate resources to meet these costs. Even when needed resources are possessed, legislators may decide that the 'opportunity cost' of a particular law-making opportunity is too high. 'Position-taking' or casework may offer a better return for the investment of scarce resources than legislative entrepreneurship. 'Profit' involves a calculation, after all, of both benefits and costs.

The costs of legislative enterprise

The costs that typically confront legislators considering whether to take advantage of a law-making opportunity can be divided into two broad types: information costs and transaction costs.[11] Information costs are the time and effort needed to acquire policy expertise. Legislative entrepreneurs must acquire not only information about a problem, but also about possible solutions. They must obtain knowledge about the extent and cause of a problem, the best way that it can be addressed and the political outcomes of such solutions.[12] Transaction costs are the time and effort needed to obtain enactment of a law.[13] Legislative entrepreneurs will need to consult colleagues, negotiate compromises and put together winning coalitions at each stage of the legislative process. They will need to persuade others that their proposed law addresses a significant problem in a competent way and will do no political harm.

The level of these costs will depend upon the characteristics of the particular law-making opportunity that interests legislative entrepreneurs. Information costs will be relatively low when an issue is either simple or the amount of knowledge available is limited. In both cases the acquisition of sufficient information to fashion a law should not consume large amounts of time and resources. The opposite will be true when an issue is complex or the subject of considerable research. Obtaining and processing information under such circumstances will take time and resources.[14] Transaction costs will be relatively low when an issue is highly salient and unidimensional. Not only will public pressure for action facilitate attempts to enact legislation, but the 'scope of conflict' associated with the issue will be limited.[15] The converse will hold when an issue lacks saliency or is multidimensional. Low public saliency means that legislators may not be under pressure to reach agreement while the 'scope of conflict' associated with a multidimensional issue is likely to be high.

A law-making opportunity with high information and transaction costs (see Table 2.2) is unlikely to attract legislative entrepreneurs as the opportunity cost of producing legislation will usually be too large to bear. Legislators will receive a greater return on their investment of time and resources, in other words, by doing something else. Legislative production is most likely to occur when costs are low as a 'profit' will be easier to make. Even when costs are low, however, a law may not be produced if a legislative entrepreneur lacks the resources to meet such costs. Resources are essential to legislative production.

Table 2.2   *The incidence of legislative costs*

	Information costs	Transaction costs
High	Problem is complex Problem is well researched	Scope of conflict is large Problem is multidimensional Problem lacks saliency
Low	Problem is simple Little is known about problem	Scope of conflict is limited Problem is unidimensional Problem is salient

All members of Congress have some resources at their disposal. Even the most junior representative or senator has certain parliamentary rights. All have an unlimited right to introduce bills and all have equal votes in divisions. The parliamentary position of junior senators is further bolstered by extensive amending and debating rights. Junior members are also provided with offices, equipment and staff to a degree that is unknown in other national legislatures.[16] A dramatic expansion of these resources in the 1970s even led some commentators to characterize members' offices as 'legislative enterprises'.[17] For all these comparative riches, however, junior members still have fewer resources than colleagues occupying more senior positions. Although the relative power of party leaders, committee chairs and junior members has fluctuated over time, those legislators fortunate enough to occupy party or institutional positions have always had more resources than junior members. Party leaders and committee chairs have parliamentary rights that allow them to make authoritative decisions at certain stages of the legislative process, and staff resources that provide them with considerable information processing and gathering capacity.

This unequal distribution of resources in Congress means that the costs involved in law-making may present formidable 'barriers to entry' that will deny many legislative entrepreneurs access to the 'market'. Although both information costs and transaction costs can be reduced by fashioning legislation that is unambitious and non-controversial, the costs of law-making will usually be 'nontrivial'.[18] Best positioned to meet such costs are majority party leaders and committee chairs. Possession of both parliamentary authority and abundant staff means that they are well placed to assimilate information and to negotiate with other legislators. Less able to engage in legislative entrepreneurship are junior members of the majority party and most members of the minority party.[19] Denied parliamentary authority and with fewer staff, they may find it difficult to obtain information, and will certainly struggle to persuade or cajole colleagues to do their bidding.[20]

It is not impossible for junior members of the majority party and members of the minority party to become successful legislative entrepreneurs. Several studies have shown the impact that these legislators can have.[21] The need for resources to meet the costs of production, however, means that legislative entrepreneurs are most likely to be drawn from the ranks of the party and committee leadership. Laws are produced primarily by legislators occupying positions of institutional authority.

Legislative enterprise and 'market conditions'
Economic theories of enterprise postulate that 'market conditions' will be transformed by the actions of an entrepreneur. Profit will send a signal to other entrepreneurs to enter the market, and the matrix of costs and benefits associated with production will be altered as a result. Not only will competition over the resources needed for production drive costs upwards, but the increased availability of substitute products will mean that available benefits have to be divided among many entrepreneurs. To slow or stop this process, successful entrepreneurs will seek to erect 'barriers to entry' that will dissuade competitors from entering the market. Successful entrepreneurs may seek legal protection or employ economic means to maintain a monopolistic position. Competitors may respond by attempting to create niches for their products. Production may also provide opportunities for other entrepreneurs to make a profit by supplying components or catering to new demands

generated as a result of the actions of the original entrepreneur. The entrepreneurship of Henry Ford, for example, provided opportunities which numerous other entrepreneurs were able to exploit.

The idea that entrepreneurship changes market conditions is an important conceptual insight that can be usefully applied to legislative production. Law-making changes the *status quo* in several respects. Not only do laws advantage certain interests in society and disadvantage others, but they also invariably promote the development of new institutional arrangements. This means that the matrix of costs and benefits associated with an issue will be transformed as a result of legislative entrepreneurship. Production of a law will create both new incentives for further entrepreneurship, and new barriers to action. 'As politics creates policies, policies also remake politics' Theda Skocpol has noted.[22]

Legislative production will change the benefits associated with law-making on a particular issue in at least three different ways. First, the public saliency of an issue is likely to fall if a law is produced.[23] This will lead to a reassessment of the electoral benefits associated with the issue. Second, enactment of a law is likely to leave an institutional legacy that will usually provide new opportunities to garner institutional prestige.[24] Benefits may be available to those who take action to maintain the institutional structures that evolve to process a new issue. Third, and perhaps most important, the fact that laws create winners and losers will generate new incentives for legislative enterprise.[25] While some legislative entrepreneurs may seek to help groups that have been advantaged by a law to maintain their benefits, others may wish to come to the aid of disadvantaged groups.

The costs associated with law-making on a particular issue will also change if a law is enacted. Information costs are likely to rise considerably as a result of law-making. Not only will bureaucrats, academics and interest groups produce more information about an issue, but this information is likely to be increasingly contested as different groups offer competing advice as to the best way forward. Both the acquisition and assimilation of this knowledge will consume scarce legislative resources. Transaction costs will similarly rise as groups affected by a law mobilize supporters to protect their interests. Legislative entrepreneurs will find it more difficult, as a result, to obtain the majorities needed to enact significant changes to a law.

Examples of successful legislative enterprise will usually tempt other legislators into the 'market'. While some may wish to compete directly for the benefits that flow from addressing a particular issue, others may seek to exploit opportunities created by the production of the earlier law. The ability of these legislative entrepreneurs to penetrate the 'market' will depend upon how easy it is to overcome any 'barriers to entry' that the original entrepreneur is able to establish. Successful legislative entrepreneurs will seek to establish and maintain a law-making monopoly which allows them to continue making a profit.[26] The better they are able to control flows of information, define the issue, and specify alternatives, the longer they will be able to reap the benefits of their entrepreneurship.

The prominent role of committees and their subcommittees in the legislative process means that control of a panel that has jurisdiction over an issue is the key to establishing a law-making monopoly. Control of a committee and subcommittee that has jurisdiction over an issue confers tremendous informational and transactional advantages on legislative entrepreneurs wishing to legislate in that area. Not only do professional committee and subcommittee staff provide a level of policy expertise that is not readily available to non-members, but the panels also possess some 'gatekeeping' powers which can be used to control the flow and shape of legislation.[27] This latter point is particularly important. Committee jurisdictions may be viewed as a functional equivalent of patents: they bestow 'policy property rights' on a group of legislators.[28] Legislative entrepreneurs who are not in control of a relevant committee or subcommittee are unlikely to establish a law-making monopoly.

The ability of successful legislative entrepreneurs to maintain a law-making monopoly once established will depend, in large part, upon their skill in defending jurisdictional barriers from encroachment. Evidence of 'profit-making' is likely to prompt legislative entrepreneurs who control other committees to engage in 'turf battles'. Just as entrepreneurs in the business world may seek to negate patents through marginal changes in design, so predatory legislative entrepreneurs may attempt to circumvent the 'policy property rights' held by another committee by redefining an issue in terms that allow legislation to be processed in a committee under their control.[29] They are likely to be aided in this endeavour by those interest groups that have been disadvantaged by the production of a law.[30] Losers always have an incentive to change the rules under which the game is played. Interest groups that have been advantaged by the production of a law, conversely, will strive to protect the law-making monopoly that benefited them.

The success of challenges to 'policy property rights' depends primarily upon the nature of the issue and the elasticity of the predatory committee's jurisdiction. A complex, multi-dimensional issue will be easier to redefine than a simple, unidimensional one. Not all committees are equally well placed, however, to make plausible jurisdictional claims even when an issue is multi-dimensional. The broader and more elastic the existing jurisdiction of a predatory committee, the easier it will be to gain a 'seat at the table'. Law-making monopolies may also be broken by systemic changes. New external challenges or a dramatic turnover in membership may be sufficient to bring about a realignment of 'policy property rights'.[31]

'Turf battles' will inevitably erode a law-making monopoly over time and create opportunities for other legislative entrepreneurs to enter the 'market'. Any laws produced by these legislative entrepreneurs will, in turn, create new incentives for further legislation. 'Legislation unquestionably generates legislation', Woodrow Wilson noted over a century ago, 'Once begin the dance of legislation, and you must struggle through its mazes as best you can to its breathless end, – if any end there be'.[32]

The timing and shape of legislation

The production of a law is not easy. Legislative entrepreneurs have to identify an opportunity to make a 'profit', design a product that allows this 'profit' to be realized and assemble the resources needed for production. They will need to persuade colleagues that the issue they wish to address is important, that the solution they have devised is the best available, and that political good, or at least no harm, will come from enactment. Success will depend upon the saliency of the issue that legislative entrepreneurs wish to address, the level of conflict surrounding the issue, the design of the legislative product, the preferences of other legislators and the capabilities of the legislative entrepreneur. Although the legislative process is too complex and chaotic to allow precise predictions about the production of legislation, some observations about the timing and shape of laws can be made if a conceptual framework that treats laws as goods is adopted.

The timing of legislation depends, in the first instance, upon a law-making opportunity being brought to the attention of a legislator. Initial interest in an issue is likely to be sparked when it is obviously visible, highly salient or vigorously promoted by powerful interest groups. Some issues explode on to the legislative consciousness as a result of some 'catalytic event'; others take time to permeate through layers of disinterest. The legislator's decision to engage in law-making activity on a particular issue is subjective and impossible to predict with any accuracy. Entrepreneurship is more likely to occur, however, in certain circumstances than others. A possibility to make a 'profit' is likely to be perceived when an issue is important to constituents, is perceived as nationally important and has low costs associated with it.

The shape of legislation will be determined to a large extent by the nature of the 'profit' that the legislative entrepreneur wishes to obtain from action on an issue. Distributive policy laden with particularistic benefits is likely to be designed if the intention is simply to enhance electoral prospects. 'Pork-barrelling' is a well-known means of courting constituents. Distributive policy has a further advantage of low costs. 'Throwing money at a problem' is not only easily understood, but usually arouses little sustained conflict as long as the 'pork' is widely distributed.[33] Regulatory policy is more likely if the intention is to make good public policy. Legislators wishing to address a problem in society will usually try to manipulate the behaviour that causes the problem. A disadvantage of regulatory policy is that both information and transaction costs are likely to be high. Knowledge is needed about the efficacy of various regulatory tools, and levels of conflict will often be high.

Different legislative benefits and costs are associated with different regulatory tools, and the legislative entrepreneur will seek to employ those tools that maximize pertinent benefits but minimize costs.[34] Legislators wishing to enhance re-election prospects will be tempted by tools which promise obvious short-term gains but postpone costs into the future.[35] Those wishing to make good public policy may be more willing to forgo short-term gains and choose tools that promise long-term policy success. The choice of tools will be mediated, however, by legislative costs.[36] Both information and transaction costs may be reduced if legislation is designed which employs tools familiar to all. Learning about new solutions, and persuading colleagues that they work, requires resources that the legislative entrepreneur may not have to hand.[37]

Information costs and transaction costs may be reduced further by delegating authority to an agency. Rather than devote resources to learning about a complex, highly technical issue, a legislative entrepreneur may prefer to design a law which specifies a broad goal and leaves the particulars to a bureaucrat to fathom out.[38] This has the further advantage of being a useful blame avoidance strategy.[39] Legislators can blame the bureaucracy when problems are not resolved. Greater discretion may also be given to bureaucrats in order to overcome problems in obtaining agreement on specific legislative formulations.[40] Obtaining agreement on a general, perhaps vague, goal is often easier than securing agreement on the precise means by which that goal will be achieved.[41]

Enactment of a law will depend upon the ability of legislative entrepreneurs to garner support for their products. The ease with which this can be achieved is contingent upon the skills of the legislators, the design of the law, the saliency of the issue and the characteristics of the membership. Legislative production is most likely to end in enactment when a skilled entrepreneur who occupies a position of parliamentary authority is able to design a product that addresses a highly salient issue in a way that minimizes conflict. The nature of the legislative process suggests that laws will usually specify general goals, employ familiar regulatory tools and delegate considerable authority to the bureaucracy.

The legislative benefits and costs of air pollution control

The key to understanding the production of air pollution control legislation is the matrix of benefits and costs associated with the issue at a particular time. Many of the benefits flow from public perceptions about the nature of the problem. Air pollution has been regarded variously over time as a sign of economic progress, a local nuisance and a major national problem. Opportunities to reap electoral rewards or secure praise for tackling a major public problem have risen and ebbed as a result. Other benefits derive from the creation of institutional structures. These have remained fairly constant. The costs flow from the characteristics of the issue. Air pollution control has many of the attributes of a public good, requires the assimilation of complex and uncertain technical information, cannot be easily contained within a single policy dimension and affects a large number of interests. These costs have tended to rise as a result of increased government activity.

Legislative benefits of air pollution control

Improved re-election prospects, an enhanced reputation for making good public policy, greater institutional prestige, and fame as a friend of the White House have all been associated with air pollution control since the 1940s. Poor local air quality has provided legislators with opportunities to enhance re-election prospects by supporting action to clean the air. The perception that air pollution is a national problem has allowed legislators to establish reputations for policy leadership on a major issue. The creation of institutional structures to process air pollution control issues has given legislators opportunities to gain institutional prestige. Finally, presidential interest in the issue has provided opportunities for legislators to serve the President. Not all of these benefits have been available to all legislators all of the time. Fluctuations in public opinion, the vagaries of geography and the accident of institutional position have led to considerable variation in the magnitude and range of benefits available to different legislators at different times.

Public concern about air pollution has risen and fallen over time. This has produced considerable variation in the magnitude of the electoral benefits that have been available from involvement in the issue. Before the Second World War public concern with air pollution was localized and sporadic. Few electoral incentives existed for members of Congress to fashion laws on the subject. After the Second World War a growing public awareness of the dangers posed by air pollution provided greater opportunities to reap electoral rewards from control efforts. Dramatic changes in the saliency of the issue during this period, however, have produced variation in the magnitude of the electoral benefits that have been available. The high saliency of air pollution during the late 1960s and the late 1980s produced significant electoral benefits from involvement in the issue. Concerns about the economy and energy supplies in the 1970s reduced the electoral benefits that could be reaped from championing air pollution control.

Variation in air quality across the United States means that the possibility of enhancing electoral prospects by addressing a local problem is not available to all legislators. Legislators representing constituencies blessed with pristine air will gain little in the way of direct electoral benefits from displaying an interest in air pollution whereas those representing areas with poor air quality may gain a great deal from taking action. In the decade immediately following the Second World War the areas where air pollution was a *recognized* problem included California and the environs of New York City. Increasing use of the automobile in subsequent decades made air pollution a major problem in most of the country's urban areas. The air quality of some Rocky Mountain states, none the less, remained relatively good. Legislators representing these areas do not have the same incentive to promote air pollution control measures as their colleagues from Los Angeles, New York and Denver.

    The number of institutional structures that have been created to process air pollution control issue is limited. This has severely restricted the number of legislators who are in a position to impress colleagues through the production of legislation. Since the mid-1950s air pollution control legislation has been fashioned primarily in the Subcommittee on Health and the Environment of the House Committee on Commerce, and the Subcommittee on Clean Air, Wetlands, Private Property and Nuclear Safety of the Senate Committee on Environment and Public Works.[42] Government action to control air pollution has provided legislators on these panels with recurring opportunities to show colleagues that they can produce laws as statutes have needed periodic reauthorization. The availability of benefits has been fairly constant, as a result, but few have the opportunity to enjoy them.

    Finally, the engagement of presidents with air pollution control issues has fluctuated considerably. Although presidential intervention has proved a *sine qua non* for the enactment of major air pollution control laws, few presidents have made it a priority. Only Presidents Nixon and Bush have devoted much attention to the issue. This has tended to make 'bag carrying' for the administration a reactive rather than proactive operation. Opportunities to curry favour by working to secure passage of air pollution control legislation close to the administration's heart have been few and far between. The more usual function has been to dilute or obstruct proposals with which the administration disagrees.

    A significant feature of the various benefits that have been available from legislative action to control air pollution is their different elasticities.[43] Electoral and presidential 'bag carrying' benefits have been relatively elastic while institutional benefits have been more inelastic. Incentives have always been available to a few legislators to craft air pollution control laws, but the type of benefits that would generate widespread legislative enterprise have been available rather infrequently.

Legislative costs of air pollution control

The legislative costs associated with air pollution control have risen since the 1940s. Information costs have soared as the amount of technical knowledge that needs to be assimilated to fashion legislation has grown without becoming any less controversial. The fundamental tasks of identifying the extent of a problem, isolating causes and evaluating potential solutions have become especially difficult. Transaction costs have also increased. Persuading colleagues to accept specific legislative proposals to control air pollution has become difficult as disputes about the science have raged and the economic costs of action have become apparent. Interests mobilized by previous laws have made it difficult to enact new laws.

The information costs associated with air pollution control have changed beyond all recognition since the end of the Second World War. In the early 1950s little policy expertise was needed to fashion air pollution control legislation because little was known about the problem and the ambition of proposed solutions was limited. Assimilating available knowledge was relatively easy. Increased research and greater ambition in later decades created more significant barriers to entry. The wish to do more to control air pollution meant that legislative entrepreneurs had to obtain and assimilate increased amounts of complex and uncertain technical information about the problem and potential solutions. High information costs began to restrict entry into the market in the late 1960s and have continued to do so ever since. Floor participation has also been structured by the technical complexity of air pollution control issues. Few members have the information to challenge committee expertise on the issue.[44]

The transaction costs associated with air pollution control have followed a similar trajectory to information costs. Although the need to persuade colleagues that the federal government should become involved in controlling air pollution posed a problem to early legislative entrepreneurs, the limited ambition of their legislation ensured that conflict was kept to a minimum. Few legislators objected to the federal government promoting research or helping the states. Subsequent efforts to expand the role of the federal government, however, increased the transaction costs associated with the issue. Groups who believed that they would suffer as a result of government action mobilized to counter proposals. Transaction costs soared, in particular, following enactment of the Clean Air Act Amendments 1970 as increased government regulation dramatically expanded the scope of conflict associated with the issue. Persuading colleagues to accept new legislation has become correspondingly more difficult.

An interesting feature of the legislative costs associated with air pollution control is that they are far more inelastic than the benefits. The information costs that need to be overcome to produce legislation are high and inelastic. It is impossible to reduce the amount of knowledge that exists about a problem. Transaction costs can fall if public demand for legislation is strong enough to force compromise, but generally have continued to rise as more aspects of American life have come under the purview of new air pollution control laws. These high and relatively inelastic costs play a major role in structuring the production of air pollution control legislation. High costs mean that considerable benefits need to be available to tempt legislative entrepreneurs into the 'market'. Rare have been the occasions on which such benefits have been readily available.

Conclusion

The language of economics provides a means to impose some order on a chaotic law-making universe. Appropriation of terms such as 'profit', 'benefits' and 'costs' allows law-making to be conceptualized in a way in which the timing and shape of legislation can be understood. Understood not explained. Although certain expectations about the timing and shape of legislation can be generated when law-making is conceptualized as a form of production, the choice and form of legislation can only be properly explained by an examination of the context in which individual legislators make decisions. Case studies allow the importance of different variables to be uniquely specified in a way that is impossible using aggregate data.

Notes

1 Gerry Stoker 'Introduction' in David Marsh and Gerry Stoker (eds), *Theory and Methods in Political Science* (Basingstoke: Macmillan, 1995), p.18.

2 The idea that laws can be treated as goods is central to economic theories of the law. See Richard A. Posner *Economic Analysis of Law* 3rd edition (Boston: Little, Brown, 1986) pp.496–8.

3 See David E. Price 'Professionals and "Entrepreneurs": Staff Orientations and Policymaking on Three Senate Committees' *Journal of Politics* (1971), 33:316–36; Eric Uslaner 'Policy Entrepreneurs and Amateur Democrats in the House of Representatives: Toward a More Party-Oriented Congress?' in Leroy N. Rieselbach (ed.), *Legislative Reform* (Lexington, MA: Lexington Books, 1978); John W. Kingdon *Agendas, Alternatives, and Public Policies* (Boston: Little, Brown, 1984); Nelson W. Polsby *Political Innovation in America* (New Haven, CN: Yale University Press, 1984; Burdette Loomis *The New American Politician* (New York: Basic Books, 1988); Carol S. Weissert 'Policy Entrepreneurs, Policy Opportunists, and Legislative Effectiveness', *American Politics Quarterly* (1991), 19:262–74.

4 Kenneth Koford 'Different Preferences, Different Politics: A Demand-and-Structure Explanation' , *Western Political Quarterly* (1989), 42:15.

5 See Mark Casson *The Entrepreneur: An Economic Theory* (Oxford: Robertson, 1982); Israel M. Kirzner *Discovery and the Capitalist Process* (Chicago: University of Chicago Press, 1985).

6 See Mark Schneider and Paul Teske 'Toward A Theory Of The Political Entrepreneur: Evidence From Local Government', *American Political Science Review* (1992), 86:737–47; Michael Laver 'Political Solutions to the Collective Action Problem', *Political Studies* (1980), 28:195–209.

7 See Christopher J. Bailey 'Congress and the Crisis of Legitimacy' in Philip John Davies and Frederic A. Waldstein (eds), *Political Issues in America Today* (Manchester: Manchester University Press, 1996) especially pp.174–8.

8 Seminal studies include Richard F. Fenno *Congressmen in Committees* (Boston: Little, Brown, 1973); David R. Mayhew *Congress: The Electoral Connection* (New Haven, CN: Yale University Press, 1974); Morris P. Fiorina *Representatives, Roll Calls, and Constituencies* (Boston: Heath, 1974); Kenneth A. Shepsle *The Giant Jigsaw Puzzle: Democratic Committee Assignments in the Modern House* (Chicago: University of Chicago Press, 1978); John W. Kindon *Congressmen's Voting Decisions* 3rd edition (Ann Arbor, MI: University of Michigan Press, 1989); R. Douglas Arnold *The Logic of Congressional Action* (New Haven, CN: Yale University Press, 1990); Richard L. Hall *Participation in Congress* (New Haven, CN: Yale University Press, 1996).

 9 Hall *Participation in Congress*, p.77.
10 See Robert M. Stein and Kenneth N. Bickers *Perpetuating the Pork Barrel: Policy Subsystems and American Democracy* (Cambridge: Cambridge University Press, 1995).
11 See Hall *Participation in Congress*, pp.86–7.
12 The distinction between 'programmatic' or 'policy' information and 'political' information is common in the literature. A good discussion of the distinction between the two types of information can be found in Mark A. Peterson 'How Health Policy Information is Used in Congress' in Thomas E. Mann and Norman J. Ornstein (eds), *Intensive Care* (Washington, DC: Congressional Quarterly Press, 1995), pp.83–8. The empirical reality of the distinction is questioned in Keith Krehbiel *Information and Legislative Organization* (Ann Arbor, MI: University of Michigan Press, 1991), pp.67–68.
13 Murray J. Horn *The Political Economy of Public Administration* (Cambridge: Cambridge University Press, 1995), p.14.
14 See John S. Dryzek *Discursive Democracy* (Cambridge: Cambridge University Press, 1990), chapter 3.
15 E. E. Schattschneider *The Semi-Sovereign People* (Hinsdale, IL: Dryden Press, 1960).
16 Michael J. Malbin 'Delegation, Deliberation, and the New Role of Congressional Staff' in Thomas E. Mann and Norman J. Ornstein (eds), *The New Congress* (Washington, DC: American Enterprise Institute, 1981), p.135.
17 See Robert Salisbury and Kenneth Shepsle 'US Congressman as Enterprise' *Legislative Studies Quarterly* (1981), 6:559–76.
18 Hall *Participation in Congress*, p.87.
19 Junior and minority party senators are better placed than their counterparts in the House to become legislative entrepreneurs because of their greater institutional resources.
20 An excellent account of the problems of being in the minority is William F. Connelly and John J. Pitney *Congress's Permanent Minority? Republicans in the House* (Lanham, MD: Rowman and Littlefield, 1994). See also Christopher J. Bailey *The Republican Party in the US Senate 1974–1984* (Manchester: Manchester University Press, 1988).
21 See Loomis *The New American Politician*.
22 Theda Skocpol *Protecting Mothers and Soldiers* (Cambridge, MA: Harvard University Press, 1992) p.58.
23 See Anthony Downs 'Up and Down with Ecology – The "Issue-Attention Cycle"', *Public Interest* (1972), 28:38–50.
24 B. Guy Peters and B. Hogwood 'In Search of the Issue-Attention Cycle', *Journal of Politics* (1985), 47:239–53.

25 See Douglas Dion 'The Robustness of Structure-Induced Equilibrium', *American Journal of Political Science* (1992), 36:476.

26 Frank R. Baumgartner and Bryan D. Jones *Agendas and Instability in American Politics* (Chicago: University of Chicago Press, 1993) p.6.

27 See Krehbiel *Information and Legislative Organization*.

28 David C. King 'The Nature of Congressional Committee Jurisdictions', *American Political Science Review* (1994), 88:48.

29 See William H. Riker *The Art of Political Manipulation* (New Haven, CN: Yale University Press, 1986); Deborah A. Stone 'Causal Stories and the Formation of Policy Agendas', *Political Science Quarterly* (1989), 104:281–300; David A. Rochefort and Roger W. Cobb 'Problem Definition, Agenda Access, and Policy Choice', *Policy Studies Journal* (1993), 21:56–71

30 See Jack L. Walker 'Setting the Agenda in the US Senate' *British Journal of Political Science* (1977), 7:423–45; Bryan D. Jones, Frank R. Baumgartner and Jeffrey C. Talbert 'The Destruction of Issue Monopolies in Congress', *American Political Science Review* (1993), 87:657–72.

31 See Roger H. Davidson and Walter J. Oleszek 'Adaptation and Consolidation: Structural Innovation in the US House of Representatives', *Legislative Studies Quarterly* (1976), 1:37–66.

32 Woodrow Wilson *Congressional Government* (Baltimore: Johns Hopkins University Press, 1981, original edition published in 1885), p.195.

33 See Theodore Lowi 'Decision Making vs Policy Making: Toward an Antidote for Technocracy', *Public Administration Review* (1970), 30:314–25; Theodore Lowi 'Four Systems of Policy, Politics and Choice' *Public Administration Review* (1972), 32:299–310.

34 The literature on regulatory tools is extensive. A sample includes Christopher Hood *The Tools of Government* (London: Macmillan, 1984); Richard F. Elmore 'Instruments and Strategy in Public Policy', *Policy Studies Review* (1987), 7:174–86; and Anne Schneider and Helen Ingram 'Behavioral Assumptions of Policy Tools', *Journal of Politics* (1990), 52:510–29.

35 See James Q. Wilson 'The Politics of Regulation' in James W. McKie (ed.), *Social Responsibility and the Business Predicament* (Washington, DC: Brookings, 1974).

36 See Morris P. Fiorina 'Legislative Choice of Regulatory Form' *Public Choice* (1982), 39:45–6.

37 Stephen H. Linder and B. Guy Peters 'The Logic of Public Policy Design: Linking Policy Actors and Plausible Instruments', *Knowledge and Power* (1991), 4:129.

38 Patricia W. Ingraham 'Toward More Systematic Consideration of Policy Design', *Policy Studies Journal* (1987), 15:617.

39 See Arnold *The Logic of Congressional Action*.

40 See Matthew D. McCubbins and T. Page 'A Theory of Congressional Delegation' in Matthew D. McCubbins and Thomas Sullivan (eds), *Congress: Structure and Policy* (Cambridge: Cambridge University Press, 1987).
41 See Posner *Economic Analysis of Law*, p.513.
42 The name of these subcommittees and committees has changed over time. These are their latest incarnations.
43 I should like to thank my colleague Jon Herbert for this observation.
44 C. Lawrence Evans *Leadership in Committees* (Ann Arbor, MI: University of Michigan Press, 1991), pp.161–2.

3
Congressional interest in air pollution control

The level and nature of congressional interest in air pollution control has changed dramatically since the 1940s. Aggregate indicators of legislative activity such as bill introductions and committee hearings reveal an awakening of interest in the late 1940s and 1950s, a rapid increase in activity in the 1960s, slightly lower levels of activity in the 1970s, and a return to high levels of activity in the 1980s and 1990s. Not shown in these simple indicators of activity are changes in the nature of congressional efforts to control air pollution during this period. Research and financial assistance to the states was the primary purpose of most legislative activity until the mid-1960s, directing the states to take action to control air pollution became the main thrust of policy development during the late 1960s, and efforts to expand or reduce the role of the federal government in controlling air pollution have dominated activity since enactment of the Clean Air Act Amendments 1970.

These broad changes in the level and nature of congressional interest in air pollution control conform to the pattern of legislative activity that would be expected if law-making is conceptualized as a form of production. Congressional interest in controlling air pollution control was initiated by a few legislative entrepreneurs who fashioned unambitious laws to minimize the transaction costs of entry into a new policy domain. Further action followed as even the limited ambition of laws such as the Air Pollution Control Act 1955 left an institutional legacy replete with law-making opportunities. Incremental adjustments in policy ensued as new legislative entrepreneurs seized the chance to garner institutional prestige. A rapid rise in the public saliency of the issue in the late 1960s, however, provided the conditions for a radical change in policy. The prospect

of securing enormous electoral benefits from establishing a reputation as a policy leader on the issue prompted a law-making competition which produced the Clean Air Act Amendments 1970.
Enactment of the 1970 Amendments established the basic 'market
conditions' that have since shaped legislative activity on the issue.
High information and transaction costs created by the mobilization
of competing interests within the policy domain have led to considerable activity but made it difficult to produce laws. This character-
ization of the development of congressional interest in air pollution
control employs a slightly different language but is none the less
consistent with the analysis of events found in earlier studies by
Charles O. Jones and by E. Donald Elliot, Bruce A. Ackerman and
John C. Millian.[1] Both studies depict several phases in the development of air pollution control policy. Jones talks about different
phases in the acquisition of knowledge about the problem while
Elliot, Ackerman and Millian focus on the incentives that prompt
legislative action. Common to the two studies is the idea that law-
making is an evolutionary process. Laws have both 'ancestors' and
'descendents' to employ the language of Woodrow Wilson.[2]

The evolutionary nature of law-making means that it is important to map general trends in some detail. Although case studies are
necessary to understand the precise timing and shape of particular
laws, the use of aggregate data to establish patterns of law-making
activity provides a necessary broader picture. Without such contextualization all that would remain of a study of congressional efforts
to control air pollution would be a series of dislocated legislative
incidents.

Levels of congressional interest

Levels of congressional interest in air pollution control have grown
and widened since the first bill was introduced in 1949. Originally
the concern of a few legislators from heavily polluted states like California, New York and Pennsylvania, an interest in controlling air
pollution began to ripple across the country in the 1960s as the
saliency of the issue increased and the multi-dimensional nature of
the problem became apparent. Not only were more bills introduced
and more committee hearings conducted, but the number of legislators introducing bills and the number of committees holding hearings also increased as members engaged in 'position-taking' or

struggled for control of the issue. Interest fell briefly in the immediate aftermath of enactment of the Clean Air Act Amendments 1970, but soon stabilized at a level higher than that found during most of the 1960s. Periodic bursts of enthusiasm have subsequently occurred which generally match the public saliency of the issue.

Bill introductions

Although bills addressing the problem of air pollution in Washington, DC, had been introduced in Congress during the Progressive Era, the start of congressional interest in air pollution as a national issue can be dated to 1949.[3] Galvanized into action by an air pollution episode in Donora, Pennsylvania, in December 1948, two local Representatives responded to the concerns of their constituents and introduced legislation in Congress to promote research into the problem. Although no further action was taken on these two bills, they paved the way for other legislators to turn to the federal government for help in controlling air pollution. Leading demands for the federal government to provide some assistance to the states were members of the Californian delegation. The growing problem of automobile pollution in California, particularly Los Angeles, led to consistent agitation for federal financial and technical help. Similar demands soon began to be aired by Representatives from New York City and its surrounding environs.

The number of air pollution control bills introduced in Congress (see Figure 3.1) remained low until the intervention of President Eisenhower in 1955 provided a stimulus for an unprecedented outburst of legislative activity. Levels of activity were greatest in the House because the compact nature of urban constituencies generated demands for action that were not articulated across populations of entire states. The number of bills introduced in the House increased sevenfold in the 84th Congress (1955–56) as members of the Californian and New York delegations were joined by legislators representing other urban areas in demanding action. Enactment of the Air Pollution Control Act 1955 satisfied immediate demands for the federal government to assume a more prominent role in conducting research into air pollution. After falling to levels found in the early 1950s in the 85th Congress (1957–58), however, the number of air pollution control bills introduced in the House began to rise as increased evidence of the extent of the problem became available. Bill introductions even jumped in the Senate in the 88th

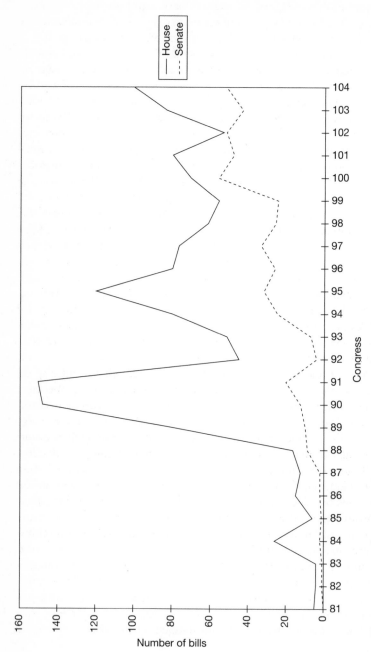

Figure 3.1 *Number of air pollution control bills introduced, by Congress*

Congress (1963–64) with the growing recognition that the problem of air pollution was not simply confined to urban areas. Enactment of the Clean Air Act 1963 flowed from this increased concern.

The number of air pollution control bills introduced in Congress did not fall in the immediate wake of enactment of the Clean Air Act 1963, but continued to rise as more and more legislators responded to the growing public saliency of the issue. Although bill introductions rose steadily in the Senate during the late 1960s, an explosion of activity took place in the House. The number of air pollution control bills introduced in the House in the 89th Congress (1965–66) was six times greater than introduced in the previous Congress. Over the next four years the number of bill introductions rose even further as environmental issues captured the public and political imaginations. Ten times as many air pollution control bills were introduced in the 91st Congress (1969–70) as in the 88th Congress. Levels of activity were less pronounced in the Senate where a strong perception that the issue was the domain of Senator Edmund Muskie (Democrat, Maine) served to deter rivals. Nevertheless, bill introductions were twice as high in the Senate during the 91st Congress than four years earlier.

A fall in the number of air pollution control bills introduced in Congress followed enactment of the Clean Air Act Amendments 1970, but significantly, did not decline to the levels of the early 1960s. In the House, bill introductions fell to about a third of the number that had been introduced in the 91st Congress before beginning to rise slowly. Although a brief explosion of activity occurred in the 95th Congress (1977–78), the number of air pollution control bills introduced in the House remained reasonably constant throughout the 1970s and 1980s. In the Senate, bill introductions fell more dramatically in the immediate aftermath of passage of the 1970 law, but then rose to a level that remained constant until the late 1980s. The increased public saliency of environmental issues towards the end of that decade prompted a rapid rise in bill introductions in the Senate. Over twice as many air pollution control bills were introduced in the Senate during the 100th Congress (1987–88) than had been introduced in the 91st Congress. The determination of a new Republican majority in the 104th Congress (1995–96) to provide regulatory relief prompted a further burst of activity, particularly in the House.

The number of legislators introducing air pollution control bills

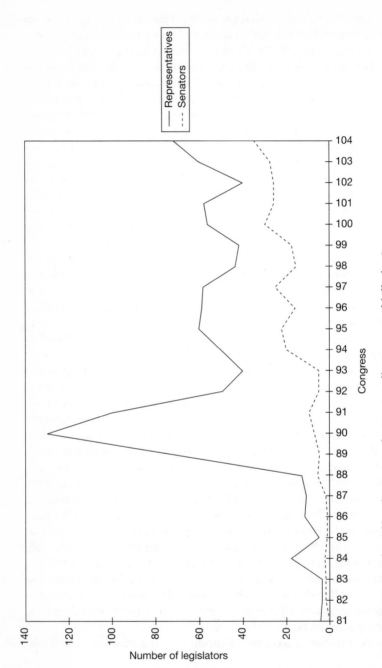

Figure 3.2 *Number of legislators introducing air pollution control bills, by Congress*

in Congress (see Figure 3.2) since the 1940s also increased as the issue assumed a *national* dimension. The early domination of the Californian and New York delegations was gradually dissipated as interest in the issue spread across the country in the 1960s. In the 90th Congress (1967–68) approximately 30 per cent of House members introduced an air pollution control bill. Enactment of legislation provided a further spur to activity as some legislators campaigned to increase the role of the federal government in controlling air pollution while others tried to obtain regulatory relief for industry. Only in the 93rd Congress (1973–74), the 99th Congress (1986–86) and the 102nd Congress (1991–92) did the number of legislators introducing air pollution control bills in the House fall below 10 per cent of the membership. In the Senate, the number of legislators introducing bills remained well over 10 per cent of the membership from the 94th Congress (1975–76) onwards.

The motivation of most of those who introduced air pollution control bills was almost certainly 'position-taking'. The vast majority simply introduced a bill, made a speech and promptly forgot about the issue. Only eleven Representatives and nine Senators introduced more than ten air pollution control bills in three Congresses or more (see Table 3.1). The majority of these legislators, significantly, were members of the congressional committees with primary jurisdiction over clean air. Of the eleven Representatives who fall in this category seven were members of the Committee on Energy and Commerce. Staggers and Dingell chaired the Committee while Rogers and Waxman both chaired the subcommittee with direct jurisdiction over the issue. The figures are even more striking in the Senate. Only Senator Gore was not a member of the Committee on Environment and Public Works. Randolph, Stafford, Baucus and Chafee all chaired the Committee while Muskie chaired the subcommittee with jurisdiction over the issue of air pollution.

The fact that so many of the legislators who introduced air pollution control bills over a sustained period of time were members of just two committees is testimony both to the resources, opportunities, and obligations conferred by membership of a panel with primary jurisdiction over an issue. Committees provide members, particularly their chairs, with considerable staff resources and parliamentary authority. These may be exploited to dominate legislative proceedings and shape policy objectives. Without such institutional advantages it is difficult for a legislator to secure and

Congress and air pollution

Table 3.1 *Legislators who introduced over ten air pollution control bills in three or more Congresses*

Senators		Representatives	
F. Lautenberg (D. NJ)	23	J. Dingell (D. MI)	34
M. Baucus (D. MT)	19	G. Brown (D. CA)	28
G. Mitchell (D. ME)	18	J. Scheuer (D. NY)	16
E. Muskie (D. ME)	18	J. Florio (D. NJ)	16
J. Randolph (D. WV)	18	P. Rogers (D. FL)	15
R. Stafford (D. VT)	17	L. Farbstein (D. NY)	13
D. Durenberger (R. MN)	15	H. Staggers (D. WV)	12
J. Chafee (R. RI)	12	W. Dannemeyer (R. CA)	12
A. Gore (D. TN)	11	H. Waxman (D. CA)	11
		N. Rahall (D. WV)	11
		E. Koch (D. NY)	10

Note: D. = Democrat
   R. = Republican

maintain a meaningful role in developing policy. Legislators with an interest in air pollution control policy, but lacking a seat on the appropriate committee, may decide to exploit law-making opportunities provided by their own committee assignments.

Committee activity
No institutional barriers stand in the way of a legislator who wishes to introduce an air pollution control bill. House and Senate rules allow members to introduce legislation virtually at will. Committee activity, in contrast, is conditioned to a certain extent by jurisdictional patterns. Although any committee may hold an investigative or oversight hearing on any subject, a committee may only hold legislative hearings on those bills that have been referred to it.[4] Bill referrals are determined formally by the Speaker of the House and the Majority Leader in the Senate on the basis of the descriptions of committee jurisdictions provided in the rules of each chamber and precedent. 'Statutory' and 'common law' jurisdiction are the terms that David C. King has used to describe these respective sources of jurisdiction.[5] The House and Senate Parliamentarians, in practice, usually determine which bills are sent to which committees.

The sudden stirrings of interest in air pollution in the 81st Congress (1949–50) raised a jurisdictional dilemma for the House Parliamentarian who had responsibility for referring the five air pollution control bills to a committee. The fact that air pollution had not been recognized as a national issue when committee jurisdictions had been codified in the Legislative Reorganization Act 1946 meant that no explicit grant of 'statutory' jurisdiction over the issue existed. Nor had any concrete precedent been established in earlier bill referrals that might serve as the basis for 'common law' jurisdiction. All that the Parliamentarian could do under such circumstances was define the issue in a way that was congruent with existing grants of 'turf'. The five air pollution control bills introduced in the 81st Congress, as a result, were referred to the House Committee on Interstate and Foreign Commerce which had been granted jurisdiction over 'public health and quarantine' by the Legislative Reorganization Act 1946. A similar logic informed the decision of the Senate Parliamentarian in 1951 to refer the first air pollution control bill to be introduced in that chamber to the Senate Committee on Labor and Welfare. Senate Labor's lack of interest in the issue, however, allowed the Committee on Public Works to claim jurisdiction by building upon its existing jurisdiction over water pollution. In 1955 the Committee's Subcommittee on Flood Control – Rivers and Harbors held a hearing on 'Water and Air Pollution Control' and reported legislation that formed the basis for the Air Pollution Control Act 1955.[6] The action established Senate Public Works as the original authorizing committee of the main air pollution control law in the United States.

The basic contours of committee activity on air pollution were established by these initial grants of jurisdiction. The assignment of 'policy property rights' to House Commerce and Senate Public Works meant that a committee wishing to become involved in controlling air pollution had either to conduct investigative hearings, or else draft legislation in such a way that it would fall within the purview of the committee. Investigative hearings can be regarded to a certain extent as a form of 'position-taking'. They offer a relatively cost-free way of displaying interest in a subject. Perhaps more significantly, however, such hearings can often prepare the ground for jurisdictional challenges. Investigative hearings provide a means for legislative entrepreneurs to reconnoitre the landscape surrounding an issue. An issue like air pollution may be explored in an investigative hearing to find an 'angle' that will allow the issue to be defined in terms that fit the jurisdiction of the committee. Inviting evidence from witnesses who have been denied access or who feel alienated from other committees may well offer a way to discover desired new vistas.

Little committee activity on air pollution control issues took place in either the House or the Senate during the 1950s and early 1960s (see Figures 3.3 and 3.4). A few hearings on air pollution control legislation were conducted by subcommittees of the House Committee on Interstate and Foreign Commerce and the Senate Committee on Public Works. Investigative hearings into the problem of air pollution were also conducted by subcommittees of the House Committee on Science and Aeronautics, the House Committee on Government Operations, the House Committee on Appropriations, the House Select Committee on Small Business and the Senate Committee on the District of Columbia. Levels of committee activity increased dramatically towards the end of the 1960s, however, as the increased public saliency of the issue prompted greater congressional interest in air pollution. Both the number of legislative and investigative hearings rose to new levels. As many hearings on air pollution took place in the 91st Congress (1969–70) as in the previous eight Congresses.

Part of the increase in levels of committee activity during the late 1960s can be explained by the newly kindled activism of House Commerce's Subcommittee on Public Health and Welfare under Representative (hereafter Rep.) Rogers and Senate Public Work's Subcommittee on Air and Water Pollution under Senator Muskie. Both Chairmen were determined to use their institutional positions to fashion policy on air pollution. Part of the increase can also be explained by the determination of other committee and subcommittee chairmen either to engage in position-taking or to seize some jurisdiction over a highly salient issue. Maiden interest in air pollution was shown by the Senate Committee on Interior and Insular Affairs, the Senate Committee on Commerce, the Senate Committee on the Judiciary, the House Committee on Interior and Insular Affairs, and the House Committee on Merchant Marine and Fisheries. Eight committees in total conducted investigative hearings into air pollution during the 91st Congress. (see Table 3.2, which shows all hearings).

Levels of committee activity declined in the immediate aftermath of passage of the Clean Air Act Amendments 1970 but bounced back in the 93rd Congress (1973–74) as congressional committees began to investigate the effectiveness of the law. The inquiry was led

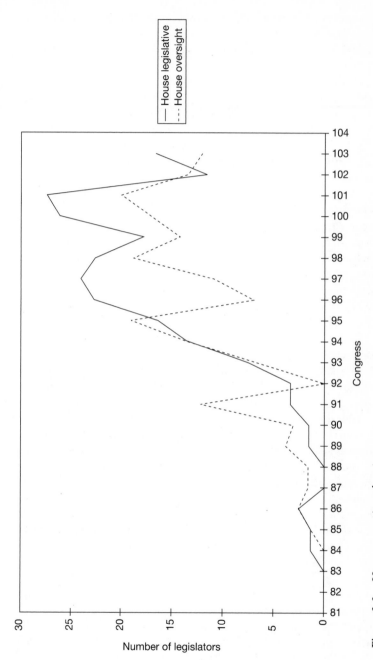

Figure 3.3 *House committee hearings*

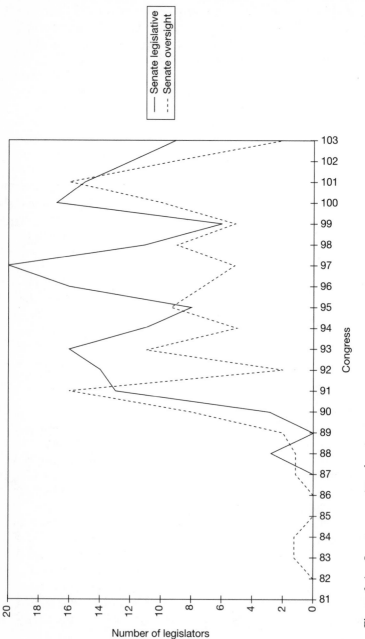

Figure 3.4 *Senate committee hearings*

by House Commerce's Subcommittee on Public Health and Welfare, and Senate Public Work's Subcommittee on Air and Water Pollution, but the broad regulatory impact of the 1970 law provided opportunities for other committees to hold investigative hearings. Six committees in addition to House Commerce and Senate Public Works held investigative hearings into air pollution during the 93rd Congress. Conducting its first hearing into air pollution was the House Committee on Banking and Currency.

The number of committees conducting hearings on air pollution control issues continued to rise during the 1970s as legislative entrepreneurs took advantage of the multidimensional nature of the issue to fashion legislation that changed the pattern of bill referrals. Particularly important in this process was the energy crisis of the mid-1970s which opened up an entirely new dimension to the issue of air pollution. The number of committees being referred air pollution control bills doubled in both the House and the Senate between the 92nd Congress (1971–72) and the 95th Congress (1977–78). Referred air pollution control bills for the first time in this period were the House Committee on the District of Columbia, the House Committee on Interior and Insular Affairs, the House Committee on Agriculture, the House Committee on Foreign Affairs, the House Committee on Merchant Marine and Fisheries, the House Committee on Education and Labor, the House Committee on Small Business, the Senate Committee on Interior and Insular Affairs, the Senate Committee on Agriculture and the Senate Committee on Foreign Relations (see Table 3.3).

Levels of committee activity remained high in the 1980s and 1990s as new dimensions to the issue were open up. Although House Commerce and Senate Public Works retained primary jurisdiction over air pollution, particularly over clean air legislation, a large number of other committees had grabbed some control over the issue. Virtually all congressional committees had conducted a hearing of some sort on air pollution by the mid-1990s.

The pattern of committee activity is similar in many respects to that of bill introductions. Both show an increase and a broadening of activity. Although more air pollution control bills were introduced by more legislators, and more committee hearings were conducted by more committees, a handful of legislators and a couple of committees formed the main focus of activity. Levels of committee activity, however, do not exhibit the peaks and troughs of bill introductions.

Table 3.2 *Oversight/investigative hearings on air pollution by congressional committee*

	81st	82nd	83rd	84th	85th	86th	87th	88th	89th	90th
House										
Commerce	—	—	—	—	—	1	—	—	—	—
Ways & Means	—	—	—	—	—	—	—	—	—	—
Science	—	—	—	—	—	—	—	—	1	—
Interior	—	—	—	—	—	—	—	—	—	—
Public Works	—	—	—	—	—	—	—	—	—	—
Banking	—	—	—	—	—	—	—	—	—	—
Agriculture	—	—	—	—	—	—	—	—	—	—
Judiciary	—	—	—	—	—	—	—	—	—	—
Foreign Affairs	—	—	—	—	—	—	—	—	—	—
Armed Services	—	—	—	—	—	—	—	—	—	—
Merchant Marine	—	—	—	—	—	—	—	—	—	—
Education	—	—	—	—	—	—	—	—	—	—
Govt Ops	—	—	—	—	1	—	—	—	—	1
District of Columbia	—	—	—	—	—	—	—	—	—	—
Small Business	—	—	—	1	—	—	—	—	—	—
Appropriations	—	—	—	—	—	1	—	—	—	—
Senate										
Labor	—	—	—	—	—	—	—	—	—	—
Public Works	—	—	—	—	—	—	—	3	—	2
Interior	—	—	—	—	—	—	—	—	—	—
Commerce	—	—	—	—	—	—	—	—	—	—
Finance	—	—	—	—	—	—	—	—	—	—
Banking	—	—	—	—	—	—	—	—	—	—
Govt Ops	—	—	—	—	—	—	—	—	—	—
Judiciary	—	—	—	—	—	—	—	—	—	—
Agriculture	—	—	—	—	—	—	—	—	—	—
Armed Services	—	—	—	—	—	—	—	—	—	—
Foreign Relations	—	—	—	—	—	—	—	—	—	—
Budget	—	—	—	—	—	—	—	—	—	—
Small Business	—	—	—	—	—	—	—	—	—	—
Aero/Science	—	—	—	—	—	—	—	—	—	—
DC	—	—	—	—	—	—	—	—	—	1
Appropriations	—	—	—	—	—	—	—	—	—	—

91st	92nd	93rd	94th	95th	96th	97th	98th	99th	100th	101st	102nd	103rd
—	2	4	2	3	8	4	3	5	12	5	4	5
—	—	—	—	—	—	—	—	—	—	1	6	4
1	1	1	7	8	5	9	7	4	4	6	—	2
1	—	1	—	2	1	—	2	2	3	—	—	—
—	—	—	1	—	1	1	2	1	2	2	—	—
—	—	1	—	—	—	—	1	—	—	1	—	—
—	—	—	—	1	—	1	—	1	—	—	—	1
—	—	—	—	—	—	—	—	—	—	—	—	—
—	—	—	—	—	—	1	—	1	1	1	1	—
—	—	—	—	—	—	—	1	—	—	1	—	—
1	—	—	—	—	—	—	—	—	1	—	—	—
—	—	—	—	1	1	—	2	1	—	1	—	—
1	—	1	3	1	2	5	3	2	2	—	1	3
—	—	—	—	—	—	—	—	—	—	—	—	—
—	—	1	—	—	—	1	2	—	—	—	—	1
—	—	—	—	—	1	—	—	—	—	—	—	—
—	—	—	—	—	1	—	—	—	—	—	1	—
3	4	11	6	2	4	10	4	7	12	3	2	6
1	4	4	2	—	3	1	3	1	2	5	2	—
2	—	—	1	1	—	—	—	1	—	1	2	—
—	—	—	—	—	—	—	—	—	—	—	—	—
—	1	—	—	—	1	—	—	—	—	—	5	1
—	—	—	—	—	—	5	—	—	—	1	—	—
1	1	—	—	—	—	—	—	—	—	—	—	—
—	—	—	—	—	—	—	—	—	—	—	—	—
—	—	—	—	1	—	—	—	—	—	—	—	—
—	—	—	—	—	—	—	—	—	—	1	—	—
—	—	—	—	—	1	—	—	—	—	—	—	—
—	—	—	—	—	2	—	—	—	—	—	—	—
—	—	—	1	—	—	—	—	—	—	—	—	—
—	1	—	—	—	—	—	—	—	—	—	—	—
—	—	—	—	1	1	—	—	—	—	—	—	1

Table 3.3 *Air pollution bill referrals*

						Congress							
	81st	82nd	83rd	84th	85th	86th	87th	88th	89th	90th	91st	92nd	93rd
House													
Commerce	5	4	3	7	2	7	9	8	20	36	79	27	44
Ways & Means	—	—	1	14	3	6	4	4	62	82	53	18	2
Science	—	—	—	—	—	1	—	—	—	—	—	—	1
Interior	—	—	—	—	—	—	—	—	—	1	—	—	—
Public Works	—	—	—	—	—	—	—	2	2	—	7	1	1
Banking	—	—	—	1	—	—	—	—	—	—	1	1	1
Agriculture	—	—	—	—	—	—	—	—	—	—	1	—	—
Judiciary	—	—	—	—	—	—	—	—	1	7	6	1	1
Foreign Affairs	—	—	—	—	—	—	—	—	—	—	—	—	—
Armed Services	—	—	—	—	—	—	—	—	—	—	—	—	—
Merchant Marine	—	—	—	—	—	—	—	—	—	—	—	—	—
Education	—	—	—	—	—	—	—	—	—	—	—	—	—
Govt Ops	—	—	—	—	—	—	—	—	—	—	—	—	—
District of Columbia	—	—	—	—	—	—	—	—	—	—	—	1	—
Small Business	—	—	—	—	—	—	—	—	—	—	—	—	—
Rules	—	—	—	1	—	—	—	—	—	—	—	—	—

Table 3.3 (contd)

	Congress												
	81st	82nd	83rd	84th	85th	86th	87th	88th	89th	90th	91st	92nd	93rd
Senate													
Labor	—	1	—	—	—	1	—	—	—	—	—	—	—
Public Works	—	—	—	1	—	2	2	6	5	4	7	2	7
Interior	—	—	—	—	—	—	—	—	—	—	1	4	4
Commerce	—	1	—	—	—	—	—	1	—	—	4	—	—
Finance	—	—	1	1	1	—	—	1	3	5	4	—	—
Banking	—	—	—	—	—	—	—	—	—	—	—	—	—
Govt Ops	—	—	—	—	—	—	—	—	—	—	—	—	—
Judiciary	—	—	—	—	—	—	—	—	1	3	2	1	—
Agriculture	—	—	—	—	—	—	—	—	—	—	—	—	—
Armed Services	—	—	—	—	—	—	—	—	—	—	—	—	—
Foreign Relations	—	—	—	—	—	—	—	—	—	—	—	—	—
Budget	—	—	—	—	—	—	—	—	—	—	—	—	—
Small Business	—	—	—	—	—	—	—	—	—	—	—	—	—
Aero/Science	—	—	—	—	—	—	—	—	—	—	—	—	—

Table 3.3 (contd)

House	94th		95th		96th		97th		98th		99th	
	S1	*J2*	*S*	*J*	*S*	*J*	*S*	*J*	*S*	*J*	*S*	*J*
Commerce	44	12	50	9	37	16	53	11	31	8	27	8
Ways & Means	3	5	16	4	7	8	6	1	1	3	8	4
Science	10	6	16	1	2	5	1	6	5	3	4	6
Interior	3	1	—	1	3	11	—	—	—	2	4	1
Public Works	5	1	8	4	5	11	—	2	2	3	—	3
Banking	—	1	1	6	—	4	—	—	—	1	—	—
Agriculture	1	—	5	2	2	1	2	—	1	1	1	2
Judiciary	—	2	—	1	2	—	1	2	1	2	—	2
Foreign Affairs	1	—	6	1	1	1	1	1	1	2	—	1
Armed Services	—	2	—	—	—	3	1	1	1	1	—	—
Merchant Marine	—	2	2	1	—	3	—	—	1	—	—	1
Education	—	—	1	1	1	—	1	—	3	1	1	1
Govt Ops	—	—	—	2	1	3	2	—	2	—	—	—
DC	—	—	—	1	1	1	—	—	—	—	—	—
Small Business	—	—	2	—	—	—	1	—	3	—	—	—
Rules	—	—	—	—	—	1	—	2	—	—	—	—

Table 3.3 (contd)

	94th S1	94th J2	95th S	95th J	96th S	96th J	97th S	97th J	98th S	98th J	99th S	99th J
Senate												
Labor	—	2	1	—	1	—	—	—	2	—	—	1
Public Works	12	2	17	—	12	2	22	1	16	—	16	1
Interior	2	—	2	—	4	—	3	—	1	—	—	—
Commerce	4	2	1	—	2	1	1	—	1	—	—	—
Finance	1	1	6	—	3	1	4	—	3	—	5	1
Banking	—	—	2	—	—	—	—	—	—	—	—	—
Govt Ops	1	1	1	—1	—	—	—	2	1	1	—	4
Judiciary	—	1	—	—	1	—	—	—	1	—	—	1
Agriculture	1	—	1	—	—	—	1	—	1	—	—	—
Armed Services	—	1	—	—	—	—	—	—	—	—	—	—
Foreign Relations	—	—	2	—	—	—	1	—	—	—	2	—
Budget	—	—	—	—	—	—	—	1	—	—	—	—
Small Business	—	—	—	—	—	—	1	—	—	—	—	—
Aero/Science	—	1	—	—	—	—	—	—	—	—	—	—

Table 3.3 (contd)

House	100th		101st		102nd		103rd		104th	
	S	*J*	*S*	*J*	*S*	*J*	*S*	*J*	*S*	*J*
Commerce	35	20	47	18	17	12	39	8	49	11
Ways & Means	6	10	6	9	7	5	6	6	5	9
Science	2	11	4	10	4	7	3	5	1	7
Interior	—	4	2	3	2	1	2	2	5	3
Public Works	—	5	—	7	1	5	7	4	10	9
Banking	1	3	—	5	—	2	1	4	—	3
Agriculture	1	5	—	4	—	2	—	2	—	2
Judiciary	—	2	—	—	—	1	—	2	—	3
Foreign Affairs	1	8	1	5	4	4	4	4	2	3
Armed Services	—	—	—	4	1	3	2	4	—	4
Merchant Marine	—	6	—	2	1	3	2	3	—	—
Education	2	1	—	5	1	1	4	7	2	—
Govt Ops	—	4	1	3	—	2	—	4	—	1
DC	—	1	—	—	—	—	—	2	—	—
Small Business	1	1	—	1	—	—	—	2	—	1
Rules	—	—	—	1	—	—	1	—	—	—
Post Office	—	—	—	—	2	—	2	3	—	—

Table 3.3 (contd)

	100th S	100th J	101st S	101st J	102nd S	102nd J	103rd S	103rd J	104th J
Senate									
Labor	—	—	1	—	3	—	3	—	—
Public Works	30	—	25	—	—	26	—	18	27
Interior	4	—	2	—	—	7	—	1	3
Commerce	6	—	2	—	—	1	1	3	9
Finance	4	—	7	—	—	6	1	3	5
Banking	1	—	—	—	—	1	—	1	—
Govt Ops	—	1	—	—	—	—	2	3	—
Judiciary	—	—	3	—	—	2	1	1	1
Agriculture	—	—	2	—	—	—	1	—	1
Armed Services	—	—	—	—	—	1	1	5	3
Foreign Relations	3	—	4	—	1	6	1	2	2
Budget	—	—	—	—	—	—	—	—	—
Small Business	1	—	—	—	—	—	1	—	—
Aero/Science	—	—	—	—	—	—	—	—	—
Indian Affairs	—	—	—	—	—	1	—	—	—
Veterans' Affairs	—	—	—	—	—	—	—	1	—

Notes: S Single
        J Joint

The number of committee hearings rises steadily from the late 1960s onwards, whereas the number of bill introductions varies quite considerably. These levels of committee activity provide some evidence that concern about air pollution rapidly became institutionalized.

The nature of congressional interest

Measures of legislative activity provide some evidence about the way that congressional interest in controlling air pollution has varied over the decades, but fail to capture changes in the nature of that involvement. Congressional efforts to control air pollution have deepened, broadened and fragmented since the 1940s. Simple one-page bills designed to help the states control 'air pollution' have been replaced by bills that take hundreds of pages to specify levels of control for particular air pollutants. Conflict and division has accompanied this process. The development of a strong regulatory regime to control air pollution has had an impact upon almost all sections of America. Bills have been introduced to provide regulatory relief to selected industries, more witnesses have demanded the right to a sympathetic hearing before committees, and legislators have become more uncertain in their support for air pollution control efforts. An expansion in the 'scope of conflict' surrounding the issue has inexorably followed the development of policy.

The deepening and broadening of legislation

The ambition of the air pollution control bills introduced in Congress during the 1950s was determined by a lack of knowledge about the extent of the problem and a belief that states and local governments were responsible its control. Although a few bills sought to provide tax relief for the purchase of air pollution abatement equipment, the majority simply sought to increase the level of financial and technical assistance that the federal government gave states and local governments. The laws that were enacted during this period fully reflected this limited sense of air pollution control. Both the Air Pollution Control Act 1955 and the Clean Air Act 1963 affirmed that primary responsibility for controlling air pollution resided with the states and authorized money for demonstration projects, grants-in-aid to state and local government air pollution control agencies, and research. The 1963 law also gave the Secretary of the Department of Health, Education, and Welfare (HEW) authority to take legal action against polluters causing interstate pollution.

Demands for the federal government to play a greater role in controlling air pollution grew during the 1960s as evidence of both the extent of the problem and the incapacity of the states to deal with it became available. One result was the introduction of an increasing number of bills designed to expand the regulatory purview of the federal government. The pace of change, however, depended largely upon the source of the air pollution. Although the Air Quality Act 1967 pre-empted the authority of every state except California to set automobile emission standards and required them to meet national standards, the same law directed the states to set ambient air quality standards rather than establish national standards for stationary sources (see Table 3.4). The Secretary of HEW was authorized to act against stationary sources of air pollution only in time of 'imminent and substantial' danger to public health.

Table 3.4 *The development of air pollution control laws*

	Air Pollution Control Act (1955) Clean Air Act (1963)	Air Quality Act (1967)	Clean Air Act (1970)	Clean Air Act (1977) Clean Air Act (1990)
Depth of federal role	Very shallow	Shallow	Deep	Mixed
	– research	– research	– research	– research
	– funding	– funding	– funding	– funding
		– state standards	– federal standards	– federal/state standards
Width of federal role	Narrow	Widening	Wide	Wide
	– air pollution	– air pollution	– air pollution	air pollution
		– automobile emissions	– automobile emissions	– automobile emissions
		– industrial	– criteria pollutants	– criteria pollutions
			– NSPS	– NSPS
			– hazardous pollutants	– toxic pollutants
Regulatory means	Not applicable	Not applicable	– command	– command
			– technology	– technology
				– economic

High levels of public concern about the environment in the late 1960s and clear evidence of the failure of the states to comply with the standard setting provisions of the Air Quality Act combined to generate further pressure on the federal government. The incremental adjustments that had characterized the development of policy over the previous fifteen years were abandoned, however, as President Nixon and Senator Muskie turned the issue of air pollution control into a political blood sport. With congressional support for an expansion of federal responsibility evident from the introduction of a large number of bills to establish national emission standards, President Nixon and Senator Muskie competed with each other to produce a tough new law. The structure of air pollution control in the United States was changed as a result, with the enactment of the Clean Air Act Amendments 1970. The Administrator of the Environmental Protection Agency (EPA) was required to set National Ambient Air Quality Standards (NAAQS) for six pollutants, to promulgate New Source Performance Standards (NSPS) to control the emissions of fourteen specific pollutants from newly constructed facilities and to identify and regulate hazardous air pollutants.

Enactment of the Clean Air Act Amendments 1970 changed the scope of conflict associated with the issue of air pollution control. Bills to provide regulatory relief began to be introduced in Congress as groups sought to challenge the ambition of the new law. Against the backdrop of the oil crisis, laws containing waivers for automobile exhaust emission standards were passed in 1973, 1974 and 1976. Further relief was provided in the Clean Air Act Amendments 1977 which extended many of the deadlines for compliance with emission standards. The deepening and widening of federal control, however, continued even amidst episodes of regulatory relief. New restrictions on industrial plants were imposed in parts of the country with clean air in an effort to limit any deterioration of air quality. The country was divided into three classes of air quality districts. No deterioration of air quality would be permitted in districts categorized as Class I, specified increments of additional pollution would be permitted in Class II districts, and no restrictions on pollution would be imposed in Class III districts as long as NAAQS were met.

Efforts to provide regulatory relief to groups disadvantaged by the Clean Air Act continued during the late 1970s and early 1980s.

Legislation to provide relief to the steel industry was enacted in 1981, and an amendment to the fiscal 1984 Housing and Urban Development Appropriation Act stopped the EPA from imposing economic penalties on communities that had not achieved the air quality standards required by the 1977 Amendments. The focus of congressional efforts to control air pollution started to change as public concern about the problem began to increase in the late 1980s. Large numbers of bills were introduced to strengthen existing regulatory arrangements and to address new issue such as acid rain and global climate change. The result of this effort was enactment of the Clean Air Act Amendments 1990. Although this law gave the states greater control over the regulation of new sources of pollution, hazardous air pollutants and the prevention of serious deterioration, the primacy of the federal government in controlling air pollution was confirmed. New federal controls were imposed on automobile emissions, toxic substances, and sulphur dioxide, while the states were prohibited both from enacting their own standards for emissions from aircraft and regulating appliances to protect the stratospheric ozone layer.

The focus of congressional efforts to control air pollution switched to the problem of indoor air pollution in the wake of enactment of the 1990 Amendments. Attention reverted to traditional concerns by the mid-1990s, however, as evidence of the effectiveness of the new law became available. This evidence was seized upon by the new Republican majority in the 104th Congress (1995–96) to launch an attack on the Clean Air Act. Large numbers of bills were introduced to provide regulatory relief and even repeal entire sections of the law. Despite these efforts, no major changes in policy were enacted.

Division and conflict
The deepening and broadening of federal responsibility for controlling air pollution changed the politics surrounding the issue in Congress. Little division or conflict was associated with the issue while the main thrust of congressional efforts to control air pollution was devoted to helping the states. The Air Pollution Control Act 1955 passed with relatively little debate or controversy. Efforts to expand the role of the federal government, on the other hand, generated considerable division and conflict. Perceptions that the Clean Air Act 1963 presaged an expansion of federal authority led

to divisions in floor votes on passage in the House. Although the overwhelming votes in favour of final passage of laws such as the Clean Air Act Amendments 1970, 1977 and 1990 suggests limited disagreement, such votes mask the division and conflict that characterized earlier phases of the legislative process. Committee hearings reveal a wide range of witnesses providing contested testimony, and voting patterns on floor amendments show considerable disagreement about the means and ends of air pollution control.

The number of witnesses giving evidence on air pollution control issues before congressional committees increased dramatically in the mid-1960s (see Figure 3.5) as pressure mounted for the federal government to play a more active role in dealing with the problem. A fivefold increase in the total number of witnesses giving evidence, and a doubling of the average number of witnesses per hearing, accompanied consideration of the Clean Air Act 1963 in the 88th Congress (1963–64). A further doubling of the total number of witnesses giving evidence occurred four years later when the 90th Congress (1967–68) discussed the Air Quality Act 1967. The most prominent leap in numbers, however, accompanied consideration of the Clean Air Act Amendments 1970 in the 91st Congress (1969–70). Although the average number of witnesses per hearing declined from the level found in the 88th Congress because of an increase in the number of hearings conducted, the total number of witnesses trying to inform legislators was four and half times greater than six years earlier. These witnesses divided fairly equally between pro-environment organizations and pro-business organizations.[7]

Enactment of the 1970 law changed the nature of interest representation in hearings on air pollution. In the period before 1970 the total number of witnesses giving evidence in each Congress was associated with consideration of major legislation. Numbers rose dramatically in the 84th Congress (1955–56), the 88th Congress (1963–64), the 90th Congress (1967–68) and the 91st Congress (1969–70) when major laws were discussed and enacted. In the period after 1970 the total number of witnesses remained high as groups responded to the regulatory regime established by the Clean Air Act Amendments 1970. Particularly noteworthy is the changed balance of pro-environment and pro-business witnesses in the two periods. Pro-environment witnesses outnumbered pro-business

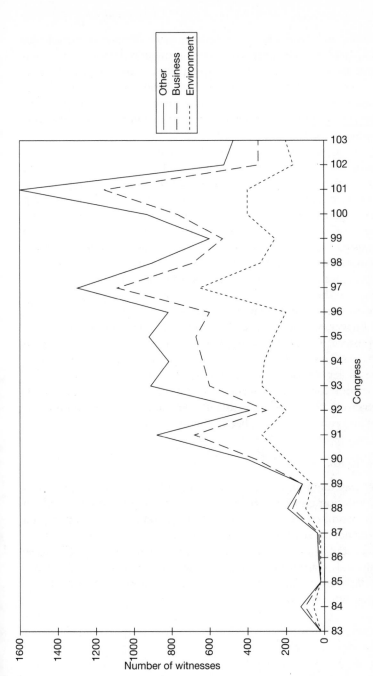

Figure 3.5 *Number and type of witnesses appearing at air pollution control hearings*

witnesses in hearings on air pollution in each Congress before 1970. After 1970 pro-business witnesses outnumbered pro-environment witnesses in seven out of twelve Congresses. This change in the pattern of representation suggests that enactment of the Clean Air Act Amendments 1970 prompted pro-business interests to mobilize to protect their interests in a way that they had not considered necessary previously.

Further evidence of the conflict and divisions over air pollution control policy that began to emerge after 1970 can be seen in amending activity. Contested floor amendments to air pollution control legislation, where more than 10 per cent of the membership voted against the majority, were extremely rare in the decades before 1970. After 1970 they became much more frequent. Sixteen contested floor amendments took place during consideration of the Clean Air Act Amendments 1977 and eighteen during consideration of the Clean Air Act Amendments 1990. Amending activity was greater in the Senate primarily because of the more open amending process that exists in that chamber.

The increased levels of conflict associated with air pollution control after 1970 placed a premium upon negotiation and compromise. The result was a slowing in the production of air pollution control legislation as information and transaction costs soared. Laws took longer and longer to design, package and enact as legislators found it increasingly difficult to assimilate contested information and resolve conflicts between competing interests.

Conclusion

Aggregate data on the level and nature of congressional interest in air pollution control provides important evidence about trends in activity and concerns. Much needed contextualization is provided by the data. Such broad paint strokes tell little, however, about the choice and timing of particular laws. Case studies which allow the value and relationship of a wide range of variables to be described are the only way in which the production of specific laws can properly be understood.

Notes

1 Charles O. Jones *Clean Air* (Pittsburgh: University of Pittsburgh Press, 1975); E. Donald Elliot, Bruce A. Ackerman and John C. Millian 'Toward a Theory of Statutory Evolution: The Federalization of Environmental Law', *Journal of Law, Economics, and Organization* (1985), 1:313–40.

2 Woodrow Wilson *Congressional Government* (Baltimore: Johns Hopkins University Press, 1981), p.194.

3 A data set of air pollution control bills was created by searching the indices of the *Congressional Record* under the term 'air pollution'.

4 A data set of committee hearings was created by searching the *Congressional Information Service* database of committee activity using 'air pollution' as a key word.

5 David C. King 'The Nature of Congressional Committee Jurisdictions', *American Political Science Review* (1994), 88:48–62.

6 US Senate, Committee on Public Works, Subcommittee on Flood Control – Rivers and Harbors, *Hearing*, 'Water and Air Pollution Control', 84th Congress, 1st session, 25 April 1955.

7 Witnesses were coded on the basis of the criteria set out by Paul Sabatier as pro-environment if they were members of the 'clean air coalition', pro-business if they were members of the 'economic efficiency coalition' and other/uncodable if they did not seem to fit either category. See Paul A. Sabatier 'An Advocacy Coalition Framework of Policy Change and the Role of Policy-Oriented Learning Therein', *Policy Science* (1988), 21:141–2.

4
Policy awakening, 1949–63

Interest in air pollution began to emerge in Congress in the years between the end of the Second World War and the assassination of President John F. Kennedy. The first air pollution control bills were introduced in 1949, the first committee hearings to investigate the problem were held in 1954, the first law was enacted in 1955, minor reauthorizations followed in 1959 and 1962, and passage of the Clean Air Act occurred in 1963. Institutional structures also evolved to gather and process information about the problem. In the House of Representatives, the Subcommittee on Health and Safety of the Committee on Interstate and Foreign Commerce assumed primary responsibility for the issue. In the Senate, the Committee on Public Works created a Special Subcommittee on Air and Water Pollution in 1963 to back up its claim to jurisdiction over the issue. Between 1945 and 1963, in short, Congress discovered air pollution and began to do something about the problem.

The spark that ignited this period of policy awakening was a catastrophic air pollution episode in Donora, Pennsylvania in 1948. The considerable publicity given to the episode provided an opportunity for local politicians to pander to public concern through posturing and symbolic action. Air pollution control bills were introduced in the House by members of the Pennsylvanian delegation to serve electoral needs. The fuel that fed the fire of congressional interest, however, was located primarily on the other side of the country. The growing problem of smog in Los Angeles generated a powerful and persistent incentive for members of the Californian delegation to promote a federal role in controlling air pollution long after the impact of Donora had faded. Pressure from Californians ensured that interest in the issue continued to grow throughout the 1950s, and provided the impetus that led to enactment of the first air pollution control laws.

Most studies of air pollution control have glossed over this early period. Bruce A. Ackerman and William T. Hassler do not mention either the Air Pollution Control Act 1955 or the Clean Air Act 1963 in their study of air pollution control.[1] Richard E. Cohen begins his account of 'Early Clean-Air Politics' in 1963.[2] Gary C. Bryner devotes two paragraphs to the period before 1970.[3] The main exceptions to the headlong rush towards the later years are studies by Arthur C. Stern, Randall B. Ripley, J. Clarence Davies, James E. Krier and Edmund Ursin, and Charles O. Jones.[4] The most important of these studies are the latter two. Krier and Ursin highlight the importance of California in these years of policy awakening. They show that the needs of that state drove much of the development of early federal air pollution control policy. Jones takes a slightly different angle. In his book *Clean Air* he shows that this early period was significant in terms of 'problem identification and definition'.[5] Congressional committees held hearings to explore the nature and scope of the problem; laws were passed to authorize research into different aspects of air pollution. Knowledge grew and perceptions began to change as a result. Legislators started to appreciate both the need to address the problem of air pollution and the level of support that was available should they decide to take action.

The reason why most studies have glossed over the early years of congressional interest in air pollution control is that the laws enacted during the period did little beyond authorize studies. 'By today's standards, [the Air Pollution Control Act 1955] did extraordinarily little to actively work toward clean air' Kent E. Portney has correctly noted.[6] Judging significance simply in terms of the content of legislation, however, means that important aspects of policy development are missed. First, and perhaps most obviously, the enactment of laws with limited ambition helped to secure a federal beachhead in a policy arena that had previously been the preserve of state and local governments. They paved the way for the more ambitious laws that were to follow. Second, the period saw the emergence of the legislative structures that served to institutionalize concern about air pollution and would shape decision-making in the future. And, finally, the process of 'problem identification and definition' that Jones describes helped to set in motion forces that would generate future action. The studies and reports that were commissioned during this period were submitted to Congress and demanded a response that an increasing number of legislators were willing to provide.

Adoption of a broad perspective allows the significance of the early years of Congress's interest in air pollution to become apparent. Important areas that demand closer examination include the origins of congressional interest in air pollution, the nature of early initiatives, the effect that federalism had on the choice of solutions, the way that legislative structures evolved and the long-term consequences of the early action. The intention is to improve understanding of the early evolution of air pollution control law in the United States, analyze the factors that determined the pace of legislative production, and show how the seeds of later developments were sown in this period of awakening.

First stirrings

The first stirrings of congressional interest in air pollution became apparent in the late 1940s as evidence began to emerge about the extent of the problem and the failure of existing methods of control. A small number of legislators, particularly members representing Californian constituencies, began to appreciate the electoral rewards that might be achieved through policy entrepreneurship on the issue. Entry into this new policy arena was made awkward, however, by two factors. First, knowledge about the problem was limited. Although a non-scientific understanding that smoke contributed to ill health had been available since the days of the Roman Empire, little was known about other forms of air pollution.[7] Second, smoke abatement was regarded as part of the 'police powers' of the states and local governments.[8] The constitutional authority of the federal government to take action to control air pollution was uncertain as a result. Both factors structured early policy choices. Bills were introduced to improve 'problem identification', and considerable effort was taken to ensure that constitutional sensitivities were not offended. A lack of institutional power, however, made enactment a difficult task. Proponents of a federal role in air pollution control lacked the clout to secure easy passage of their legislation in this period. The policy entrepreneurs recognized a market for air pollution control laws, but found it difficult to assemble the necessary resources for legislative production.

Early abatement efforts

Air pollution is not a modern phenomenon. The *conquistadores* complained about 'smog' in the Los Angeles Basin as early as 1542 when a thermal inversion trapped the smoke from Native American camp fires.[9] Later travellers reported similar tales of air pollution caused by domestic burning of fossil fuels in cities such as Philadelphia and New York. Rapid industrialization after the American Civil War magnified the problem many times over. Steelworks, chemical plants and other factories began to pump thick black smoke into the skies of America's industrial cities. Although no emissions data is available for this period, an idea of the extent of the problem can be gleaned from Upton Sinclair's graphic description of the smoke that came from Chicago's stockyards and slaughterhouses as

> thick, oily, and black as night. It might have come from the center of the world, this smoke, where the fires of the ages still smoulder. It came as if self-impelled, driving all before it, a perpetual explosion. It was inexhaustible; one stared, waiting to see it stop, but still the great streams rolled out. They spread in vast clouds overhead, writhing, curling; then, uniting in one great river, they streamed away down the sky, stretching a black pall as far as the eye could reach.[10]

The only protection that Americans had against air pollution for most of the nineteenth century was litigation. Suits based on common law concepts such as trespass, nuisance and injury could be brought to seek compensation for injury caused by smoke emissions.[11] Common law suits, however, often failed to achieve their purpose. Not only did the plaintiff have the difficult task of proving that an injury was the fault of a particular polluter, but the courts usually upheld public interest defences based on the need to promote economic growth.[12] Even in the early decades of the twentieth century, this doctrine still held sway in many courtrooms. Typical was the opinion of a New York judge in a 1931 case that air pollution from fifty coke ovens constituted a 'petty annoyance' to a neighbouring home-owner and was 'indispensable to progress'.[13] 'In the transition from an agricultural to an industrial economy', Peter C. Yeager has argued, 'the law came to support the increasingly organized interests of manufacturers and cities as against the rights of individual persons to fair use of natural resources'.[14]

Concern about the inadequacies of the common law and a growing awareness of the damage to health caused by smoke were seized upon by progressive reformers in the late nineteenth century. Members of civic leagues and women's organizations, in particular, began to demand government action to control smoke emissions. The result was the adoption of smoke abatement laws in cities across the industrial heartland of the country.[15] Chicago and Cincinnati passed ordinances in 1881 to regulate smoke emissions from furnaces.[16] The Chicago ordinance declared that: 'the emission of dense smoke from the smoke-stack of any boat or locomotive or from any chimney anywhere within the city shall be … a public nuisance'.[17] Cleveland, Pittsburgh and St Paul passed smoke abatement ordinances that prohibited the release of 'dense', 'black' or 'grey' smoke in the last decade of the nineteenth century. A further eighteen cities, including Detroit, Milwaukee, New York and Philadelphia, followed suit in the first decade of the twentieth century. Other cities were soon to act. Between 1910 and 1930 a further twenty-eight cities, including most major population centres outside the old Confederacy, adopted smoke abatement ordinances.

Little appreciation that air pollution was anything other than a local problem was apparent during the period before the Second World War. On the few occasions when higher levels of government did take action, the focus was still predominantly on local concerns. Ohio passed a law in the late nineteenth century designed to regulate steam boilers in Cleveland and Cincinnati. Massachusetts and Rhode Island similarly passed laws to control smoke in Boston and Providence in 1910 and 1912 respectively. Albany County, NY, and Erie County, NY, were the only counties to pass smoke abatement laws before 1930. Even the very limited actions of the federal government at this time had predominantly a local focus. The US Bureau of Mines published guidelines on how to prevent excessive emissions of smoke from coal-burning equipment in 1912 and a model smoke abatement ordinance in 1930.[18] The latter was intended as a guide to help local governments draft legislation.

The widespread belief that air pollution was a local problem effectively limited congressional interest in the issue before the Second World War to a sporadic concern about the quality of the air of Washington, DC. The only air pollution law passed by Congress during this period was an 1899 resolution to control smoke emissions in the capital city. The committees on the District of Columbia in the House and Senate conducted the only hearings on air pollution: the Senate Committee on the District of Columbia held hearings in 1905 and 1907, and the Subcommittee on Public Health, Hospitals and Charities of the House Committee on the District of Columbia held a hearing in 1935.[19] Witnesses at these hearings came predominantly from Washington, DC. No fewer than thirty-four of the forty-two witnesses who gave evidence at the three hearings represented local concerns.

Early congressional interest

Interest in air pollution first began to emerge in Congress in the late 1940s after a particularly acute air pollution episode in Donora, Pennsylvania which killed twenty people and caused 6,000 cases of illness in October 1948.[20] Representative Augustine B. Kelley (D. PA) whose 27th District included Donora, and Rep. Herman P. Eberharter (D. PA) whose 32nd District included some of the worst polluted areas of neighbouring Pittsburgh, responded to the concerns of constituents and introduced bills 'to provide research into the health effects of air pollution' in the 1st session of the 81st Congress (1949).[21] Rep. Robert J. Corbett (R. PA), who represented the 30th District just upstream of Donora, introduced a similar bill a year later.[22] Corbett's bill called for greater research on 'the health hazards and methods of preventing pollution'. No action was taken on any of these bills.

The interest shown in air pollution by the three Pennsylvanian legislators did not last long beyond the immediate outpouring of public concern that followed the Donora incident. Only Rep. Corbett would introduce another air pollution control bill in Congress.[23] Perhaps the best interpretation of the actions of the three, therefore, is to regard the introduction of the bills as an example of symbolic politics – or what David Mayhew has termed 'position-taking'.[24] The bills were introduced simply to send a message to constituents and did not signal any real effort to address the problem of air pollution. None of the three made any statement on the floor of the House urging colleagues to support the bills, and there is no evidence that they sought other means to persuade recalcitrant colleagues to take action on the measures. Such 'position-taking' was not without one important consequence, however. The emphasis on public health in the bills ensured that they were referred to the House Committee on Interstate and Foreign Commerce (House Commerce) which had been granted jurisdiction over 'public health and quarantine' by the Legislative Reorganization Act 1946. These referrals were significant because they established the precedents upon which committee jurisdictions are partially based.[25] The result was that House Commerce became the main venue for the consideration of air pollution control issues in the House of Representatives for the next four decades or so.[26]

Greater commitment to addressing the problem of air pollution was shown by Rep. James J. Murphy (D. NY) whose 16th District included Staten Island and some of the worst polluted areas of lower west Manhattan.[27] Following the lead of Rep. Kelley and Rep. Eberharter, he introduced a bill in 1950 that also sought to promote research into the problem of air pollution.[28] Unlike the Pennsylvanians, however, Rep. Murphy worked to secure passage of an air pollution control bill. In a speech to the House he declared that: 'There is a real and urgent need for immediate research about these health effects from air pollution, but at present the Public Health Service is unable to do it because of lack of funds'.[29] When no legislative action occurred on the 1950 bill, he introduced two further bills the following year.[30] Both bills were referred to House Commerce. Previous air pollution control bills had died in committee, and Rep. Murphy took to the floor of the House to urge action on his bills. In a speech he reported his 'earnest endeavour to obtain a hearing before the Committee on Interstate and Foreign Commerce' and requested support.[31] Such badgering finally paid off. In 1952 House Commerce reported one of Rep. Murphy's bills.[32] HJ Res 218 (1951) was passed by the House on 2 July 1952 and sent to the Senate where it was referred to the Senate Committee on Interstate and Foreign Commerce (Senate Commerce).[33] Senate Commerce reported the bill on 3 July 1952 without alteration, but it was defeated the following day on the floor when Senator Herman Welker (R. ID) objected to the unanimous consent agreement under which the measure was being considered.[34] Senator Welker claimed that Section (b) of the bill, which stated that 'The Secretary of the Interior, and the Surgeon General, shall [render] every effort insofar as practicable to aid such State and local agencies in discharging their [air pollution control] responsibilities', would lead to a dramatic and costly expansion of federal authority.[35]

Although the early air pollution control bills introduced in the aftermath of the Donora incident were important in signalling congressional interest in the problem and establishing the referral

precedents that would shape the development of institutional structures, the twenty deaths and 6,000 cases of illness in Donora had
relatively little impact on the long-term development of policy. To
quote Arthur C. Stern: the incident 'caused a ripple of concern but
was soon forgotten'.[36] Similar in most respects to the many air pollution episodes that had cursed the country's industrial centres for
at least fifty years, the Donora incident did little to shake the prevailing belief that air pollution was a periodic, local problem that
could be addressed adequately by local governments.[37] Much more
important in inducing a change of policy was the growing problem
of air pollution in California. Los Angeles had begun to suffer from
frequent and persistent episodes of a brownish, hazy smog in the
early 1940s.[38] Blamed initially on emissions from wartime industrial
plants, and then on emissions from household furnaces, the even-
tual identification of automobile exhausts as the main precursors of
this new form of air pollution dramatically altered the contours of
the problem and cast doubt on local efforts at control.[39] Traditional
methods of air pollution control were not appropriate and local
governments were unwilling to take the politically unpalatable
action of curbing automobile use or investing in new mass transit
systems. An expensive search soon began for a technological solution to the problem.

The cost of finding a means of curbing exhaust emissions provided a strong incentive for members of Californian congressional
delegation to seek financial aid from the Federal Government. Rep.
Helen G. Douglas (D. CA) was the first to act. Prompted by the need
to find a popular issue to boost her flagging campaign against
Richard Nixon for a vacant US Senate seat, she introduced a bill in
1950 to provide for federal research into methods of preventing air
pollution.[40] Although no action was taken on the bill, and Rep. Douglas failed in her bid for the Senate, her bill was a harbinger of things
to come. With smog beginning to affect other Californian cities and
towns besides Los Angeles, the problem threatened to overwhelm
both local and state capabilities, and prompted other Californian
legislators to follow the lead of Rep. Douglas. The traditional path
of seeking to promote federal research into air pollution was taken
in bills introduced by Rep. Morris C. Poulson (R. CA) in 1953, and
Representatives Gordon L. McDonough (R. CA), Edgar W. Hiestand (R. CA) and James D. Roosevelt (D. CA) in 1955.[41] A different
path was pioneered by Senator Thomas H. Kuchel (R. CA). Fors-

aking efforts to promote research, Senator Kuchel introduced a bill in 1954 to provide tax relief for the purchase of air pollution control equipment.[42]

The ideological spectrum covered by these Californians was broad. Representatives (hereafter Reps) Hiestand and McDonough were conservatives, Rep. Poulson and Senator Kuchel were moderates, and Reps Roosevelt and Douglas were liberals. What they did have in common was a belief that air pollution control was a good political issue in California. Rep. Poulson introduced his air pollution control bill, in fact, as part of a successful campaign for mayor of Los Angeles that promised tough action to deal with smog. He claimed that Fletcher Bowron, the mayor of fifteen years, had done nothing to address the problem of air pollution in Los Angeles.[43] Not all of the Californians, however, were quite as opportunistic as Rep. Poulson. Rep. Roosevelt introduced further air pollution control bills in 1957 and 1961.[44] Rep. McDonough did likewise in 1957, 1959 and 1961.[45] But the most important role was undoubtedly played by Senator Kuchel who was at the forefront of efforts to enact air pollution control legislation in the 1950s.

Two obstacles hindered the early efforts of the Californian congressional delegation to increase the role of the federal government in controlling air pollution. First, the prevailing belief in Congress was that air pollution control was a state and local government responsibility. To many, the example provided by Oregon, which in 1951 passed a law that established a comprehensive air pollution control programme, offered a more acceptable way forward than increased federal involvement.[46] Second, none of the Californians interested in air pollution control issues occupied a position of institutional power. Most were relatively junior members. Rep. McDonough was first elected in 1947, Rep. Hiestand in 1952 and Rep. Roosevelt in 1955. Senator Kuchel was appointed to office in 1952 by Governor Earl Warren. At a time when junior members of Congress were expected to be seen and not heard, the lack of seniority enjoyed by proponents of an increased federal role in controlling air pollution was an obstacle to success. Control over the fate of legislation was also made difficult by the fact that none of the Californians served on a committee with an obvious claim to jurisdiction over air pollution. Both Rep. McDonough and Rep. Hiestand served on House Banking, and Rep. Roosevelt on House Education and Labor. Senator Kuchel served on Senate Public Works and

Senate Interior. To compound matters further, the fact that all apart from Rep. Roosevelt were Republicans made it difficult to exercise power when the Democrats controlled Congress. Majority status was a luxury that the Republicans enjoyed only during the 83rd Congress (1954–55).

Draftmanship and rhetoric were employed in efforts to alleviate and circumvent fears that state and local government power would be usurped by the enactment of federal air pollution control legislation. Legislation was designed that fell clearly within the existing purview of the federal government. Few could deny that the federal government had a right to conduct research, use the federal tax structure to engineer change, or even provide subsidies for certain types of activity. Senator Kuchel made this point in a 1954 speech to the Senate: 'While I recognize that the enforcement of controls are problems for the community and the State, it is in the field of taxation that the Federal Government may well be of assistance.'[47] Other speeches made in support of legislation constantly stressed that nothing was being proposed that would diminish the responsibility of lower levels of government. Speaking in favour of her 1950 resolution, for example, Rep. Douglas stressed that: 'Primary responsibility and authority for effective action rest with State and local governments, because the needs for control of air pollution vary from locality to locality'.[48] Little was said or proposed, in short, to suggest that the federal government should do anything other than support prevailing air pollution control arrangements.[49] Too few members, however, were convinced of the need for any federal role.

A lack of institutional power compounded the problems faced by proponents of an increased role for the federal government in controlling air pollution. Bills could be designed to fit prevailing views, speeches made to emphasize their compatibility with existing arrangements, but once introduced and referred to a committee little was likely to happen without the support of a sympathetic chair. Under such circumstances, two basic options were available. First, an effort could be made to bypass the committee system altogether by offering an air pollution control measure as a floor amendment rather than a bill. This option was easier in the Senate than in the House because of the former's relatively open amending process. Second, an air pollution control bill could be drafted in a way that allowed it to be referred to a different committee with a more sympathetic chair. 'A bill's phraseology can effect its referral and hence its chance of survival', note Roger H. Davidson and Walter J. Oleszek, 'This political fact of life means that members make artful use of words when crafting legislation'.[50] Both options would be tried by Senator Kuchel.

Frustrated at the prospect of air pollution control bills disappearing without trace in unsympathetic committees, Senator Kuchel joined with Senator Homer E. Capehart (R. IN), who had become Chairman of the Senate Committee on Banking and Currency (Senate Banking) following the Republican takeover in the elections of November 1952, to try a different legislative tactic in 1954. Rather than introduce a bill, the two offered an amendment to the Housing Act 1954 that would both promote research into air pollution, and provide loans and tax incentives for businesses to install control equipment. Senator Capehart defended the proposed amendment in a speech to the Senate in which he stressed that nothing was being suggested that would abrogate local responsibility for controlling air pollution:

> Essentially, by the very nature of the problem, the air pollution nuisance is interstate in character. Its control, however, is a local problem. By that I mean any program to be effective must originate at the local level and have the full and united support of all segments of the local economy.[51]

A few days later he provided a justification for treating air pollution as a housing issue: 'It is shortsighted to permit air pollution to continue. Unless it is abated, we can expect the newly constructed homes of today to become the slums of tomorrow – as surely as blight follows decay'.[52] The Senate Banking and Currency Committee conducted a hearing on the amendment in April 1954 at which local air pollution control officials from Los Angeles, South Pasadena, New York, Detroit, Philadelphia and a number of other Pennsylvanian towns gave evidence.[53] None of these officials spoke against the amendment and it was accepted without debate by the Senate. The amendment was dropped, however, in Conference Committee.[54]

Defeat of the amendment to the Housing Act 1954 brought home to Senators Kuchel and Capehart the need for greater political pressure to be brought on recalcitrant colleagues. In 1954 they wrote to President Eisenhower to suggest that he convene an interdepartmental committee to investigate possible action to control air pollution.[55] Eisenhower agreed to the suggestion, and created an *ad hoc* Interdepartmental Committee on Community Air Pollution under the stewardship of the Secretary of the Department of Health, Education, and Welfare (HEW) with the Surgeon General acting as chair. The Committee's recommendation that a broad programme of federal research and technical assistance be established was accepted by the President. In his 1955 State of the Union message Eisenhower gave notice that he would soon propose 'strengthening programs to combat the increasingly serious pollution of our rivers and the growing problem of air pollution'.[56] In a Special Message to Congress on 31 January 1955 the President proposed to 'step up research on air pollution'.[57]

Administration support had an immediate effect. No fewer than twenty-four air pollution control bills were introduced in the House in 1955 – more than twice the number that had been introduced in the previous six years.[58] Not all of these bills reflected the position of the Administration. The Californian congressional delegation, in particular, sought to take advantage of the impetus created by President Eisenhower to push for financial help to control air pollution. Representatives Gerald P. Lipscomb (R. CA), Andrew J. Hinshaw (R. CA), Donald L. Jackson (R. CA), Edgar W. Hiestand (R. CA) and Gordon L. McDonough (R. CA) all introduced bills to provide tax relief for businesses that installed air pollution control equipment.[59] Rep. Hiestand went even further and introduced a second bill in 1955 to provide direct financial aid to businesses that installed air pollution control equipment.[60] Although no action was taken on any of these bills, they signalled a determination among a minority to move beyond legislation that simply authorized research.

Legislation incorporating President Eisenhower's proposals was introduced by Senators Kuchel and Capehart.[61] In an effort to establish some control over the bill's progress, Senator Kuchel drafted the legislation as an amendment to the Water Pollution Control Act 1948. This meant that the bill was referred to the Senate Committee on Public Works (Senate Public Works) on which Senator Kuchel served. Senator Kuchel then persuaded Senator Robert S. Kerr (D. OK), the chair of the Committee's Subcommittee on Flood Control – Rivers and Harbors, to hold hearings on water and air pollution in April 1955.[62] Among the witnesses who gave evidence at the small portion of the hearings that Senator Kerr allowed to be devoted to air pollution were the Mayor of Philadelphia, air pollution control officials from Los Angeles and New York, the Dean of the University of California Medical School, and representatives of the Air Pollution Control Association, the American Medical Association and the Wilderness Society. Representatives of the Manufacturing Chemists Association also gave evidence. Virtually all of the former set of witnesses stressed that local governments needed help to control air pollution while the latter witness argued that the problem was best addressed by business.

Senate Public Works reported the bill unanimously on 3 May 1955. Although the bill authorized $3 million annually for five years for air pollution research, training, and technical assistance, the report also stressed that the Committee believed that: 'it is the primary responsibility of State and local government to prevent air pollution'.[63] The same message was propounded when floor consideration took place at the end of May 1955. Speaking in favour of the bill, Senator Kuchel assured colleagues that it did not presage an expansion of federal authority:

> It is not thought that Congress has anything to do with control of air pollution through the proposed legislation or through any contemplated Federal legislation. That problem remains where it ought to remain – in the States of the Union, and in the cities and the counties of our country.[64]

No serious opposition to the bill was encountered and it passed the Senate by voice vote without dissent. House Commerce reported the bill in June 1955, but increased the authorization to $5 million for five years. The House passed the bill by voice vote on 5 July 1955, and the following day the Senate agreed to accept the bill passed by the House without further debate. President Eisenhower signed the Air Pollution Control Act 1955 into law on 14 July 1955.[65]

The Air Pollution Control Act 1955 affirmed that primary responsibility for controlling air pollution resided with the states. The opening section declared that it is

> the policy of Congress to preserve and protect the primary responsibility and rights of the States and local governments in controlling air pollution, to support and aid technical research, to devise and develop methods of abating such pollution, and to provide Federal technical services and financial aid to State and local government air pollution control agencies.[66]

The law provided for federal surveys of specific local problems upon request and for the publication of reports by the Surgeon General. It authorized $5 million to be spent on demonstration projects, grants-in-aid to state and local government air pollution control agencies, as well as for research by the Public Health Service (PHS).

Considerable care was taken in the 1955 Act to preserve the primary responsibility of state and local governments in controlling air pollution. In a speech to the National Conference on Air Pollution in 1958, Senator Kuchel told the audience that:

> Underlying all of my thinking and my conversations was a conviction that actual control over air pollution sources and causes was and must be a local and State responsibility. This view was shared by all of those who took part in framing and pushing through the Air Pollution Control Act.[67]

The intention was to limit the role of the federal government to technical and financial support of state and local government activities. Despite the care and intent to preserve the role of state and local governments, however, the very enactment of the 1955 Act presaged a long-term shift in the allocation of responsibility for controlling air pollution. Not only did the Air Pollution Control Act 1955 signal the entry of the federal government into a policy arena in which it had previously been absent, but a timetable and impetus for further action had been established. Research reports had to be submitted to Congress, and reauthorization of the law was required within five years. The process of enactment had also produced institutional 'homes' in House Commerce and Senate Public Works for the issue, and created new opportunities for committee members either to gain reputations for policy expertise or to exercise political power.

Growing concern

Enactment of the Air Pollution Control Act 1955 marked the beginning of a period of growing congressional interest in air pollution control. Continued pressure from the Californian congressional delegation, and the evidence provided by federal reports on the problem, generated a momentum for further action that a increasing number of members proved willing to accommodate as elite and public concern about environmental issues grew. Bills were intro-

duced that not only sought to extend the provisions of the 1955 Act,
but also endeavoured to expand the role of the federal government.
An enduring belief that air pollution control was primarily the
responsibility of state and local governments, however, delineated
legislative possibilities. Radical changes in the federal role proved
impossible as opposition from industrial groups and concern about
constitutional sensitivities shaped congressional action.

Momentum for action
Pressure from the Californian delegation for further federal action
to control air pollution was felt less than a year after President
Eisenhower's ink had dried on the 1955 Act. Although no air pollution control bills were introduced in 1956, a congressional panel
was persuaded to visit Los Angeles to hear about the damage that air
pollution was causing. In May 1956, the Subcommittee No. 5
(Small Business) of the House Select Committee on Small Business
held hearings in Los Angeles on the harmful economic effects of
smog on small businesses.[68] Witnesses from local nurseries attested
to the problems that air pollution caused to their operations, and
local and state officials stressed the need for greater federal support
of their activities. Further ammunition for the Californians' cause
came later that year when House Commerce's Special Subcommittee on Traffic Safety, chaired by Rep. Kenneth Roberts (D. AL), held
hearings on road accidents.[69] One witness, Clark D. Bridges of the
Council on Industrial Health, gave evidence about the air pollution
caused by automobile exhausts.[70]
    The Californian delegation continued to agitate for an enhanced
federal role in controlling air pollution in 1957. Senator Kuchel and
Rep. Lipscomb introduced bills to provide tax incentives for businesses to install air pollution control equipment.[71] Rep. McDonough and Rep. Roosevelt introduced bills to require the Secretary
of Commerce to report to Congress on air pollution.[72] No action
took place on any of these bills. Part of the problem that the Californians had to confront when urging further action was a hesitancy
to act so soon after passage of the 1955 Act. Only two other representatives introduced air pollution control bills in 1957.[73] To focus
attention on the severity of the problem in their state, the Californians persuaded Rep. L. A. Fountain (D. NC) to take the Subcommittee on Intergovernmental Relations of the House Committee on
Governmental Relations to Los Angeles for hearings on the efficacy

of federal help to control air pollution in the city.[74] State and local officials informed the Subcommittee that federal support for their efforts to control air pollution were inadequate.

The cause of the Californians was taken up the following year by Rep. Paul F. Schenck (R. OH). In 1958 Rep. Schenck introduced a bill to require the Surgeon General of the Public Health Service to publish 'standards as to the amount of unburned hydrocarbons which is safe, from the standpoint of human health ... for a motor vehicle to discharge into the atmosphere'.[75] To legitimize the new regulatory authority that his bill would have given the federal government, Schenck relied upon the precedent set in federal water pollution statutes and made use of the Constitution's interstate commerce clause.[76] The bill proposed banning cars involved in interstate commerce that failed to meet the standards established by the PHS. Hearings on Rep. Schenck's bill were conducted by the Special Subcommittee on Traffic Safety of the House Committee on Interstate and Foreign Commerce in March 1958.[77] Witnesses from Los Angeles supported the bill, but opposition from both HEW and the automobile manufacturers, however, ensured that the bill was not reported out of subcommittee. The HEW opposed the bill on the basis that the PHS did not have the knowledge to determine what concentration of hydrocarbons should be considered dangerous. Secretary Marion B. Folsom informed the Subcommittee that 'there is not now available the scientific knowledge needed to carry out the purposes of the act. We would therefore recommend that the bill not be enacted by the Congress'.[78] The automobile manufacturers dismissed the bill as unfeasible. Charles M. Heinen of the Automobile Manufacturers' Association told the Subcommittee that: 'The industry's vehicle combustion products committee has given careful consideration of the intent and purpose of HR 9368, and believes that ... it could not be implemented effectively'.[79]

Behind the opposition of HEW to the Schenck Bill was a degree of confusion and uncertainty in different parts of the executive branch about the proper role of the federal government in controlling air pollution.[80] Although the notion that the federal government should conduct research into air pollution was accepted by all, suggestions that the federal government should assume a modicum of regulatory authority were not welcomed in all corners of the executive branch. In 1957 the Surgeon General, Leroy E. Burney, created a National Advisory Committee on Community Air Pollution with a membership drawn from industry, state and local air pollution control agencies, and medical and public health officials to co-ordinate research into the problem. In 1958 the National Advisory Health Council of the PHS signalled an interest in air pollution with a call for increased research and education. The PHS vehemently opposed, however, suggestions that it should have regulatory authority. When new HEW Secretary, Arthur S. Flemming, urged that the federal government be allowed to hold hearings and make recommendations on air pollution problems at a press conference on 1 December 1958, his position was opposed by the PHS which was determined to maintain its traditional role of conducting research.

Opposition from the PHS hamstrung congressional efforts in the late 1950s to enact legislation that would enhance the role of the federal government in controlling air pollution. The unwillingness of the PHS to support legislation that did anything other than promote further research fatally wounded a renewed effort by Rep. Schenck in 1959 to regulate exhaust emissions. Although the revised Schenck bill sought to meet objections that the PHS lacked the requisite knowledge to set standards by directing the Surgeon General to conduct a year's research before promulgating regulations, the central thrust of the legislation continued to raise the organization's ire.[81] In hearings on the bill conducted by the Subcommittee on Health and Safety of the House Committee on Interstate and Foreign Commerce in July 1959, opposition from the automobile manufacturers and the PHS again ensured that no further action was taken.[82] The PHS not only repeated its earlier objections based on inadequate knowledge, but also argued that federal emission standards were not needed as air pollution was predominantly an intrastate problem. To overcome the objections of the PHS, Rep. Schenck modified his bill still further. The third version of the bill simply directed the Surgeon General to conduct a thorough study of automobile exhaust and make a report to Congress within two years.[83] Stripped of all regulatory provisions the bill progressed rapidly through Congress. The Motor Vehicle Exhaust Study Act 1960, commonly known as the Schenck Act, was signed by President Eisenhower on 8 June 1960.[84]

The regulatory authority originally sought by Rep. Schenck, to quote Charles O. Jones, 'was simply ahead of its time'.[85] Neither the PHS nor a majority in Congress were willing to accept an increased

federal role in controlling air pollution. The PHS felt that regulatory authority would threaten its reputation as 'an apolitical, highly
professional, research-oriented organization'.[86] Many members of
Congress were uncertain about the legitimacy of an increased federal role and the benefits it would bring. In a speech to a National
Conference on Air Pollution held in Washington, DC, in December
1962, Rep. Kenneth Roberts (D. AL), who in 1959 had become
Chairman of House Commerce's Subcommittee on Health and
Safety, declared that:

> I do not think the Federal Government has any business telling the
> people of say Birmingham or Los Angeles how to proceed to meet their
> air pollution problems. This was made clear in the 1955 Act ... Abate-
> ment and enforcement programs to be effective must remain the
> responsibility of local government.[87]

Rep. Roberts's reluctance to move beyond the 1955 Act made even
modest change difficult to engineer. In 1960 and 1961 the Senate
passed legislation introduced by Senator Kuchel to allow the Surgeon General to hold hearings on air pollution problems, but on
both occasions the legislation died in Roberts's Subcommittee.[88]

Efforts to extend the Air Pollution Control Act 1955 proved less
controversial. Six bills to reauthorize the 1955 law were introduced
in Congress in 1959 – all but one of them by members of the Californian delegation. Reps. Roberts, Lipscomb, McDonaugh, Chester
E. Holifield (D. CA), and John F. Shelley (D. CA) introduced legislation in the House, and Senator Kuchel introduced legislation in
the Senate.[89] The Senate acted first. In April 1959 a bill passed the
Senate which extended the 1955 law for a further four years and
provided a $7.5 million annual authorization. Roberts's Subcom-
mittee held hearings on this bill and the five House bills in May and
June 1959.[90] All four of the Californian sponsors gave evidence in
favour of their bills, but for the first time in a congressional hearing
on air pollution no witness from Los Angeles gave evidence.
Instead, the Subcommittee heard the testimony of witnesses from
New York and Kentucky who described how the 1955 law had
prompted air pollution control activity in their states. Satisfied that
the Air Pollution Control Act was achieving its goals, the Subcommittee reported out a bill which extended the 1955 law for a further two years and pegged the annual authorization at $5 million.
The bill passed the House with little debate. In a classic compro-

mise, the conference committee agreed to a four-year extension with an annual authorization of $5 million. The conference report passed both chambers as the Air Pollution Control Act Extension and was signed into law by President Eisenhower on 22 September 1959.[91]

Although the Air Pollution Control Act Extension 1959 testified to a general unwillingness to expand the air pollution control activities of the federal government, the momentum for further action continued to build as the PHS began to report its research to Congress, and the Californian delegation persisted in their efforts to secure greater federal help for their state. Two congressional committees held oversight hearings on air pollution in 1960. In February 1960, House Commerce's Subcommittee on Health and Safety held hearings on automobile emissions.[92] Reps. McDonough and Dalip S. Saund (D. CA) gave evidence to the Subcommittee about the worsening problem of air pollution in California. In March 1960, House Appropriation's Subcommittee on the Departments of Labor, HEW and Related Agencies held hearings on a PHS study into environmental health problems.[93] Growing evidence of the deleterious effects of air pollution on health was presented to the Subcommittee. Evidence of this sort was seized upon by members of the Californian delegation to justify a greater federal role in controlling air pollution. Californians authored no fewer than eight of the thirteen air pollution control bills that were introduced in the 1st session of the 87th Congress (1961). Reps. McDonough, Shelley and Roosevelt introduced bills to amend the Air Pollution Control Act 1955.[94] Senator Kuchel and Rep. James C. Corman (D. CA) introduced bills to allow HEW conduct public hearings on air pollution.[95] Reps. Lipscomb and George P. Miller (D. CA) introduced a bill to allow tax relief on air pollution control equipment, and Rep. McDonough introduced a second bill to ensure that weather reports were given to air pollution control agencies.[96]

The position of the PHS regarding the proper role of the federal government in controlling air pollution had not changed. In a hearing on air pollution conducted by the Subcommittee on Health and Safety in November 1961, Dr Richard Prindle, deputy chief of the Division of Air Pollution of the PHS, informed the Subcommittee that: 'I believe the role of the Federal Government is just as our law has outlined, provision of technical assistance, research knowledge, and the information on which a State and local government might act.'[97] Proponents of a increased federal role, however, had a powerful ally in the new president. In February 1961 President Kennedy declared in a Special Message to Congress on Natural Resources that: 'We need an effective Federal air pollution control program now.'[98] Further advocacy was to follow. In a Special Message to Congress on Health Care in February 1962 President Kennedy urged the House to pass Senator Kuchel's 1961 bill which called for HEW to organize public hearings on air pollution.[99]

Rep. Roberts introduced a bill which incorporated the Administration's proposals in March 1962.[100] The bill sought to make the Air Pollution Control Act 1955 a permanent authorization, provided for grants-in-aid to state and local air pollution control authorities, and empowered the Secretary of HEW to initiate air pollution control conferences that could make recommendations to state and local authorities. Rep. Roberts's commitment to these proposals, however, was not strong. He had agreed to introduce the legislation both to accommodate the President and to cement his own control over air pollution control legislation in the House. Although the Subcommittee on Health and Safety held hearings on the bill in June 1962, Rep. Roberts used the lack of consensus among the witnesses to suggest that further time was needed to study the proposals.[101] The Subcommittee reported in its stead a bill to extend the 1955 law for a further two years. This bill passed the House by voice vote, was accepted by the Senate, and was signed into law by President Kennedy on 9 October 1962. The Air Pollution Control Act Extension 1962 provided a $5 million annual authorization for a further two years.[102]

The Clean Air Act 1963
The Air Pollution Control Act Extension 1962 was a last hurrah for those who wished to maintain the limited role of the federal government in controlling air pollution. Within a year a shift in elite and public perceptions of the problem, increased interest group activity, and membership turnover and structural change in Congress would create an environment more receptive to arguments that the federal government should do more than promote research. Ideas that had been floating around in what John W. Kingdon has described as a 'policy primeval soup' became acceptable as changes both inside and outside Congress transformed the environment in which they were considered.[103]

Elite knowledge of air pollution changed significantly in the early 1960s. Not only had the hearings conducted by the Subcommittee on Health and Safety in the early years of the decade established that panel as a source of considerable expertise on air pollution issues, but the research mandated by the Air Pollution Control Act and the Schenck Act began to provide Congress with clear evidence of the extent of the problem, and perhaps equally important to those pressing for an enhanced federal role, the inadequacy of state control arrangements.[104] Although thirty-two states had enacted some form of air pollution control legislation by 1963, considerable variation existed in the scope and efficacy of these laws.[105] Economic competition between states and a lack of resources undermined stringency.[106] Concerns for health often came a poor second to a desire not to harm the local economy.[107] State and local spending on efforts to control air pollution amounted to only $10.1 million in 1961 and over half of that total was spent in California. Only fifteen states had some control authority over air pollutants in 1963, and fewer than six states were enforcing their air pollution laws to any extent.[108]

Increased public concern about air pollution was also apparent by the early 1960s. In part, this change in public attitudes was a product of fundamental changes in the American economy in the period after the Second World War. Samuel P. Hays has argued that increased affluence allowed a new mass middle class to emerge that placed a premium on 'quality of life' issues such as pollution.[109] The increased public concern about air pollution, however, was also sparked by short-term events that boosted the saliency of the issue. The publicity that surrounded publication of Rachel Carson's book *Silent Spring* in 1962 was one factor that raised the profile of environmental issues.[110] Another was the wide reporting of the London smog disaster of December 1962 in which up to 700 people were estimated to have been killed.

State and local politicians were the first to feel the draught created by the changing winds of public opinion. Faced with increasing demands for environmental protection, but lacking the resources to act, these politicians began to turn to the federal government for aid. Interest groups such as the US Conference of Mayors, the American Municipal Association and the National Association of Counties began to lobby forcefully for a greater federal role.[111] To such voices were added those of the Administration which began to appreciate the political capital that could be made by supporting moves to enhance the role of the federal government in controlling air pollution. Ranged against these proponents of change were industrial groups. The National Association of Manufacturers sought to maintain the *status quo* while automobile manufacturers concentrated on fighting efforts to set exhaust emission standards.

Demands that the federal government assume a greater role in controlling air pollution found a more receptive environment in Congress in 1963 than had hitherto been the case. In the House, Rep. Roberts had come to accept the need for a more active federal role. Not only had the hearings conducted by the Subcommittee on Health and Safety over the previous two years produced sufficient evidence to convince him that air pollution was a national problem requiring national action, but experience of smog in his constituency of Birmingham, Alabama, had given him an important incentive to act. In the Senate, the politics and structure of the Senate Public Works Committee had changed as a result of the deaths of Senator Dennis Chavez (D. NM), who had been Chairman since 1955, on 18 November 1962, and his successor Senator Robert S. Kerr (D. OK) on 1 January 1963. Senator Pat McNamara (D. MI), the new Chairman, created a Special Subcommittee on Air and Water Pollution under the Chairmanship of Senator Edmund Muskie (D. ME) as part of a reorganization of the Committee.[112] The reorganization gave Senator Muskie, who had long been an advocate of a greater federal role in combating water pollution, a strong institutional base to shape legislation on air pollution.

A bill to expand the role of the federal government in controlling air pollution was introduced in the Senate on 23 January 1963 by Senator Abraham Ribicoff (D. CT).[113] Ribicoff had previously served as HEW Secretary and had considerable knowledge about air pollution. His bill proposed to establish a grants-in-aid programme to help states and local governments fund air pollution control programmes, to improve federal research on air pollution and to allow the Secretary of HEW to take action to abate interstate air pollution. Slightly weaker legislation was introduced the same day by Senators Clair Engle (D. CA) and Maurine Neuberger (D. OR).[114] Although resistance to an increased federal role was still evident in the PHS, the basic provisions of the Ribicoff bill were endorsed by President Kennedy in a special message on health which was transmitted to Congress on 7 February 1963. President Kennedy stated

that: 'In light of the known damage caused by polluted air, both to
our health and to our economy, it is imperative that greater emphasis be given to the control of air pollution by communities, States,
and the Federal Government.'[115] He called for HEW to be given
authority to engage in intensive research into the causes, effects and
control of air pollution, for financial help to be given to state and
local governments, for research to be conducted into interstate and
nation-wide air pollution, and for the federal government to take
action to abate interstate air pollution along the lines of existing
water pollution control measures. Three weeks later, Rep. Roberts
introduced a bill in the House incorporating the Administration's
proposals.[116]

Progress in the House was rapid. The Subcommittee on Health
and Safety held hearings on the Roberts bill in March 1963.[117] HEW
Under Secretary Ivan A. Nestingen strongly endorsed the bill as did
state and local government groups. William J. Phillips, representing
the National Association of Counties, 'enthusiastically' welcomed
the bill, but also added that industry would be encouraged to install
control equipment if 'inclusion of the fast tax write-off were made
possible'.[118] The strongest advocates of maintaining the *status quo* in
the hearings were industry groups. Daniel W. Cannon, the representative of the National Association of Manufacturers, argued that
greater federal intervention was not needed as 'communities are
entirely capable of carrying out effective air pollution control programs without federal financial aid and federal enforcement activities'.[119] Such claims went largely unheeded, and an amended version
of the bill which reduced the size of the grants-in-aid was voted out
of the full Committee on 27 June 1963.[120] The House passed the bill
on a 273–102 roll-call vote on 24 July 1963. Democrats voted
206–10 for the bill. Eight of the ten Democratic 'nays' came from
southerners. Republicans split 67–92 for the bill. Opposition to the
bill centred primarily on fears that the federal government was
intruding on an area that constitutionally belonged to the states.

In the Senate, the newly created Special Subcommittee on Air and
Water Pollution held hearings on the Ribicoff bill in September
1963.[121] Industrial groups were much more vocal in their opposition
to federal enforcement powers in these hearings than they had been
in the House. The spokesman of the Manufacturing Chemists Association, Walter Penfield, claimed that: 'Too much stress on Federal
enforcement will discourage State and local level enforcement

people and impair their programs.'[122] The representative of the American Iron and Steel Institute, Erwin Schultze, even argued that there was no 'scientific basis' for suggesting that air pollution posed 'a mounting danger to our national health and welfare'.[123] The momentum for new legislation proved unstoppable, however, and the bill was reported out of the Public Works Committee on 7 November 1963. Floor debate consisted largely of a panegyric to the bill. Three amendments were accepted by voice vote: two offered by Senator Jacob Javits (R. NY) and one offered by Senator Maurine Neuberger (D. OR). The Javits amendments clarified the circumstances under which the Secretary of HEW could act to deal with intrastate air pollution; the Neuberger amendment dealt with patents arising out of federal research. The amended bill passed the Senate by voice vote on 19 November 1963.

The bills passed by the House and the Senate differed in minor ways. The House-passed bill authorized $85 million for fiscal years 1964–67, provided an additional $5 million each year in federal matching grants for state and local pollution control programmes, and directed the HEW Secretary to 'conduct studies' into automobile exhaust emissions. The Senate-passed bill authorized $182 million for fiscal years 1965–69, limited federal matching grants to 20 per cent of appropriated funds, and directed the HEW Secretary to establish a technical committee to review and encourage efforts to eliminate pollution from automobile exhausts. A compromise version of the legislation was fashioned in conference committee which provided an authorization of $95 million for fiscal years 1964–67, followed the Senate version in most other respects, but dropped the Neuberger amendment. The House passed the conference report by a 273–109 roll-call vote on 10 December 1963. Democrats voted 204–15 in favour of the bill. Fourteen southerners voted against passage. Republicans split 69–94 in favour of the bill. Debate was focused more on the bill's philosophy than on specific provisions. Speaking against the legislation, Rep. Robert McClory argued that the problem of air pollution should not 'persuade the Congress to initiate a vast new federal program, as is done by this bill'.[124] The Senate passed the conference report by voice vote without debate the same day. One week later the legislation was signed into law by President Johnson. With typical hyperbole, Johnson predicted that: 'Under this legislation we can halt the trend towards greater contamination of our atmosphere.'[125]

The Clean Air Act 1963, as enacted, expanded federal power in a subtle way. In language similar to that found in the Air Pollution Control Act 1955, the Clean Air Act affirmed 'that the prevention and control of air pollution at its source is the primary responsibility of States and local governments', but in a departure from the language of the 1955 Act added 'that Federal financial assistance and leadership is essential for the development of cooperative Federal, State, regional, and local programs to prevent and control air pollution'.[126] In most respects the Clean Air Act built upon the pattern that had been established in earlier air pollution control laws. The emphasis was upon expanding federal research facilities and increasing the financial assistance given to state and local governments. In a significant change from the established pattern, however, the Clean Air Act gave the Secretary of the Department of Health, Education, and Welfare (HEW) authority to take legal action against polluters causing interstate pollution.[127]

Although the Clean Air Act 1963 left primary responsibility for controlling air pollution with state and local governments, its enactment presaged an expansion of federal power. In just over a decade the legitimacy of the federal government to act in a policy domain that had previously been the reserve of state and local governments had been established through a series of non-controversial measures that concentrated upon research. The provisions of the Clean Air Act that granted the Secretary of HEW authority to take action to control air pollution in specific circumstances, however, hinted at a subtle shift in responsibility for controlling air pollution. A signal had been given that the federal government might consider pre-empting state authority to tackle the problem of air pollution.

Conclusion

The period of policy awakening provides an important insight into the origins of congressional interest in air pollution control. Although the first stirrings of interest were sparked by the Donora incident, far more important to the long-term development of policy were the efforts of some of the Californian delegation to ameliorate the worsening air pollution problem in their state. Particularly important was the policy entrepreneurship of Senator Kuchel who was responsible for virtually all major initiatives up to 1963, when he ceded leadership to those occupying positions of institutional power.

Senator Muskie and Rep. Roberts may have differed in their attitudes to air pollution control in the late 1950s, but both saw an opportunity to craft public policy and enhance their institutional reputations when they acceded to positions of power. Notable by their absence in this period of policy awakening are national environmental interest groups. The origins of congressional interest in air pollution control was independent of the activities of these groups.

Three factors shaped the pace and nature of legislative activity in the period. First, proponents of a greater federal role in controlling air pollution did not occupy positions of institutional power. Not until 1963 when Senator Muskie became Chairman of the Special Subcommittee on Air and Water Pollution was a committed environmentalists in a position to control at least part of the legislative process. Second, poor 'problem identification and definition' meant that policy-making was uncertain. The assertion of Rep. Ralph Harvey (R. IN) in the debate on the Clean Air Act 1963 that Congress was 'legislating in the unknown' was in many respects an accurate observation.[128] Third, the belief that air pollution control was the constitutional prerogative of state and local governments restricted the options available to policy-makers. Policies were often proposed on the basis of their perceived constitutional correctness rather than their efficacy. Overcoming the obstacles posed by these three factors required the intervention of the administration. Presidential support was a prerequisite for Congress to take action.

The air pollution control laws enacted in the period of policy awakening had a limited purpose. Their importance lay in the creation of institutional structures that accompanied their enactment, and the improvements in 'problem identification and definition' that followed in their wake. At the end of the period both congressional panels and bureaucracies in the executive branch had been created to deal with air pollution. A small number of legislators and bureaucrats as a result had been provided with a vested interest in further action. Ammunition to fuel such interests would soon be produced by the research mandated by the Schenck Act and the Clean Air Act. As Rep. Thomas B. Curtis (R. MO) had argued during the floor debate on the Clean Air Act 1963, the reports produced by such research constituted 'lobbying with Federal funds'.[129] Further action to increase the role of the federal government in controlling air pollution would follow evidence that the states and local governments were incapable of dealing with the problem.

Notes

1 Bruce A. Ackerman and William T. Hassler *Clean Coal/Dirty Air* (New Haven, CN: Yale University Press, 1981).

2 Richard E. Cohen *Washington At Work: Back Rooms and Clean Air* (New York: Macmillan, 1992), chapter 2.

3 Gary C. Bryner *Blue Skies, Green Politics* (Washington, DC: Congressional Quarterly Press, 1993), p.81.

4 Arthur C. Stern 'History of Air Pollution Legislation in the United States', *Journal of Air Pollution Control Association* (1982), 32:44–61; Randall B. Ripley 'Congress and Clean Air: The Issue of Enforcement, 1963' in Frederic N. Cleaveland and associates (eds), *Congress and Urban Problems* (Washington, DC: Brookings, 1969) pp.224–78; J. Clarence Davies *The Politics of Pollution* (Indianapolis: Pegasus, 1970); James E. Krier and Edmund Ursin *Pollution and Policy* (Berkeley, CA: University of California Press, 1977); Charles O. Jones *Clean Air* (Pittsburgh: University of Pittsburgh Press, 1975).

5 Jones *Clean Air*, chapter 2.

6 Kent E. Portney *Controversial Issues in Environmental Policy* (Newbury Park, CA: Sage, 1992), p.68.

7 See Peter Brimblecombe *The Big Smoke* (London: Methuen, 1987), chapter 1; Robert C. Paehlke *Environmentalism and the Future of Progressive Politics* (New Haven, CN: Yale University Press, 1989), p.24.

8 See Joseph F. Zimmerman *Contemporary American Federalism* (Leicester: Leicester University Press, 1992), pp.35–6. The Supreme Court upheld the claim that 'police powers could be used to control air pollution' in *Heron Portland Cement Co. v. Detroit* (1960), 362 US 440.

9 Arnold J. Heidenheimer, Hugh Heclo and Carolyn Teich Adams *Comparative Public Policy* 3rd edition (New York: St. Martin's Press, 1990), p.308.

10 Upton Sinclair *The Jungle* (New York: Signet, 1990, first published 1906), p.30.

11 Stern 'History of Air Pollution Legislation in the United States', p.44.

12 See R. Dale Grinder 'The Battle for Clean Air: The Smoke Problem in Post-Civil War America' in Martin V. Melosi (ed.), *Pollution and Reform in American Cities, 1870–1930* (Austin, TX: University of Texas Press, 1980), pp.83–104; and Lawrence W. Pollack 'Legal Boundaries of Air Pollution Control – State and Local Legislative Purpose and Techniques' *Law and Contemporary Problems* (1968), 33:331–57.

13 *Bove v. Donner-Hanna Coke Corp.* 142 Misc. 329, 254, NYS 403 (1931).

14 Peter C. Yeager *The Limits of Law* (Cambridge, Cambridge University Press, 1991), p.62. See also Lotte M. Wenner *One Environment Under Law* (Pacific Palisades, CA: Goodyear, 1976).

15 This paragraph and the one following rely heavily upon the account provided by Stern.

16 St Louis City Council passed an ordinance in 1876 that required industrial chimneys to be at least twenty feet high. See Paehlke *Environmentalism and the Future of Progressive Politics*, p.23.

17 Cited in Jack Bregman and Sergei Lenormond *The Pollution Paradox* (New York, Spartan Books, 1966), p.6.

18 See Ripley 'Congress and Clean Air', p.228. Carbon monoxide in automobile exhaust emissions was studied by the Public Health Service (PHS) in the mid-1920s. The PHS also carried out an investigation of crop damage in Washington state a few years later that had apparently been caused by acid rain. See Krier and Ursin *Pollution and Policy*, p.47.

19 US Senate, Committee on District of Columbia, *Hearing*, 'Hearing on the Bill (S.5108) To Amend an Act for the Prevention of Smoke in D.C. and for Other Purposes', 58th Congress, 3rd session, 16 January 1905; US Senate, Committee on District of Columbia, *Hearing*, 'Union Station, Washington DC – Proposed Application of Smoke Law to Locomotives', 59th Congress, 2nd session, 18 and 29 January 1907; US House of Representatives, Committee on District of Columbia, Subcommittee on Public Health, Hospitals, and Charities, *Hearing*, 'Smoke Control', 74th Congress, 1st session, 5 April 1935.

20 H. H. Schrenk, H. Heinmann, G. D. Clayton, W. M. Gafafer and H. Wexler 'Air Pollution in Donora, Pa. Epidemiology of the Unusual Smog Episode of October 1948', *Public Health Bulletin* (Washington DC: Public Health Service, 1949).

21 Rep. Eberharter introduced HJ Res 379 (1949); Rep. Kelley introduced HJ Res 380 (1949).

22 HJ Res 441 (1950).

23 HR 3536 (1951).

24 David R. Mayhew *Congress: The Electoral Connection* (New Haven, CN: Yale University Press, 1974), p.61.

25 US House of Representatives, Select Committee on Committees, 'Committee Reform Amendments of 1974', *Report*, 93rd Congress, 2nd session, H.Rept.93–916, p.56. See also David C. King 'The Nature of Congressional Committee Jurisdictions', *American Political Science Review* (1994), 88:48–50.

26 See Christopher J. Bailey 'Explaining the Choice of Air-Pollution Control Strategies in the United States: Some Evidence of Institutional Bias', *Environmental Politics* (1996), 5:78–81.

27 Staten Island tended to suffer from air pollution originating in New Jersey. See Rep. Murphy's statement to the floor of the House in *Congressional Record* 84th Congress, 1st session, 31 May 1955, pp.7249–50.

28 HJ Res 416 (1950).
29 *Congressional Record* 81st Congress, 2nd session, 16 March 1950, p.3486.
30 HJ Res 38 (1951); HJ Res 218 (1951).
31 *Congressional Record* 82nd Congress, 1st session, 25 July 1951, p.A4666.
32 H Rept 2359 (1952).
33 The referral to Senate Commerce was interesting. In 1951 Senator James E. Murray (D. MT) had introduced the first air pollution control bill in the Senate (SJ Res 110) and it had been referred to the Senate Committee on Labor and Public Welfare (Senate Labor). Like House Commerce, Senate Labor had been given jurisdiction over 'public health and quarantine' by the Legislative Reorganization Act of 1947. The referral of HJ Res 218 to Senate Commerce, thus, represented a change in referral patterns.
34 S Rept 2079 (1952).
35 *Congressional Record* 82nd Congress, 2nd session, 4 July 1952, p.S9314.
36 Stern 'History of Air Pollution Legislation in the United States', p.48.
37 See Davies *The Politics of Pollution*, p.51.
38 Derek M. Elsom *Atmospheric Pollution: A Global Problem* 2nd edition (Oxford: Basil Blackwell, 1992), p.196.
39 Professor Haagen-Smit of the California Institute of Technology is widely cited as being the first person to suggest that the Los Angeles smog was caused by emissions from motor vehicles. See Krier and Ursin *Pollution and Policy*, pp.6–7, 79–83.
40 HR 9379 (1950).
41 HJ Res 174 (1953); HR 3680 (1955); HR 6597 (1955); HR 6699 (1955).
42 S 3115 (1954). This bill was referred to Senate Finance. A similar bill, HR 8361 (1954), was introduced in the House by Rep. Charles J. Kersten (R. WI) and referred to Ways and Means. California adopted a scheme similar to that proposed by Senator Kuchel in 1955. See Krier and Ursin *Pollution and Policy*, p.97.
43 *New York Times* 1 March 1953, p.64.
44 HR 6541 (1957), HR 3577 (1961).
45 HR 5391 (1957), HR 3183 (1959), HR 747 (1961), HR 1189 (1961).
46 US Environmental Protection Agency *Environmental Progress and Challenges: EPA's Update* (Washington, DC: EPA, 1988), p.13. Stern notes that California did not adopt a similar law until 1957, and then only in respect to emissions from motor vehicles; Stern "History of Air Pollution Legislation in the United States', p.47.
47 *Congressional Record* 83rd Congress, 2nd session, 11 March 1954, p.3060.

48 *Congressional Record* 81st Congress, 2nd session, 10 July 1950, p.A5753.

49 One exception to this type of advocacy can be found in a speech in which Rep. Isidore Dollinger (D. NY) appears to call for federal regulatory action: '[Air pollution] is no longer a purely local matter: effects of air pollution frequently transcend State lines and so create a serious interstate problem which I maintain must now be effectively dealt with by the federal government'. *Congressional Record* 82nd Congress, 2nd session, 4 March 1952, p.A2109.

50 Roger H. Davidson and Walter J. Oleszek *Congress and Its Members* 2nd edition (Washington, DC: Congressional Quarterly Press, 1985), p.267.

51 *Congressional Record* 83rd Congress, 2nd session, 1 April 1954, p.4314.

52 *New York Times* 11 April 1954, pp.VIII, 1.

53 US Senate, Committee on Banking and Currency, *Hearing*, 'Housing Act of 1954 – Air Pollution Control Amendment', 83rd Congress, 2nd session, 13–15 April 1954.

54 *New York Times* 16 July 1954, p.9.

55 See Ripley 'Congress and Clean Air', p.230.

56 Dwight D. Eisenhower 'Annual Message to Congress on the State of the Union', *Public Papers, 1955* 6 January 1955, p.24.

57 Dwight D. Eisenhower 'Special Message to the Congress Recommending a Health Program', *Public Papers, 1955* 31 January 1955, p.221.

58 Thirteen air pollution control bills had been introduced in the House between 1949 and 1954.

59 HR 2016 (1955); HR 3554 (1955); HR 3552 (1955); HR 3553 (1955); HR 3778 (1955); HR 2417 (1955).

60 HR 3901 (1955).

61 S 928 (1955).

62 US Senate, Committee on Public Works, Subcommittee on Flood Control – Rivers and Harbors, *Hearing*, 'Water and Air Pollution Control', 84th Congress, 1st session, 22, 25, 26 April 1955.

63 Ripley 'Congress and Clean Air', p.231.

64 *Congressional Record* 31 May 1955, pp. S7249–50.

65 PL 84–159.

66 42 USC 1857a(1).

67 Thomas H. Kuchel 'Public Interest Demands Clean Air' in US Department of Health, Education, and Welfare, Public Health Service *National Conference on Air Pollution: Proceedings* (Washington, DC: GPO, 1958), p.16.

68 US House of Representatives, Select Committee on Small Business, Subcommittee No. 5 (Small Business), *Hearing* 'Air Pollution Problems', 84th Congress, 2nd session, 18, 19 May 1956.

69 US House of Representatives, Committee on Interstate and Foreign Commerce, Special Subcommittee on Traffic Safety, *Hearing*, 'Automobile and Highway Safety Promotion Programs, Review', 84th Congress, 2nd session, 16, 23 July, 8–10, 27–31 August, 25–28 September 1956.

70 *Ibid.*, p.225.

71 S 1627 (1957); HR 2463 (1957).

72 HR 5391 (1957); HR 6541 (1957).

73 Rep. John W. Byrnes (R. WI) introduced HR 1082 (1957) and Rep. Richard M. Simpson (R. PA) introduced HR 4134 (1957). Both bills sought to provide tax relief for the purchase of air pollution control equipment.

74 US House of Representatives, Committee on Government Operations, Subcommittee on Intergovernmental Relations, *Hearing*, 'Air Pollution', 85th Congress, 1st session, 31 October 1957.

75 HR 9368 (1958).

76 The Refuse Act of 1899 (30 Stat. 1121, 33 USC 401 *et seq*) relied upon the commerce clause to legitimize federal regulation of pollution in navigable interstate rivers. See Peter Rogers *America's Water* (Cambridge, MA: MIT Press, 1993), pp.94–5.

77 US House of Representatives, Committee on Interstate and Foreign Commerce, Special Subcommittee on Traffic Safety, *Hearing*, 'Unburned Hydrocarbons', 85th Congress, 2nd session, 17 March 1958.

78 *Ibid.*, p.2.

79 *Ibid.*, p.34.

80 See Ripley 'Congress and Clean Air', pp.232–3; Stern 'History of Air Pollution Legislation in the United States', p.49.

81 HR 883 (1959).

82 US House of Representatives, Committee on Interstate and Foreign Commerce, Subcommittee on Health and Safety, *Hearing*, 'Motor Vehicle Safety', 86th Congress, 1st session, 7–9 July 1959.

83 HR 3238 (1960).

84 Motor vehicle exhaust study, PL 86–493, 74 stat. 162.

85 Jones *Clean Air*, p.34.

86 Ripley 'Congress and Clean Air', p.233.

87 Quoted in James L. Sundquist *Politics and Policy* (Washington DC, Brookings, 1968), p.351.

88 S 3108 (1960); S 455 (1961).

89 HR 7476 (1959); HR 2347 (1959); HR 3183 (1959); HR 3730 (1959); HR 4466 (1959); S 441 (1959).

90 US House of Representatives, Committee on Interstate and Foreign Commerce, Subcommittee on Health and Safety, *Hearing*, 'Air Pollution Control', 86th Congress, 1st session, 19 May, 24 June 1959.

91 The Air Pollution Control Act, Extension (1959), PL 86–365, 73 stat. 646.

92 US House of Representatives, Committee on Interstate and Foreign Commerce, Subcommittee on Health and Safety, *Hearing*, 'Automobile Pollution Control Progress', 86th Congress, 2nd session, 23, 24 February 1960.

93 US House of Representatives, Committee on Appropriations, Subcommittee on Departments of Labor, HEW, and Related Agencies, *Hearing*, 'Environmental Health Problems', 86th Congress, 2nd session, 8, 9 March 1960.

94 HR. 747 (1961); HR 2948 (1961); HR 3577 (1961).

95 S 455 (1961); HR 9352 (1961).

96 HR 2493 (1961); HR 6370 (1961); HR 1189 (1961).

97 US House of Representatives, Committee on Interstate and Foreign Commerce, Subcommittee on Health and Safety, *Hearing*, 'Air Pollution Control', 87th Congress, 1st session, 27 November 1961, p.36.

98 John F. Kennedy 'Remarks to the Delegates to the Youth Fitness Conference', *Public Papers, 1961* 21 February 1961, p.117.

99 John F. Kennedy 'Special Message to the Congress on National Health Needs', *Public Papers, 1962* 27 February 1962, p.171.

100 HR 3083 (1962).

101 US House of Representatives, Committee on Interstate and Foreign Commerce, Subcommittee on Health and Safety, *Hearings*, 'Air Pollution Control', 87th Congress, 2nd session, 25 June 1962.

102 The Air Pollution Control Act Extension of 1962, PL 87–761, 76 stat. 760.

103 John W. Kingdon *Agendas, Alternatives, and Public Policies* (Boston: Little, Brown, 1984), chapter 6.

104 The Secretary of HEW delivered the report 'Motor Vehicles, Air Pollution and Health' as required by the Schenck Act to Congress in June 1962 (House Doc. 87–489).

105 Evan J. Ringquist *Environmental Protection at the State Level* (Armonk, NY: Sharpe, 1993), p.46.

106 William R. Lowry *The Dimensions of Federalism: State Governments and Pollution Control Policies* (Durham, NC: Duke University Press, 1992), p.20. See also C. K. Rowland and Roger Marz 'Gresham's Law: The Regulatory Analogy', *Policy Studies Review* (1982), 1:572–80.

107 See G. Todd Norvelle and Alexander W. Bell 'Air Pollution Control in Texas', *Environmental Law Review* (1970), 1:239–81; Joel Tarr and Bill Lamperes 'Changing Fuel Use Behavior and Energy Transitions: The Pittsburgh Smoke Control Movement, 1940–1950', *Journal of Social History* (1981), 14:561–88; Matthew Crenson *The Un-politics*

of Air Pollution: A Study of Non-decisionmaking in the Cities (Baltimore, Johns Hopkins University Press, 1971).

108 Ripley 'Congress and Clean Air', p.226.

109 Samuel P. Hays *Beauty, Health and Permanence: Environmental Politics in the United States, 1955–1985* (Cambridge: Cambridge University Press, 1987). See also Ronald Inglehart *Culture Shift in Advanced Industrial Society* (Princeton, NJ: Princeton University Press, 1990).

110 Rachel Carson *Silent Spring* (Boston, Houghton Mifflin, 1962).

111 See Ripley 'Congress and Clean Air', p.237; Stern 'History of Air Pollution Legislation in the United States', p.51.

112 See US Senate *History of the Senate Committee on Environment and Public Works*, Senate Document 100–45, December 1988, p.11.

113 S 432 (1963).

114 S 444 (1963).

115 John F. Kennedy 'Special Message to Congress on Improving the Nation's Health', *Public Papers, 1963* 7 February 1963, pp.144–5.

116 HR 4415 (1963).

117 US House of Representatives, Committee on Interstate and Foreign Commerce, Subcommittee on Public Health and Safety, *Hearing*, 'Air Pollution', 88th Congress, 1st session, 18, 19 March 1963.

118 *Ibid.*, p.143.

119 *Ibid.*, p.167.

120 HR 6518 (1963).

121 US Senate, Committee on Public Works, Special Subcommittee on Air and Water Pollution, *Hearing*, 'Air Pollution Control', 88th. Congress, 1st session, 9–11 September 1963.

122 *Ibid.*, p.230.

123 *Ibid.*, p.280.

124 *Congressional Record* 88th Congress, 1st session, 10 December 1963, p.23964.

125 Lyndon B. Johnson, *Public Papers, 1963–64* 17 December 1963, p.60.

126 42 USC 1857(a)(3–4).

127 The Secretary of HEW received three requests for federal intervention in interstate pollution abatement and initiated five interstate abatement actions on his own recognizance between 1964 and 1967. See Stern 'History of Air Pollution Legislation in the United States', p.52.

128 *Congressional Record* 88th Congress, 1st session, 10 December 1963, p.23963.

129 *Congressional Record* 88th Congress, 1st session, 24 July 1963, p.13283.

5
Policy inflation, 1963–70

Congressional interest in air pollution control broadened and deepened significantly between 1964 and 1970. Part of what happened during this period of policy inflation can be outlined with simple quantitative data. A total of ninety-seven air pollution control bills were introduced in 1970 compared to three in 1964. Fourteen different congressional panels held a total of thirty-three hearings on air pollution in 1970 whereas in 1964 one committee had held just three hearings. Major legislation was enacted in 1965, 1967 and 1970. Minor reauthorizations were passed in 1966 and 1969. Such stark indicators of activity and outputs, however, tell nothing of the changes that occurred in the nature of Congress's involvement. In six years the balance of responsibility for controlling air pollution swung towards the federal government as Congress first directed state governments to take action to deal with the problem, and then began to pre-empt their authority to control an increasing number of specific air pollutants.

The forces driving this period of policy inflation had three main sources. First, the early efforts of Congress to control air pollution generated a momentum for further action. As J. Clarence Davies has noted:

> Once the Federal government has ventured into a new field, the pace of legislation is likely to accelerate. The initial hurdle of Federal responsibility having been overcome, the search for more effective ways of accomplishing the task begins.[1]

Not only did the legislation of the late 1950s and early 1960s institutionalize concern within Congress in the form of panels with jurisdiction over the issue, but the research that the Acts engendered served to improve knowledge of both the extent of the problem and the inadequacy of existing methods of control. Second, a number of industrial groups viewed the likelihood of improved state regulation of air pollution in the wake of these laws with alarm. The prospect of each state establishing its own emission standards was sufficient to force both the automobile and coal industries to lobby for federal pre-emption of state authority.[2] Finally, growing public awareness of environmental problems generated ever greater demands for further action, and spawned a new generation of interest groups willing to put pressure on Congress to take further action.

New incentives for members of Congress to address the problem of air pollution were created as a result of these forces. The rewards associated with 'position-taking' became more apparent as public concern about the environment increased. Legislators who displayed a commitment to cleaning the air by introducing bills, making speeches, participating in committee hearings and voting in support of legislation could expect to reap electoral benefits. A few even perceived rewards of sufficient magnitude to warrant meeting the costs associated with entrepreneurship. Challenges to the monopolistic position occupied by established authorities such as Senator Muskie began to emerge as a result. Efforts were made by a variety of committee chairs to claim some jurisdiction over the issue; new policy initiatives were launched to secure the support of the public. So intense was the competition to establish leadership on the issue, particularly after President Nixon entered the fray following his State of the Union message in 1970, that traditional concerns about the prerogatives of states were largely forgotten. Legislation which had sought to persuade or cajole the states to take action to control air pollution was superseded by legislation which pre-empted much of their authority to act.

Compared to the earlier period of policy awakening, this period of policy inflation has been well served by students of air pollution control policy. Descriptions of developments during these years have been provided by Arthur C. Stern and J. Clarence Davies.[3] Significant efforts to explain the incremental policy adjustment of the mid-1960s and the radical changes in policy at the end of the decade have been made in studies by Charles O. Jones, James E. Krier and Edmund Ursin, Helen Ingram, and by E. Donald Elliot, Bruce A. Ackerman and John C. Millian.[4] The studies by Krier and Ursin and by Elliot, Ackerman and Millian emphasize the importance that policy initiatives at the state level had on the development of federal policy. Jones explains the incremental adjustments in policy as part of a continuing process of policy learning. Political competition between Senator Muskie and President Nixon is cited in all the studies as the key to understanding the 'speculative augmentation' or 'policy escalation' that was evident at the end of the decade. Elliot, Ackerman and Millian employ the device of the prisoners' dilemma to show how this competition drove both politicians to adopt policy positions that they otherwise would not have chosen.

The interest displayed in this period of policy inflation is perfectly understandable given the importance of the end product. The Clean Air Amendments 1970 has correctly been described as one of the most important environmental laws ever passed by Congress.[5] Induced by the failure of earlier 'non-interventionist' policies, the 1970 law not only shifted responsibility for controlling air pollution firmly towards the federal government, but also created a regulatory regime complete with winners and losers.[6] Improvements to the quality of America's air certainly flowed from this new interventionist policy, but the price was a dramatic expansion in the scope of conflict surrounding the issue. Those who suffered as a result of stronger regulations mobilized to lessen or minimize the impact of the new law, while those who had benefited sought to secure and expand their gains. The result was increased friction, policy gridlock, the end of the period of policy inflation and the onset of a period of policy retrenchment.

Directing the states

Pressure for further federal action to control air pollution began to build almost immediately after enactment of the Clean Air Act 1963. Reports detailing the extent of the problem and the inadequacy of existing control arrangements were produced by both the Department of Health, Education, and Welfare (HEW) and the Subcommittee on Air and Water Pollution chaired by Senator Muskie. Efforts to address the deficiencies of existing legislation, however, were hindered by the persistent belief that responsibility for controlling air pollution lay clearly with the states. Although congressional interest in the issue had been legitimized by the legislation of the late 1950s and early 1960s, the case for legislation which pre-empted state authority to act had not been established. Realization of this fact shaped congressional efforts to strengthen air pollution control until the late 1960s. The compass of legislation was initially restricted to methods and subjects which were clearly within the domain of the federal government. Few could question the legitimacy of laws that used the purchasing power of the federal government to control air pollution. Nor did many question the authority of the federal government to regulate automobiles involved in interstate commerce. Later legislation sought to accommodate the assumption of state responsibility by directing the states to take action to control air pollution. The net effect was slowly to 'nibble' away at state power.[7]

The Motor Vehicle Air Pollution Control Act 1965
One way for the federal government to avoid the obstacle posed by state responsibility for air pollution control was to legislate in areas that fell unambiguously within the domain of the federal government. Two new efforts of this sort were made in the mid-1960s: one successful, the other not. In 1964 a law was enacted that required the General Service Administration (GSA) to establish emissions standards for motor vehicles purchased by the federal government.[8] The Department of Defense was the only large purchaser of motor vehicles within the federal government not covered by the law. In 1965 the Senate passed a bill which authorized the Secretary of Health, Education, and Welfare to set both air and water pollution control standards for all federal installations.[9] No action was taken in the House. President Johnson issued an executive order on 26 May 1966, however, that directed the heads of all federal agencies to develop plans for the phased installation of equipment to control air pollution at facilities operated by their agencies.[10]

These efforts to legislate in areas completely within the domain of the federal government avoided conflict with the states, but failed to control air pollution in an effective manner. Both the evidence presented to congressional hearings, and the conclusions of research mandated by earlier laws, indicated a need for greater federal involvement. In 1964 the Special Subcommittee on Air and Water Pollution of the Senate Public Works Committee, chaired by Senator Ed Muskie (D. ME), held hearings on 'Air Pollution Control' in Los Angeles, Denver, Chicago, Boston, New York and Tampa.[11] Witnesses from state and local government agencies gave evidence to the Subcommittee about the growing problem of smog across the country. A similar picture was painted later in the year when the Subcommittee held further hearings on the technical problems associated with air pollution control.[12] A staff report published by the Subcommittee in November 1964 'Steps Toward Clean Air' emphasized the 'primary importance' of pollution from automobile exhausts and recommended that national emissions standards be established.[13] Similar conclusions were reached in the first semi-annual report on 'Automotive Air Pollution' published by the Surgeon General in January 1965 as required under the provisions of the Clean Air Act 1963.[14] The report stated that 'smog is a problem of growing national importance' and was caused primarily by automobile exhausts.

A flurry of congressional activity followed publication of the report on 'Automotive Air Pollution'. Twelve bills dealing with exhaust emissions were introduced in the House by nine different members in the first few months 1965. The geographical range of constituencies represented by these members suggests a significant change in perceptions of the scope of the problem. None was a member of the Californian delegation: three represented districts in New York, the others represented districts in Pennsylvania, New Jersey, Maryland, Florida, Arkansas and Oklahoma. All bar one were Democrats, and their average length of tenure in the House was a modest 2.27 terms. Nine of the bills called for the federal government to establish emission guidelines or standards for automobile exhausts, but three took a different tack. One bill introduced by Rep. Edward J. Long (D. MD), proposed that automobiles be equipped with devices to clean emissions; two bills introduced by Rep. Sam M. Gibbons (D. FL) called for a ban on automobiles that caused high levels of pollution.[15] The junior status of most of the members introducing these bills, however, meant that the conditions for successful policy entrepreneurship were not manifest. None of the members who introduced a bill was in a position to command the legislative resources that are necessary for enactment. No action took place on any of the bills.

The story was very different in the Senate where Senator Muskie was well positioned as Chairman of the Special Subcommittee on Air and Water Pollution to play the role of policy entrepreneur. Muskie had established a limited reputation as someone who was interested in water pollution when Governor of Maine from 1955 to 1959.[16] Not until he became Chairman of the Special Subcommittee on Air and Water Pollution in 1963, however, did he display any serious commitment to air pollution. No air pollution control bill was introduced by Muskie, for example, before he became Chairman. His commitment to the issue was undoubtedly sparked by the institutional position in which he found himself in 1963. His skill as a politician lay in recognizing and acting upon the opportunities that chairmanship of the Subcommittee provided for establishing a reputation for leadership on an issue of growing national importance. Within a few years he had become known as the foremost congressional expert on pollution.

A bill was introduced by Senator Muskie in January 1965 to establish exhaust emission standards for new automobiles.[17] Mixed reactions greeted Muskie's proposal. The automobile industry opposed the bill in public, but in private preferred the prospect of uniform national standards to the confusion that would ensue if individual states were permitted to set their own standards.[18] California had already enacted legislation which required certified pollution control devices be installed on all new cars sold in the state.[19] Exhaust emission control bills were also pending in Pennsylvania and New York. Worried by the prospect of other states joining this bandwagon, the industry came to the conclusion that uniform federal standards were better than separate standards in each state. The price of industry quiescence, however, was that the Secretary of HEW should establish the exhaust emission standards, and that the states should be pre-empted from setting standards more stringent than those found in California.

The attitude of the administration was also equivocal at first. President Johnson appeared to express support for new regulatory authority to combat pollution. His Message on Natural Beauty transmitted to Congress on 8 February 1965 not only requested amendment of the 1963 Clean Air Act to allow the Secretary of HEW 'to investigate potential air pollution problems before pollution happens … and to make recommendations leading to the prevention of such pollution', but also declared a willingness 'to institute discussions with industry officials and other interested groups leading to an effective reduction or substantial reduction of pollution from liquid fuelled motor vehicles'.[20] The promise of 'discussions', however, allowed the administration to oppose the grant of regulatory authority contained in the Muskie bill. Assistant Secretary of HEW James Quigley testified at hearings conducted by the

Special Subcommittee on Air and Water Pollution on 6 April 1965 that: 'Since [discussions] could clearly open the way to a new appraisal by all concerned of the automobile exhaust problem and action required to control it, we do not recommend enactment of regulatory legislation at this time.'[21]

The public reaction to Quigley's testimony was so adverse that the Administration moved quickly to reverse its position.[22] Quigley returned to the Subcommittee on 9 April 1965 to dispel press reports that the Administration was against exhaust emission controls:

> We favor all action that is appropriate, and if it is the judgement of the committee that legislation is appropriate at this time we want to work with the committee in making sure that legislation is ... the most effective piece of legislation that we are able to put on the books.'[23]

In a letter to the Subcommittee dated 13 April 1965 HEW Secretary Anthony J. Celebrezze confirmed that:

> We wholeheartedly endorse legislation which would provide authority for the Secretary of Health, Education, and Welfare to establish, by regulation, standards for exhaust pollutant emissions. Time limitations for the application of such standards should be sufficiently flexible to permit them to be applied as early as possible ... Testimony has indicated that, based on present information, it would be technologically feasible to apply adequate control systems to the vehicles produced in the 1968 model year.[24]

Administration equivocation ended with these statements.

The support of the Administration and ambivalent attitude of the automobile industry ensured rapid progress. Senator Muskie's bill was reported out of Committee on 14 May 1965. In deference to both industry and Administration concerns, the Committee bill abandoned the specific emission standards that were contained in the original bill, and instead gave the Secretary of HEW discretionary power to set standards. The Secretary was directed to set standards for emissions of air pollutants from new gasoline-powered vehicles after giving 'appropriate consideration to technological feasibility and economic costs'. The deadline for establishing standards was moved from 1 November 1966 to 1 September 1967. At the request of the Administration, the Committee also removed a provision to provide states with grants to inspect exhaust control devices installed on automobiles. The HEW argued that the technology to inspect such devices was simply not available. The marked-up version of Muskie's bill passed the Senate on the 18 May 1965 by voice vote and without debate.

The Senate passed bill was introduced in the House and referred to House Commerce. Hearings were held on the bill by the Sub-committee on Public Health and Welfare in June 1965.[25] Testimony at the hearings mirrored that given in the Senate. State and local government agencies provided strong support for the legislation, the administration expressed concern about some of the practicali-ties involved, and the automobile industry prevaricated. The Com-mittee reported the bill on 31 August 1965 with a few changes from the Senate version. By far the most important change was a decision to delete the 1 September 1967 deadline for establishing emission standards. The House bill simply required the Secretary of HEW to develop standards 'as soon as practicable' and to set the deadlines for compliance 'after due consideration of the period reasonable necessary for industry compliance'. On 24 September 1965, the House passed the bill by a 294–4 roll-call vote. Voting against the bill were Rep. Robert Dole (R. KA), Rep. Paul Findley (R. IL), Rep. W. R. Poage (D. TX), and Graham Purcell (D. TX). The Senate agreed to the House version by voice vote on 1 October 1965, and the Motor Vehicle Air Pollution Control Act was signed by President Johnson on 20 October 1965.[26]

'[Air pollution] has become a health problem that is national in scope … We made a hopeful beginning toward solving this problem with the Clean Air Act 1963. Today, with the signing of the Clean Air Act Amendments … we are redoubling our efforts' claimed Pres-ident Johnson when he signed the bill.[27] The most important provi-sions of the Act were those authorizing the Secretary of HEW to set emission standards for all new motor vehicles. Although no statu-tory deadline was established for the promulgation of such stan-dards, an important step had been taken towards national exhaust emission standards. The legislation did not explicitly specify that federal standards pre-empted state standards, but the legislative his-tory appeared to support pre-emption.[28] Other provisions of the Act recognized the international dimension of air pollution for the first time. The Secretary of HEW was directed to call a conference of state and local air pollution agencies if pollution originating from that area affected a foreign country, and was given the power to bring a legal suit to abate air pollution affecting another country if voluntary action was not forthcoming. Like previous air pollution control statutes, the Act also authorized research into the problems of sulphur dioxide and motor exhaust. A total of $3.98 million was authorized for the purposes of the Act.

The Air Quality Act 1967
Pressure on Congress to take further action mounted inexorably in the wake of the enactment of the 1965 Act. Not only did the Surgeon General highlight the continuing problem of air pollution caused by motor vehicles in his second, third and fourth semi-annual reports to Congress, but President Johnson added his weight to demands for new legislation. In a Special Message to Congress on 23 February 1966 Johnson stated that the Clean Air Act 1963 and the Motor Vehicle Air Pollution Control Act 1965 had provided 'new tools to help attack' air pollution, but also argued that further legislation was needed 'to improve and increase federal research, financing, and technical assistance to help states and local governments take the measures needed to control air pollution'.[29] Further pressure came from increasing evidence of public concern about air pollution. Although opinion poll data on public attitudes to air pollution before 1969 is limited, Opinion Research Corporation polls show that the percentage of respondents who believed that air pollution was a 'very or somewhat serious problem' increased from 28 per cent in 1965 to 48 per cent in 1966.[30] What Anthony Downs characterized as the 'alarmed discovery' of the problem had begun.[31]

The result of such pressure was a burst of congressional activity. Sixty air pollution control bills were introduced in the House in 1966 by fifty-six different representatives. The geographical range of constituencies represented by these members shows that concern about air pollution was rapidly becoming national. Although twenty-five of the representatives hailed from California, New York or Ohio, the other thirty-one representatives were distributed among twenty-one states. Nine representatives came from Pacific Coast or Rocky Mountain states, eleven came from Northeastern or Mid-Atlantic states, eleven came from Southern or Border states and twenty-five came from Midwestern or Plains states. Concern about air pollution also crossed party lines. Thirty-three of the representatives who introduced air pollution control bills in 1966 were Republicans; the remaining twenty-three were Democrats.

No fewer than fifty-five of the sixty bills introduced in 1966 proposed to give tax relief for the purchase of air pollution control equipment. Three bills proposed to provide businesses with grants to purchase abatement equipment.[32] One bill sought to repeal the limits on grants to the states contained in the Clean Air Act 1963.[33] The other required the Secretary of HEW to publish emission standards in the *Federal Register*.[34] The large number of bills providing tax relief on air pollution control equipment can be explained by three factors. First, tax relief was particularly salient in 1966. President Johnson had proposed legislation in September 1966 to suspend for one year the 7 per cent tax investment credit that business could claim for investing in new equipment and machinery. Second, the bills offered a legislator a relatively low cost means of 'position-taking'. They required little investment in gathering information, and did not alienate business interests. James E. Krier and Edmund Ursin have even suggested that such bills 'appear to have been little more than transfer payments designed to quiet industry objections to pollution control'.[35] Third, the purport of the bills fell clearly within the domain of the federal government. No legislator could be accused of stepping on the toes of state and local governments.

Earlier bills to provide tax relief for the purchase of air pollution control equipment had disappeared without trace in an unsympathetic House Committee on Ways and Means. Between 1949 and 1965 a total of forty-four such bills had been introduced in the House, but none had been acted upon. The only tax relief that businesses could claim for purchasing air pollution control equipment was the 7 per cent tax investment credit contained in the Revenue Act 1962. This allowed businesses to claim a credit against tax liability of up to 7 per cent of investments in new and used machinery, including air pollution control equipment.[36] A suggestion that air and water pollution control equipment be exempted from the suspension of the tax incentive credit that President Johnson had proposed was initially rejected by House Ways and Means on an 11–14 vote. The large number of bills introduced in 1966 to retain the tax investment credit for pollution control equipment, however, forced the Committee to reconsider. Rep. Wilbur Mills (D. AK), Chairman of House Ways and Means, offered an amendment on the floor to exempt air and water pollution control equipment from the suspension of the tax investment credit. The amendment was adopted on a 330–2 roll-call vote. Only Rep. Robert L. Leggett (D. CA) and

Rep. Paul C. Jones (D. MO) voted against the amendment. The exemption for pollution control equipment was accepted without debate during Senate consideration of the bill.

Six air pollution control bills were introduced in the Senate in 1966. Two sought to provide tax relief for the purchase of air pollution control equipment; others sought to advance research into automobile propulsion, improve the waste management systems of the federal government and approve an Illinois-Indiana Air Pollution Control Compact.[37] The final bill of the six, introduced by Senator Muskie, sought to reauthorize the Clean Air Act 1963.[38] Authorization of the Clean Air Act was due to expire in 1966 and the Muskie bill aimed to do little more than prolong its life. The bill authorized a new programme of maintenance grants to state and local agencies, removed the existing limitation that no more than 20 per cent of the total appropriated under the Act each year could be used for grants to support state, local and regional air pollution control programmes, increased the fiscal 1967 authorization for the Act to $46 million and provided open-ended authorizations for fiscal 1968–73.

The limited purview of the bill ensured an almost complete absence of opposition. No witness spoke against the legislation at hearings conducted by the Subcommittee on Air and Water Pollution in June 1966.[39] Some disquiet about the nature of the authorization was evident when the Public Works Committee conducted its mark-up and a number of amendments were accepted. The Committee voted to eliminate the open-ended authorizations for fiscal 1968–73, and added language to provide specific authorizations of $70 million for fiscal 1968 and $80 million for fiscal 1969. Reported out of Committee on 7 July 1966, the bill passed the Senate five days later by a 80–0 roll-call vote. House passage was equally unproblematic. The Subcommittee on Public Health and Welfare of House Commerce conducted perfunctory hearings on the Senate passed bill on 27 September 1966 at which just five witnesses gave evidence.[40] Two changes to the bill were made during full committee mark-up. House Commerce reduced the authorizations to $39 million for fiscal 1967, $62 million for fiscal 1968, and $71 million for fiscal 1969, and added language to ensure that federal grants would not become a substitute for state and local funds. Reported out of Committee on 1 October 1966, the bill passed the House three days later by voice vote. Differences between the two

128 *Congress and air pollution*

versions of the bill were rapidly resolved in conference. The Senate
authorization of $46 million was accepted for fiscal 1967, and com-
promise reached on authorizations of $66 million for fiscal 1968
and $74 million for fiscal 1969. The conference report was passed
by voice votes in the House on 13 October 1966 and in the Senate
a day later. President Johnson signed the bill into law on 15 October 1966.[41]

Enactment of the 1966 Amendments did little to assuage
demands for greater federal involvement in controlling air pollution. An air pollution episode in New York City which killed an estimated eighty people certainly provided proof that the problem was
still acute.[42] The Johnson Administration, in particular, demanded
further action.[43] Opening a National Conference on Air Pollution
organized by the PHS in December 1966 Vice-President, Hubert H.
Humphrey, pointed to the inadequacies of existing methods of control: 'There is another problem relating to local government and its
part in air pollution control: standards of control vary greatly from
city to city and from State to State'.[44] A similar message was articulated in the keynote speech to the Conference given by Secretary of
HEW, John Gardiner:

> State and local governments have been slow in seizing the opportuni-
> ties for action. In particular, they have failed to establish the regional
> approaches demanded by a problem that ignores traditional state
> boundaries ... Lack of uniform air quality and emission standards
> serves as a deterrent both to States and communities and to industry.[45]

President Johnson also expressed support for a stronger federal role
in controlling air pollution. In his 1967 State of the Union Address
he declared that: 'We should vastly expand the fight for Clean Air
with a total attack on pollution at its source ... we should set up
"Regional Airsheds" throughout this great land'.[46] Finally, in a message to Congress on 'Protecting Our National Heritage' on 30 January 1967, Johnson called for new legislation to be enacted that
would establish national emissions standards for major industrial
sources of pollution.[47]

Further pressure for federal intervention came from the soft coal
industry which was threatened by increasingly strict air pollution
regulation in the Northeast.[48] The industry had been unable to stop
the New York City Council from adopting a pollution control programme in 1965 that prohibited the use of coal in domestic heating

appliances and severely restricted other uses of coal with a high sulphur content.[49] New York, New Jersey, Pennsylvania and Connecticut also announced plans to combat air pollution in December 1966 that threatened the coal industry.[50] To compound matters, the Secretary of HEW published a report on 'Air Quality Criteria for Sulphur Oxides' in March 1967 that appeared to pose a mortal threat to the coal industry. The report stated that virtually all major American cities were exposed to unhealthy levels of sulphur dioxide and recommended reducing the reliance upon soft coal. Faced with the prospect of losing major markets for its products, the industry turned to the federal government for help. Two things were demanded by the soft coal industry: federal pre-emption of state authority and greater research into abatement technologies.

The increased saliency of air pollution produced a correspondingly high level of congressional activity. A record 149 air pollution control bills were introduced in the House in 1967 by 130 different representatives. The geographical distribution of the constituencies represented by these members shows a further expansion in concern about air pollution. The 130 representatives who introduced air pollution control bills in 1967 came from thirty-five different states. Forty-five came from Northeastern or Mid-Atlantic states, thirty-six came from Midwestern or Plains states, twenty-seven came from Southern or Border states and twenty-two came from Pacific Coast or Rocky Mountain states. Concern about air pollution also continued to cut across party lines. Fifty-four of the representatives who introduced air pollution control bills in 1967 were Democrats and seventy-six were Republicans.

The vast majority of the bills that were introduced sought to provide additional tax relief to businesses that purchased air pollution control equipment: a choice of legislation that should come as no surprise given a general paucity of information about air pollution among a cohort that had just discovered the issue. No fewer than 107 bills of the 149 bills fell into this category. The Administration's call for greater federal involvement in establishing emission standards was reflected, however, in a significant number of bills. A total of thirty-one bills sought to establish air regions and set standards. Other bills sought to relax further the grant requirements found in the 1966 reauthorization of the Clean Air Act, sponsor research into alternative propulsion systems, and authorize the Mid-Atlantic Air Pollution Control Compact that had been signed between New

York, New Jersey, Connecticut and Pennsylvania.

Activity in the Senate was again less frenetic. A total of eleven air pollution control bills were introduced in the chamber in 1967. Five of the bills sought to extend the tax relief available for the purchase of air pollution control equipment, three proposed to approve various regional compacts, one sought to promote research into alternative propulsion methods for automobiles and another proposed to offer various economic incentives to industry to encourage air pollution control. A bill incorporating the Administration's proposals, the Air Quality Act 1967, was introduced by Senator Muskie on 31 January 1967.[51] The Administration's bill authorized the Secretary of HEW to establish enforceable, uniform control levels for specific pollutants in various industries. Responsibility for enforcing these standards was to be given to regional commissions, appointed by the HEW Secretary, with jurisdiction over interstate areas or airsheds. To address the problem of pollution caused by automobile exhaust emissions, the bill required the registration of all fuel additives used in interstate commerce with HEW. Increased research on the health effects of fuel additives was also authorized.

The automobile industry used the hearings on the bill to urge for the explicit pre-emption of state authority to set exhaust emission standards. Industry witnesses told Senator Muskie's Subcommittee on Air and Water Pollution that they supported the general thrust of the bill, but felt that an amendment was needed which clearly specified that only the federal government could be allowed to establish national exhaust standards. Thomas C. Mann, president of the Automobile Manufacturers Association, told the Subcommittee that the industry would welcome 'a series of stated goals, projecting what will be required of the industry as far ahead as 1975 or 1980'.[52] A similarly positive statement was made by Harry F. Barr, a vice-president of General Motors, who stated that 'we have turned the corner as far as motor vehicle emissions are concerned'.[53] He confidently predicted that the industry would be able to reduce exhaust emissions by 60 per cent in 1968. Support for federal pre-emption also came from HEW Secretary John W. Gardiner who warned of 'confusion' and 'duplication' if the states were not expressly prohibited from establishing their own standards.[54] Such arguments were sufficient to persuade Senator Muskie of the need for additional language, and an amendment was added during Subcommittee mark-up which prohibited all of the states, apart from

California, from setting exhaust emission control standards. The exemption for California was granted after Senator George Murphy (R. CA) managed to persuade his colleagues that air pollution in his state was so severe that more rigorous controls were needed than were being contemplated at the federal level.

The degree of conflict surrounding the issue of national exhaust standards during Senate consideration of the bill was limited. Knowledge of the problem was high as a result of the research man-dated by earlier laws, the constitutional right of Congress to regu-late a good that was clearly involved in interstate commerce was not challenged, the Administration supported the provisions, and the industry fought hard for federal pre-emption of state standards. Only the exemption for California was questioned, but the industry believed that House Commerce would prove a more sympathetic battlefield to fight that battle than Senator Muskie's Subcommittee. The proposals for national emission standards for stationary sources of air pollution contained within the bill were much more contro-versial. Knowledge of the problem was not well developed, the con-stitutional position was more ambiguous, most industrial groups opposed national standards and, perhaps just as significant, Senator Muskie was unconvinced as to their efficacy.

Although Muskie had introduced the bill on behalf of the Administration to maintain his institutional position as 'Mr Pollu-tion', he had long opposed national emission standards as unworkable. Muskie believed that such standards would be impossible to set given the variation in local conditions in differ-ent parts of the United States.[55] Support for Muskie came from old enemies. National standards were regarded by many industrial groups as inflexible and costly. In testimony at congressional hear-ings on the bill these groups consistently argued against national standards. A spokesman for the steel industry told the Subcom-mittee on Air and Water Pollution, chaired by Senator Muskie, on 8 May 1967 that standards should vary in different areas, depend-ing upon population density, topography and other factors.[56] J. O. Julson of the American Paper Institute counselled the Subcommit-tee to substitute regional 'control arrangements' for the 'nation-wide emission standards as currently proposed'.[57] Charles B. Avila, representing the Edison Electric Institute, claimed that national standards were not 'an effective method of achieving' the air qual-ity 'we all desire'.[58] Opposition to national standards was also expressed by the US Chambers of Commerce and the National Association of Manufacturers.

The weight of testimony against national emission standards at the hearings, and Senator Muskie's own misgivings about their efficacy, provided Senator Jennings Randolph (D. WV), Chair of Senate Public Works, with an opportunity to orchestrate significant changes in the language of the bill during full committee mark-up. Several amendments offered by Randolph were accepted by the Committee that altered the thrust of the legislation. The most important amendment deleted the Administration's request for authority to set national emission standards and substituted language that required the states to set standards. Other amendments sought to protect the soft coal industry that was so important to West Virginia. One amendment proposed that advisory committees containing representatives of various government departments and business be created to broaden the technical advice available to the Secretary of HEW. Elliot, Ackerman and Millian have suggested that: 'Advisory committees within the federal bureaucracy promised to be a far more hospitable forum for the coal industry than the politics of state and local legislatures'.[59] Another amendment proposed that special emphasis be given to the development of methods to control pollution caused by 'the combustion of fuels'. The promotion of new abatement technology obviously represented a better way to tackle air pollution to a senator from West Virginia than laws that restricted the use of coal. Appropriations of $375 million for research on fuels were authorized by the Committee for fiscal years 1968–1970. A further $325 million was authorized for pollution control grants, development of air quality criteria, establishment of quality standards and enforcement procedures over the same period.

Stripped of its most controversial provisions, the Air Quality Act encountered no opposition on the floor of the Senate. No amendments were offered, no senator spoke against passage, and the bill passed on a 88–0 roll-call vote on 18 July 1967. Debate consisted mainly of hymns of praise to those involved in drafting the bill. Senator Randolph congratulated Muskie's leadership and called the bill 'the most significant step toward pollution abatement' in the nation's history.[60] Senator John Sherman Cooper (R. KY), ranking minority member of Senate Public Works, praised Muskie, Randolph, and Senator J. Caleb Boggs (R. DE) – the ranking minority member of the Subcommittee – for their work. He stated that he had 'never seen … a better demonstration of the Committee legislative process than in … the consideration and development of this measure'.[61] Senator Muskie was slightly more subdued. He cautioned that passage of the bill would not solve 'the air pollution problems of the nation … with one fell swoop', but added that it would create 'a national program of air quality' in which the states would 'retain the primary responsibility to determine the quality of air they desire'.[62]

An effort was made by the Administration to persuade the House to accept national emissions standards during consideration of the Senate bill and a companion House measure.[63] The electoral defeat of both Rep. Roberts and Rep. Schenck in 1964, however, meant that House Commerce lacked the expertise at the time to challenge seriously the evidence presented by industrial groups and conclusions arrived at in the Senate.[64] Qualified support for the Senate version was a common theme at hearings held by House Commerce. The spokesman of the American Petroleum Institute, P. N. Gammelgard, told the Committee that 'air pollution problems should be handled by the lowest level of government capable of dealing adequately with them' and supported the Senate's rejection of national emission standards.[65] In more imaginative language, the National Association of Manufacturers told members of the Committee that the national standards approach to the pollution problem was

> very reminiscent of the legendary Procrastes who made all persons to fit in his iron bed. If they were too short to fit it, he stretched their legs. If they were too tall, he chopped their legs off to fit … air pollution control problems … are too variable and too complex to be subjected to a Procrustean approach.[66]

Against such a backdrop, the Administration's efforts to reverse the Senate's rejection of emission standards were doomed.

The automobile industry used the forum provided by the hearings to voice concerns about the exemption given to California in the Senate bill. Thomas C. Mann, speaking for the industry, called for federal regulation of exhaust emissions, and stressed that the industry would find it difficult to comply with a multitude of diverse state requirements for new cars. He argued that the exemption given to California was unnecessary as the proposed federal standards were the same as those in force in the state.[67] House Commerce proved a more sympathetic forum than Muskie's Subcommittee for such arguments. The Committee's jurisdiction over matters of commerce meant that it always attracted some members anxious to promote and protect the interests of industry, and in the person of Rep. John Dingell (D. MI) the automobile manufacturers had someone willing and able to champion their cause. With a constituency that included parts of Detroit, Rep. Dingell had good reason to protect the American automobile industry whenever possible.

Although Rep. John E. Moss (D. CA) and Rep. Lionel Van Deerlin (D. CA) argued that the prospect of worsening air pollution in southern California made it imperative that the state be permitted to promulgate stricter exhaust emission standards than provided at the federal level, the arguments of Rep. Dingell prevailed on the Committee. Not only was Rep. Dingell highly skilled at committee politics, but the absence of an acknowledged air pollution expert on House Commerce undermined the opposition's advocacy. The Committee reported legislation that accepted the general thrust of the Senate bill, but which deleted the language that exempted California from the requirement that the states conform to federal exhaust emission standards. Other significant changes included the elimination of the $375 million programme for research into controlling pollution caused by fuel combustion, and the reduction of the total authorization from $700 million to $428.3 million for fiscal years 1968–70.

Rep. Moss sought to reverse his defeat in Committee by offering an amendment during floor debate to restore the language of the Senate passed bill which permitted California to enforce stricter exhaust emission standards than those promulgated by the federal government. Speaking in support of the amendment Rep. Charles H. Wilson (D. CA) stressed that California needed stronger standards than those envisaged in the bill.[68] Rep. Dingell countered that the proposed federal standards would 'fully and adequately protect the health and welfare of people everywhere, not just in California, but everywhere in the United States'.[69] The task for Rep. Dingell was to persuade sufficient members that he was motivated by a goal other than to protect the automobile industry. In this he failed. The Moss Amendment was accepted on a 152–58 teller vote with the entire Californian delegation voting in support. Further amendments offered by Rep. Charles S. Joelson (D. NJ) and Rep. Theodore R. Kupferman (R. NY) to allow other states to adopt stricter exhaust emission standards, however, were defeated. No other state was regarded as having an acute air pollution problem that warranted special treatment. An amendment offered by Rep. Richard D. McCarty (D. NY) to allow the Secretary of HEW to establish national emission standards for stationary sources of pollution was also defeated.

Restoration of the California waiver meant that the bill which eventually passed the House on a 362–0 roll-call vote differed from the Senate passed bill in two main areas: research on fuel combustion and overall level of authorization. A compromise worked out in conference agreed to the reduced authorization contained in the House bill, but earmarked $125 million for research into methods of reducing the pollution caused by fuel combustion. The conference report was agreed by voice vote in both chambers and signed into law by President Johnson on 21 November 1967. Although President Johnson praised the Air Quality Act, he offered a subdued assessment of its likely success:

> But for all that it will do, the Air Quality Act will never end pollution. It is a law – and not a magic wand … that will cleanse ours skies. It is a law whose ultimate effectiveness rests out there with the people of this land – on our seeing the damnation that awaits us if the people do not act responsibly to avoid it and curb it.[70]

The Air Quality Act 1967, as enacted, directed the states to set ambient air quality standards, and provided for federal intervention only if a state had failed to take action after fifteen months. Such provisions mirrored those found in the Water Quality Act 1965 which also sought to force the states to act to combat pollution.[71] The Air Quality Act 1967 further authorized the Secretary of HEW, in time of 'imminent and substantial' danger to public health from air pollution, to seek a court injunction against the continued emission of such pollutants as might be necessary to protect the public. Other provisions authorized the Secretary to designate air quality control regions throughout the country, provided full federal funding for regional control commissions to be established by state governors and established a two-year programme of research into fuels and vehicles.[72] The Act also prohibited any state other than California from establishing automobile exhaust standards.[73] All other states had to meet national standards. A total of $428.3 million was authorized for the purposes of the Act.

Enactment of the Air Quality Act 1967 signalled the beginning of the end of state primacy over matters of air pollution control. Although Senator Muskie argued on the Senate floor that the states would 'retain the primary responsibility to determine the quality of air they desire', the Act authorized a significant expansion in federal regulatory authority.[74] Control over mobile sources of pollution, where the constitutional authority of Congress and knowledge of the problem were strongest, had passed completely from the states to the federal government. Control over stationary sources of pollution remained with the states, but the option of inaction had been removed. 'What began in 1955 with simple grants-in-aid to state and local governments', in the words of Paul R. Portney, had 'evolved to the point where those recipients were being given very specific responsibilities by the federal government to combat air pollution problems'.[75]

Federal primacy

Dissatisfaction with the control arrangements established by the Air Quality Act 1967 was soon to emerge. Evidence presented at a number of congressional committee hearings revealed that only limited progress was being made in the battle against air pollution. The procedures of the Air Quality Act were regarded as cumbersome, many states were unable or unwilling to meet the responsibilities that had been assigned to them and economic development continued to pose new problems.[76] Little was actually new about this litany of deficiencies. Similar observations had been expressed soon after the enactment of practically every other air pollution control law. What was new was the backdrop against which the litany was chanted. Environmental protection was a highly salient issue in the late 1960s and the competition for policy leadership was fierce. Challenges to Senator Muskie's authority as 'Mr Pollution' emerged both from within Congress as others sought to assume the mantle of leadership, and from the White House as President Nixon sought to neutralize the appeal of a potential rival for the presidency. A result of such competition was a dramatic change in the nature of air pollution control law. The Clean Air Amendments 1970 not only preempted much of the authority of the states, but also expanded the range of pollutants to be controlled.

Inflationary pressures

Evidence that the Air Quality Act was failing to achieve its purpose began to emerge in hearings conducted by a variety of congressional committees in 1968. The Subcommittee on Science, Research, and Development of the House Committee on Science and Astronautics (House Science), chaired by Rep. Emilio Q. Daddario (D. CN), conducted a general review of the progress that had been made in air and water pollution abatement in March 1968.[77] Another set of hearings on the effects of air pollution on public health were conducted by the Subcommittee on Air and Water Pollution, chaired by Senator Muskie, in July 1968.[78] The Subcommittee on Research and Technical Programs of the House Committee on Government Operations, chaired by Rep. Henry Reuss (D. WI), held hearings on the efficacy of the federal government's research into sulphur oxide pollution in September 1968.[79] Although the focus of each hearing was different, the evidence presented to the three subcommittees revealed that the health effects associated with air pollution were worse than had previously been thought, that the research mandated by federal law was not being carried out adequately, and that the efficacy of existing control arrangements were being undermined by a media-specific approach to pollution control.

An effort to remedy some of the deficiencies in research that had been revealed by the three subcommittee hearings was made in bills introduced by Senator Randolph and Rep. Staggers in 1969.[80] Both bills sought to reauthorize Section 104 of the Air Quality Act which required the Secretary of HEW to conduct research on the control of air pollution from automobile exhausts. The two bills encountered no opposition. Senate Public Works reported the Randolph bill on 2 July 1969, and it passed the Senate by voice vote on 8 July 1969. The bill authorized $90 million for research on exhaust emissions for fiscal 1970. Perfunctory hearings on the Staggers bill were conducted by the Subcommittee on Public Health and Welfare on 19 June 1969 at which only three witnesses from HEW gave evidence.[81] House Commerce reported the Staggers bill and it passed the House by a 332–0 roll-call vote on 4 September 1969. The House version of the bill authorized $18.7 million for research. Both chambers agreed to a compromise authorization of $45 million worked out in conference committee, and President Nixon signed the bill into law on 5 December 1969.[82]

Apart from some heated exchanges over an amendment offered

by Rep. Leonard Farbstein (D. NY) the debate on the Staggers bill
was cursory. No member objected to the principle of authorizing
further research into air pollution, and all were willing to accept the
level of authorization suggested by House Commerce. An amendment offered by Rep. Farbstein to prohibit the manufacture and sale
of automobiles with internal combustion engines after 1 January
1978, however, was not met with such equanimity. Rep. Farbstein
argued that the automobile manufacturers should assume responsibility for clearing up pollution by making engines that would not
produce harmful smog.[83] Support came primarily from members
representing districts with acute air pollution problems. Rep.
George E. Brown (D. CA) accused the automobile manufacturers of
duplicity: 'They have actually conspired over the last 10 years ... to
avoid doing anything about controlling this problem'.[84] Rep. Roman
C. Pucinski (D. IL) noted that special interests like the automobile
industry always found a way to slow progress.[85] Support for the
automobile industry was provided by the Michigan delegation. Rep.
James Harvey (R. MI) told the House that: 'You can knock it all you
want ... but this industry means an awful lot ... and I would consider that very carefully before we tamper with writing standards
that could affect it on the floor of this House'.[86] Such economic
arguments were telling. Few members wished to cast a vote that
might cause serious damage to an industry that directly and indi-
rectly provided one in seven jobs in America. The amendment was
defeated on a 22–99 standing vote.

   The 1969 reauthorization was essentially a holding operation.
Evidence of policy failure was provided at various committee hearings conducted in 1969 which suggested that more drastic revision
of the law was required. The Subcommittee on Public Health and
Welfare, chaired by Rep. John Jarman (D. OK), held a hearing on
federal research into fuels and automobiles in June 1969.[87] Three
witnesses from HEW reported that progress was not as rapid as
required. The Joint Committee on Atomic Energy, chaired by Rep.
Chet Holifield (D. CA), held a hearing on the pollution caused by
electricity generation in October 1969.[88] Perhaps not unsurprisingly,
the Committee learned of the dangers of generating electricity by
burning fossil fuels. A more general overview of progress was conducted by the Subcommittee on Air and Water Pollution in same
month.[89] Held in St Louis, Missouri, Senator Muskie learned first
hand of the problems that state and local officials were experienc-

ing in meeting the responsibilities they had been given under the Air Quality Act. The most important hearings, however, were probably those conducted by the Subcommittee on Public Health and Welfare into the progress of federal air pollution control efforts in December 1969.[90] Orchestrated by Rep. Paul G. Rogers (D. FL), who was allowed to chair the hearings, both the evidence presented and the cross-examination of witnesses were far more critical than had been the case before Senator Muskie's Subcommittee.

A key witness at the hearings conducted by the Subcommittee on Public Health and Welfare was Dr Jesse L. Steinfeld, Acting Surgeon General. Dr Steinfeld revealed that only limited progress had been made in implementing the 1967 Act.[91] He predicted that automobile exhaust emissions of carbon monoxide and hydrocarbon would be reduced to the levels prevailing in the 1950s by the end 1970, but that emission levels would begin to rise again if standards were not tightened because of increasing numbers of automobiles on America's roads. Progress in controlling other pollutants was not so sure. Dr Steinfeld disclosed that the states had been very slow to take the action that was required under the Air Quality Act. The Subcommittee learned that no state had met its obligations in their entirety. Part of the problem was the complexity of the procedures created by the 1967 Act and inadequate funding at the federal level. Much of the problem stemmed, however, from a lack of resources and commitment at the state level.

The increasing availability of grants that resulted from enactment of federal legislation during the 1960s had encouraged both state and local governments to establish air pollution control programmes. Municipal and county governments, in particular, had taken vigorous action to attract federal financial aid. Between 1960 and 1970 the number of municipal governments that had enacted air pollution control legislation increased from eighty-four to 107, and the number of county governments with such legislation increased from seventeen to eighty-one.[92] State governments also took action to attract federal funds. By 1970 every state had adopted a state-wide air pollution control law in one form or another.[93] As the hearings conducted by the Subcommittee on Public Health and Welfare in December 1969 had revealed, however, the overall effectiveness of these laws was a matter of considerable debate. Most states simply did not have the resources both to set emission standards and devise state implementation plans, and some proved susceptible to pressure from large industries to take a relaxed view of the responsibilities they had been given under the Air Quality Act.

Senator Muskie responded to the evidence of policy failure by introducing bills that sought to improve the effectiveness of the Air Quality Act. In December 1969 he introduced a bill to extend federal regulation of emission standards to vessels, aircraft and other vehicles.[94] In March 1970 he introduced a bill which sought to improve the implementation of the Air Quality Act by providing federal agencies with greater authority and resources.[95] The problem confronting Senator Muskie was that public concern about the environment had outstripped the sort of incremental adjustments contained in the two bills. Rival policy entrepreneurs were also posing an increased challenge to Senator Muskie's leadership on the issue.

The late 1960s saw public concern about the environment rise to unprecedented heights. Catastrophic events such as an oil spill off the coast of Santa Barbara in January 1969, and the inflaming of Cleveland's Cuyahoga River when a sailor dropped a cigarette into its waters in the summer, served as a catalyst for an emerging environmental movement. Not only did membership of traditional groups such as the Sierra Club, the National Audubon Society, the Wilderness Society and the National Wildlife Federation increase dramatically, but new groups such as Friends of the Earth, the Environmental Defense Fund and the Natural Resources Defense Council were also established.[96] Increased public concern about air pollution was also reflected in opinion polls. The percentage of respondents in Opinion Research Corporation polls who viewed air pollution as a 'somewhat serious' or 'very serious' problem rose from 55 per cent in 1968 to 69 per cent in 1970.[97] Equally important, the saliency of the issue also reached a new high. Pollution was regarded as the second most serious problem facing the nation in 1970.[98] Public concern about the environment reached a crescendo with the celebration of Earth Day on 22 April 1970.

The high saliency of the issue prompted a new wave of bill introductions as members sought to prove to their constituents that they were concerned with the quality of the air. A total of sixty-seven air pollution control bills were introduced by fifty-three representatives in the House, and ten bills by eight senators in the Senate in 1969. Bills were introduced by representatives hailing from twenty-five different states. Bills were introduced by seventeen representatives from Northeastern or Mid-atlantic states, sixteen representatives from Midwestern or Plains states, ten representatives from Southern or Border states and ten representatives from Pacific Coast or Rocky Mountain states. The eight senators who introduced bills came from seven different states. Concern about air pollution continued to cross party lines. In the House, twenty-three of the representatives who introduced air pollution control bills were Democrats and thirty were Republicans. In the Senate, five of the senators who introduced bills were Democrats and three were Republicans.

Little change is evident in the content of the bills that were introduced in 1969. Consideration of the Tax Reform Act 1969 provided members with little policy expertise a simple opportunity to introduce legislation.[99] No fewer than forty-two of the air pollution control bills introduced in the House and three of those introduced in the Senate sought to maintain or provide greater tax relief for businesses that installed control equipment. The cumulative effect of the introduction of such a large number of bills ensured that the 7 per cent investment tax credit for pollution control facilities was retained while other forms of amortization were repealed. Other air pollution control bills also ploughed familiar furrows. Two bills sought to ban the internal combustion engine.[100] Six bills sought to increase research into low emission vehicles.[101] Four bills sought to provide increased grants to the states.[102] Six bills simply sought to approve interstate air pollution control compacts.[103] Only a few bills sought to change the structure of federal air pollution control efforts. Continued uncertainty about the desirability of national emission standards is shown in the fact that only six bills were introduced which sought to direct the Secretary of HEW to establish such standards for stationary sources of air pollution.[104]

Bill introductions remained at a high level in 1970. A total of eighty-seven air pollution control bills were introduced in the House by fifty-four representatives. The geographical distribution of the constituencies represented by these members again provides evidence that a concern with air pollution had spread beyond California and New York. The fifty-four representatives came from twenty states distributed fairly evenly across the country. Sixteen representatives came from northeastern or Mid-Atlantic states, nine came from Southern or Border states, nineteen came from midwestern or plains states, and ten came from Pacific Coast or Rocky Mountain states. Thirty-two of the representatives were Democrats and twenty-two were Republicans. Seven bills were introduced in the Senate by six senators. Three of these senators were Democrats and three were Republicans.

Some of the bills introduced in 1970 were very similar to those introduced in 1969. Bills to ban the internal combustion engine, increase grants to states and improve research into various aspects of air pollution, were introduced in 1970. Some significant changes in the purview of many bills can also be identified. The number of bills that sought to increase tax relief on air pollution control equipment dropped to seven as passage of the Tax Reform Act 1969 knocked the wind out of the sails of such efforts. Advocates of using the tax system to control air pollution instead introduced bills to tax automobiles that failed to meet exhaust emission standards, or to increase the tax on leaded gasoline.[105] A large number of the bills introduced in 1970 sought to revise the Clean Air Act to improve its effectiveness. No fewer than thirty of the bills introduced in the House and three of those introduced in the Senate sought to overhaul, in one way or another, the basic structure of federal air pollution control efforts. A further eleven bills sought to establish national emission standards for stationary sources of air pollution.

Although the vast majority of those who introduced legislation were undoubtedly motivated simply by a desire to stake out a position on a highly salient issue, a small number were motivated by an ambition to play a more significant role in shaping policy. The problem confronting the ambitious few, however, was that considerable 'barriers to entry' limited opportunities for entrepreneurship. Not only had the information costs associated with policy-making escalated, but the transaction costs had risen as well. Information costs had been driven up by increased research which revealed the complexity of the problem. Policy entrepreneurship required a command of the subject that was becoming ever more difficult and expensive in terms of resources to acquire. Transaction costs had been driven up by the establishment of institutional venues with jurisdiction over air pollution issues. Opportunities for shaping policy were limited if a legislator was not a member of the Subcommittee on Public Health and Welfare in the House or the Subcommittee on Air and Water Pollution in the Senate.

The travails of Rep. Farbstein illustrate well the problems that such 'barriers to entry' can present. Elected in 1956 from a district with an air pollution problem, Rep. Farbstein made a strong effort to establish a reputation for policy leadership on air pollution control issues in the 1960s. He introduced a bill in 1965 to control air pollution from federal installations.[106] In 1967 he introduced a bill to establish air regions.[107] He introduced two further bills in 1969: one to use the highway trust fund for air pollution control purposes; the other to ban the internal combustion engine.[108] In 1970 he introduced no fewer than ten air pollution control bills.[109] Rep. Farbstein's ability to shape policy, however, was limited by his lack of an adequate institutional base. Not being a member of House Commerce, he lacked the 'seat at the table' that was necessary to play a meaningful role in making policy. He made an attempt to influence the agenda in December 1969 by conducting *ad hoc* hearings on automobile pollution with a number of other New York Democrats, but these hearings were soon overshadowed by those held by the Subcommittee on Public Health and Welfare.[110]

Rep. Farbstein's lack of an adequate institutional base meant that he posed no serious threat to the primacy established by Senator Muskie over air pollution control policy. Others were not so easy to ignore. In the House, Rep. Daddario used his position as Chairman of House Science's Subcommittee on Science, Research, and Development to promote the concept of ecology.[111] In the Senate, Senator Henry Jackson (D. WA), Chairman of Senate Interior, posed a real threat to Senator Muskie's leadership after authoring the National Environmental Policy Act (NEPA) 1969. Other predatory chairmen circled ominously in the background. Senator Warren G. Magnusson (D. WA), Rep. Morris Udall (D. AZ), Rep. John Blatnik (D. MN), and Rep. John Dingell (D. MI) all recognized the 'profit' that might be obtained from establishing a reputation for leadership on such a highly salient issue.[112] Rep. Rogers also posed a threat as the prime mover on the Subcommittee on Public Health and Welfare.

A new dimension was added to the battle for leadership on air pollution control policy in early 1970 when President Nixon entered the fray. Motivated by the desire to tap into a highly salient issue, and undermine the position of a potential front-runner for the 1972 Democratic presidential nomination, President Nixon sought to establish his credentials as an environmentalist.[113] In his 1970 State of the Union Address Nixon declared that: 'The great question of the seventies is, shall we surrender to our surroundings, or shall we make our peace with nature and begin to make reparations for the damage we have done to our air, to our land and to our water?'[114] He called for increased research into the design of automobile engines, tighter standards for exhaust emissions and new regulations for stationary sources of air pollution. The stage had been set for a radical change in air pollution control policy.

The Clean Air Amendments 1970
President Nixon sent a special message on the environment to Congress on 10 February 1970 which identified air pollution as the most serious environmental problem facing Americans, and made a number of proposals to remedy perceived defects in the Air Quality Act 1967.[115] Nixon made two proposals for legislation to tighten controls on automobile exhaust emissions. He called for better procedures to test automobile exhaust emissions and for the regulation of fuel additives. Perhaps more significantly, Nixon called for the regulation of stationary sources of pollution. He proposed 'that the Federal government establish nation-wide air quality standards, with the States to prepare within one year abatement plans for meeting those standards', and that 'designation of interstate air quality control regions continue at an accelerated rate'.[116] He also proposed 'that the Federal government establish national emissions standards for facilities that emit pollutants extremely hazardous to health, and for selected classes of new facilities which could be major contributors to air pollution'.[117] To improve enforcement of the air pollution control laws, Nixon proposed 'that Federal authority to seek court action be extended to include both inter- and intrastate air pollution situations', and to increase the fine for noncompliance with air pollution standards to $10,000 per day.[118] Bills incorporating these proposals were introduced in the House by Rep. Harley O. Staggers (D. WV) and Rep. William L. Springer (R. IL), and in the Senate by Minority Leader Senator Hugh Scott (R. PA) on 18 February 1970.[119]

Initial action on the proposals took place in the House where Rep. Rogers was anxious to build upon his growing reputation for leadership on the issue.[120] Hearings on the Administration bill were conducted by the Subcommittee on Public Health and Welfare, with Rep. Rogers again serving as Chairman, in March and April 1970.[121] Virtually all the witnesses agreed that the arrangements for controlling air pollution that had been established by the Air Quality Act were not working. Suggested solutions, however, fell into two broad types. A number of witnesses argued that an expansion of federal authority was required. Rep. Abner J. Mikva (D.Ill) declared that: 'The present approach of Federal coordination of air pollution control standards and state enforcement of them is not working. Air pollution requires an interstate solution: Federal standards, Federal enforcement, and private remedies in Federal courts when enforcement fails'.[122] This solution was opposed by industrial groups who argued that the best way to improve the control of air pollution would be to limit the authority of the federal government. Herbert S. Richey, a member of the board of directors of the United States Chambers of Commerce, told the Subcommittee that: 'To avoid delays in air pollution control programs increased responsibility should be given to local and state air pollution agencies.'[123]

Advocates of national emission standards outnumbered champions of state and local governments at the hearing. Although eighteen of the twenty-five witnesses who gave evidence to the Subcommittee represented industrial organizations, Herbert S. Richey was one of only five who spoke for industries likely to be affected by national emission standards. The other thirteen witnesses represented either the automobile industry or the petroleum processing industry, and their main concerns were the provisions of the bill pertaining to the testing of automobile engines and the regulation of fuel additives. Representatives of the automobile industry generally welcomed the Administration's proposals. Paul F. Chenea, a vice-president of General Motors, declared that: 'General Motors endorses extension of the Clean Air Act and urges that test procedures be improved.'[124] Donald A. Jensen, director of Ford's emissions office, even offered a suggestion for improving testing procedures: 'The present system of testing should be replaced by one in which each production run of cars is sampled and the entire run held up for testing and adjustment if non-compliance is found'.[125] This co-operative attitude was regarded cynically by some. Lawrence E. Blachard, executive vice-president of the Ethyl Corporation, noted drily that: 'The air pollution control proposal before the Subcommittee would give the Secretary of Health, Education and Welfare the authority to regulate the composition of fuels and fuel additives used in automobiles but would impose no additional requirements on the automobile manufacturers'.[126]

An attempt was made by Rep. Lionel Van Deerlin (D. CA), Rep. Richard L. Ottinger (D. NY), and Rep. Robert O. Tiernan (D. RI) in Committee mark-up to tighten the provisions of the bill pertaining to exhaust emissions, but the allies of the automobile industry on the committee were easily able to ward off the trio's efforts. The only change made to the section on automobile emissions was to adopt the proposal made by Donald A. Jensen that automobiles be tested straight off the assembly line. Rep. David Satterfield (D. VA) was also successful in protecting the interests of the Ethyl Corporation, which had its headquarters in his district, when he persuaded the Committee to accept an amendment that weakened the fuel standards provision contained in the bill.[127] In most other respects, however, the bill reported out of Committee was tougher than the original Administration bill.[128] Rep. Rogers ensured that the provisions on air quality standards and state implementation plans were stricter than desired by the Administration. New provisions were also added to make each state an air quality region, establish standards for aircraft emissions, and oblige federal facilities to comply with the air pollution control requirements of federal, state and local governments.

The bill reported by House Commerce marked a significant shift in the development of federal policy towards air pollution. The bill proposed both to deepen and widen federal control of air pollution. It authorized the Secretary of HEW to establish national air quality standards for any pollutants determined to endanger public health or welfare; required each state to specify what action it would take to meet such standards; and required the HEW Secretary to establish emission standards for new stationary sources where emissions were extremely hazardous or endangered public health or welfare. Emission standards for aircraft and aircraft engines were to be established, federal agencies directed to comply with all federal, state, interstate and local emission standards, and federal agents permitted to inspect any establishment believed to have infringed pollution control regulations. The only provisions that marked time rather than moving ahead were those dealing with pollution from automobiles. The bill required new automobiles to be tested as they came off the production line to see if they met exhaust emission standards, required the HEW Secretary to study fuel additives and authorized additional research into means of measuring automobile exhaust emissions. A total of $200 million was authorized for fiscal

1971, $250 million for fiscal 1972, and $325 million for fiscal 1973.

The House debated the bill on 10 June 1970, just a week after it had been reported out of Committee. Although the bill received broad bipartisan support, the provisions on automobile emissions and fuel standards proved contentious, and a number of amendments were offered that sought to make the bill less palatable to the automobile and fuel industries. All of the amendments were defeated. The most radical amendment was offered by Rep. Farbstein. Claiming that the bill 'appears to bend over backward to accommodate the auto industry', Farbstein offered an amendment to phase out the internal combustion engine.[129] The amendment was defeated by voice vote. Rep. Van Deerling offered an amendment which proposed establishing voluntary inspection of exhaust emission control devices after 4,000 miles. The automobile manufacturer would be obliged to correct any defect found in the test. This amendment was also rejected by voice vote. A similar fate befell Rep. Tiernan's amendment to restore the fuel standards language of the Administration bill. Rep. John P. Saylor (R. PA) offered an amendment to give all states the authority to set tougher exhaust emission standards than those promulgated by the federal government. The amendment was defeated on a 50–66 teller vote. A final amendment to tighten provisions on exhaust emission standards was defeated by voice vote. Rep. Daniel E. Burton (R. NY) offered an amendment which would have applied California's standards across the country.

Four amendments were offered to other sections of the bill. The only amendment to be accepted was one offered by Rep. Staggers which clarified the authority of the HEW Secretary. An amendment offered by Rep. Ken Hechler (D. WV) which sought to increase the authorization in the bill from $775 million to $7.75 billion was defeated by voice vote. Rep. William F. Ryan (D. NY) offered two amendments to the section of stationary sources which would have dramatically changed the nature of the bill. The first sought to delete a requirement that the Secretary of HEW take 'economic feasibility' into consideration when setting standards; the second attempted to substitute 'the deterioration of the quality of the environment' for 'endangerment of the public health or welfare' in the provision for setting standards. Both these amendments were defeated by voice vote. The bill was finally passed by the House on a 374–1 roll-call vote. Only Rep. Glenn C. Cunningham (R. NE) voted against passage.

The ease with which floor amendments to the bill were defeated reveals both the parliamentary and informational advantages possessed by the reporting committee. First, Chairman Staggers and Rep. Rogers had managed to obtain a 'modified' rule from the House Committee on Rules which gave less than a day's notice of floor action and restricted authority to offer amendments.[130] An objection from Rep. Farbstein that the rule failed to provide sufficient time to consider such complex legislation was to no avail. The rule obtained by Chairman Staggers and Rep. Rogers was approved by a 335–40 roll-call vote. Second, the bill's managers were able to take advantage of the asymmetry in information that existed between the committee and those proffering amendments. Rep. Rogers was able to undermine support for the Van Deerlin amendment by producing evidence that questioned the feasibility of the proposal. This enabled him to pronounce that: 'we do not have the testing devices'.[131] Chairman Staggers was similarly able to deflect the Burton Amendment with a claim that the Committee had considered and rejected the idea as impracticable.[132]

The confidence and assurance displayed by Rep. Rogers in guiding the bill through the House was not initially matched in the Senate. Whereas Rep. Rogers had been more than willing to use the Administration's proposals as a vehicle to address what were widely perceived as glaring defects in the Air Quality Act, Senator Muskie was much less willing to both criticize legislation that he had authored and concede the value of a proposal originating in the Nixon White House. Not only did Senator Muskie continue to have reservations about the efficacy of national emission standards, but as a leading contender for the 1972 Democratic presidential nomination he was also anxious not to provide President Nixon with the slightest opportunity to claim credit for leadership on a highly salient issue. Such concerns, combined with the fact that Senator Muskie was also distracted by running for re-election in Maine in 1970, ensured that progress on the bill was much slower in the Senate than it had been in the House.

The Subcommittee on Air and Water Pollution conducted hearings in March and April 1970 on the Administration's bill and the rival bills that had been introduced by Senator Muskie in December 1969 and March 1970.[133] The range of witnesses giving evidence to the Subcommittee was broadly similar to that which had appeared before the House Subcommittee. Five witnesses from the Administration, three from state governments, seven from the fuel industry, five from other industrial groups and two from the automobile industry gave evidence. The number of environmental groups testifying, however, was greater than in the House. Representatives of five environmental interest groups, including the Environmental Defense Fund, gave evidence to the Subcommittee on Air and Water Pollution whereas the House Subcommittee had heard only from Denis A. Hayes, co-ordinator of Environmental Action.

The evidence given to the Subcommittee on Air and Water Pollution was, not unsurprisingly, similar in most respects to that heard by Rep. Rogers and his colleagues. Administration officials and representatives of environmental groups urged the Subcommittee to consider national emission standards. Ruth Weiner, representing Colorado Citizens for Clean Air Inc., stated simply that: 'There should be national emission standards.'[134] The standard bearers of most industrial groups disagreed. Herbert S. Richey repeated the opposition of the US Chambers of Commerce to national emission standards. He declared that industry opposed 'national emissions standards because they are not responsive to the needs and demands of local conditions'.[135] A similar point was made by Fred E. Tucker of the National Steel Corporation: 'The company opposes national emission standards for stationary sources because some areas require more restrictive control than others to meet a specified air quality'.[136] Representatives of the fuel industry also voiced their opposition to the proposed regulation of fuel additives. Eneas D. Kane, president of Chevron Research Company, told the Subcommittee that: 'The Federal Government's role in automotive pollution control should focus on setting standards for vehicle emissions rather than attempting to regulate fuel composition'.[137] A representative of the Manufacturing Chemists Association, Willard F. Bixby, stated that: 'Legislation to regulate fuel composition and additive use is premature'.[138]

Not all the evidence heard by the Subcommittee covered familiar ground. One day of the hearings was devoted to the different methods that could be employed to achieve desired air pollution control goals. A number of witnesses stressed that means needed to be found to force control activity should either the Administration fail to implement the law properly or particular industries seek to avoid

their responsibilities. Professor James W. Jeans of the University of
Missouri argued that this could be achieved by establishing environmental 'property rights': 'The Clean Air Act should be amended
to enunciate the right of each individual to an unpolluted environment.'[139] Establishing such rights would create a powerful incentive
for industry to limit emissions, he argued, as individuals exposed to
pollution would be able to take legal action against those identified
as infringing their right to an unpolluted environment. A similar
point was articulated by Bernard S. Cohen of the American Trial
Lawyers Association: 'Federal regulatory agencies have complained
about the lack of funds and staff to adequately police and regulate
industry for air pollution. The availability of private damage actions
will cause preventive measures to be taken by industry.'[140] The idea
of using citizen suits to force compliance with environmental laws
was well received by Senator Muskie who had often complained
about the failure of successive administrations to implement the Air
Quality Act properly.

Little happened in the immediate aftermath of the hearings.
Diverted by his re-election campaign and other distractions, Senator Muskie failed to match the early pace set by Rep. Rogers in the
House. Publication of a report into air pollution by the Ralph Nader
organization in May 1970, however, finally prompted Senator
Muskie to focus his energies on the pending legislation.[141] The
report severely criticized both the role that Senator Muskie had
played in drafting the Air Quality Act and his continued passivity
when confronted with evidence of policy failure. Galvanized into
action by the prospect of providing President Nixon with valuable
political ammunition, Senator Muskie began to take action to
recover his reputation for leadership on the issue. In a number of
press conferences and speeches made in the summer 1970 he
alluded time and time again to the fact that he was authoring legislation that was even more uncompromising than that advocated by
the Administration.[142]

The Subcommittee on Air and Water Pollution finally reported a
bill to the Committee on Public Works for consideration on 25
August 1970. Tougher than both the Administration's bill and the
House-passed bill, its provisions revealed just how much Senator
Muskie had been stung by criticism of his leadership. For the first
time, Senator Muskie conceded the need for national standards to
control pollution from stationary sources. The Subcommittee bill

required the Secretary of HEW to establish national air quality standards for specific pollutants that would provide 'an adequate margin of safety ... requisite to protect human health'. No account was to be taken of economic feasibility when setting these standards. The bill also established a new category of extremely hazardous pollutants which were to be banned entirely. The provisions on mobile sources of pollution were no less stringent. A 90 per cent reduction in automobile exhaust emissions was required by 1975, and the Secretary of HEW was authorized to prohibit the use of any fuel in commerce which might endanger public health. To promote compliance with the legislation, citizens were authorized to bring suits for violation of standards, and the penalties for violation of the law were set at $25,000 per day.

Senator Muskie's purpose in proposing national standards based solely on the criteria to protect human health was not only to assuage public demands for greater protection, but also to establish standards that would have a good chance of surviving legal challenges. Writing twenty years later, Senator Muskie stated that: 'I was convinced that strict federal air pollution regulation would require a legally defensible premise. Protection of public health seemed the strongest and most appropriate such premise'.[143] The reference to 'economic feasibility' contained in the House-passed bill was believed to offer an open invitation to industry groups to challenge in the courts whatever standards were eventually promulgated by the Secretary of HEW. The requirement that automobiles reduce their exhaust emissions by 90 per cent by 1975 was put in the bill after Leon G. Billings, Senator Muskie's main environmental aide, asked John Middleton, Commissioner of the National Air Pollution Control Agency, how much automobile emissions would have to be reduced to achieve the goal contained in the Air Quality Act that states reduce their pollution by 50 per cent.[144]

Committee discussion of the bill centred on the 1975 deadline for achieving a 90 per cent reduction in exhaust emissions from automobiles. The Subcommittee bill had not contained any provision for an extension of the deadline, but after heavy lobbying by the automobile industry Senate Public Works agreed on a 10–3 vote to permit a one-year extension. The Committee also added a provision allowing for judicial review of any decision made by the Secretary of HEW regarding extensions. Other changes made by Senate Public Works involved setting specific deadlines for the establishment and implementation of national air quality standards. Although the Committee reported the bill unanimously on 11 September 1970, two Republicans expressed minor reservations. Senator Robert Dole (R. KS) recommended a congressional review of the automobile exhaust emission deadline rather than a judicial review. Senator Edward J. Gurney (R. FL), proposed that automobile manufacturers be granted the possibility of a two year extension rather than a single year.

Senate Majority Leader Mike Mansfield moved swiftly to schedule debate on the bill. Little more than a week after the bill had been reported out of committee, Senator Muskie took the floor of the Senate to open debate. He told the chamber that a tough bill was needed to protect the health of Americans, and took particular care to defend the provisions pertaining to automobile exhaust emission standards: 'Detroit has told the nation that Americans cannot live without the automobile. This legislation would tell Detroit that if that is the case, then they must make an automobile with which Americans can live'.[145] Primary opposition to the provisions came from Senator Robert P. Griffin (R. MI) who was anxious to protect the interests of his home state. He termed the 1975 deadline for achieving a 90 per cent reduction in exhaust emissions as 'brinkmanship – an industry pivotal to the US economy is to be required by statute to meet standards which the Committee itself acknowledges cannot be met with existing technology'.[146] With the public clamouring for rigorous action against air pollution, however, few senators were swayed by tales of woe from the automobile industry. Amendments to soften the impact of the deadline were introduced by Senator Dole and Senator Gurney, but both were defeated on roll-call votes. Only a few minor and clarifying amendments were accepted before the bill as a whole was passed on a 73–0 roll-call vote.

The Senate bill differed from the House bill in a number of important respects. First, the provisions on emissions from stationary sources, automobile exhaust emission standards and fuel additives were tougher in the Senate version than in the House version. Second, the House version made no mention of citizen suits to spur adequate implementation. Finally, the Senate version authorized $1.27 billion over three years for the purposes of the bill compared to $775 million in the House version. The House version was tougher than the Senate version only in provisions on air quality regions and emissions from aircraft. No provision of the original Administration bill was tougher than that found in the Senate version. In authoring and guiding such a bill through the Senate, Senator Muskie had managed to reclaim his reputation for policy leadership on air pollution control issues. Both Rep. Rogers and President Nixon had ultimately been outflanked.

The compromise bill that was reported out of conference on 17 December 1970 reflected Senator Muskie's reclaimed authority as 'Mr Pollution'. At virtually every point of dispute the House conferees acceded to the views of the Senate. The conference accepted the Senate's provisions, with minor adjustments, on stationary sources, fuel additives, air quality regions and citizen suits. An authorization of $1.1 billion over three years was also much closer to the Senate version than the House version. Senate conferees, in turn, agreed to the provisions in the House version regarding emissions from aircraft. The only significant concession made by Senator Muskie concerned the establishment of the automobile exhaust emissions deadlines. Heavy lobbying by the Administration and the industry had persuaded Rep. Jarman that the deadlines needed to be more flexible, and Senator Muskie was forced to compromise slightly to make progress.[147] Not only did the conference specify what emissions were to reduced by 90 per cent, it also extended the period in which automobile manufacturers could apply for an extension to the deadline. Reductions in exhaust emissions of carbon monoxide and hydrocarbons had to be achieved by 1975, and nitrogen oxides by 1976. Automobile manufacturers were permitted to request an extension of the 1975 deadline on or after 1 January 1972 rather than 1 January 1973 as specified in the Senate bill.

Both the House and Senate passed the conference bill by voice vote on 18 December 1970. Although debate in the Senate revealed widespread support for the bill, a comment by Senator Thomas F. Eagleton (D. MO) criticizing the efforts of the Administration to weaken the provisions on automobile exhaust emissions ruffled some Republican feathers. General support for the bill was also apparent in the debate in the House. A note of discord was introduced by Rep. Ryan who criticized both Chairman Staggers and Rep. Rogers for producing an 'inadequate' original bill, but there was no serious challenge to the compromise worked out in conference. The bill was signed into law by President Nixon on 31 December 1970. Nixon described the bill as 'the most important piece of legislation … dealing with the problem of clean air that we have this year and the most important in our history'.[148] Although Nixon noted the bipartisan effort that had led to the bill's passage and specifically thanked Senator Randolph, Senator Cooper and Congressman Springer, the role of Senator Muskie as the primary author went unacknowledged. The White House failed to extend an invitation to attend the signing ceremony to the Senator.

The Clean Air Amendments 1970, as finally enacted, directed the Administrator of the newly created Environmental Protection Agency (EPA) to set National Ambient Air Quality Standards (NAAQS) for carbon monoxide, ozone, particulate matter, hydrocarbons, sulphur dioxide and lead. Primary standards were required to protect human health and secondary standards to protect the wider environment. Each state was required to adopt plans (state implementation plans, or SIPs) to implement, maintain and enforce those standards. States had to submit their SIPs to the EPA for approval within nine months of NAAQS being set. Authority was granted to the Administrator to amend unsatisfactory SIPs and to impose implementation plans on states which had not submitted their own. The Clean Air Amendments 1970 also required motor vehicle emissions of carbon monoxide and hydrocarbons to be reduced by 90 per cent from 1970 levels by 1975, and emissions of nitrogen oxides to be reduced by 90 per cent from 1971 levels by 1976. Other provisions sought to control the emission of fourteen specific pollutants from newly constructed facilities by requiring the promulgation of New Source Performance Standards (NSPS), expanded research into air pollution, provided additional funds to the states and authorized citizens or groups to bring suits in federal courts against either the Administrator for failure to perform specified duties, or alleged polluters, including the federal government.

Enactment of the Clean Air Amendments 1970 changed the structure of air pollution control in the United States. 'In an attempt to avoid reliance upon the voluntary cooperation of the states, the Clean Air Amendments 1970 enlarged the role of the federal government and gave greater definition to the responsibilities of the states' noted two observers.[149] Not only was a federal role in controlling air pollution established that rendered 'quite hollow the statutory catechism that pollution control is primarily a state problem', but the provisions pertaining to hazardous pollutants and pollution from new sources indicated both a broadening as well as a deepening of federal authority.[150] To quote Kent E. Portney: 'Although the title of the Act suggests incremental changes this legislation marked a very new and different approach to air pollution control.'[151] The Act established the primacy and extended the interest of the federal government in matters of air pollution control.

Conclusion

The development of air pollution control law between 1964 and 1970 reveals the policy inflation that may occur when 'profits' are sufficiently high to generate competition among policy entrepreneurs. Lured into the policy 'market' by the promise of electoral rewards, the opportunity to make policy on an issue of national importance or the chance to enhance institutional prestige, a 'bidding war' between entrepreneurs led to the abandonment of the incremental style of policy-making that had characterized the development of air pollution control law since 1955. Constitutional niceties and technical feasibility were forgotten in the competition to satisfy public demands for greater protection from air pollution. Legislation was enacted which not only deepened but also widened the role of the federal government in controlling air pollution. The authority of the states was largely pre-empted as a wide range of pollutants were brought under the control of federal agencies.

The regulatory regime that was created as a result of this policy inflation changed the scope of the conflict surrounding the issue of air pollution control. Whereas the limited purview of earlier air pollution control laws had generated little conflict, the 'speculative augmentation' of the Clean Air Amendments 1970 produced distinct winners and losers. On the one hand, environmental groups were given a boost. Enactment of the law both provided the emerging environmental movement with a victory that could be used to foster recruitment, and opened new avenues for interest group activity through its provisions for citizen suits. On the other hand, many industrial groups were left in a worse position. Automobile manufacturers and utility companies faced the prospect of increased costs as a result of the 1970 law. Sandwiched between the environmentalists and the industrial groups was the newly created EPA. Required to implement a law which Charles O. Jones has described as 'policy beyond capacity', the EPA faced not only technical difficulties in establishing standards, but also had to deal with the constant threat of legal action from environmentalists and industry.[152]

Demands for changes to the regulatory regime established by the Clean Air Amendments 1970 emerged almost as soon as the ink of President Nixon's signature had dried. Environmentalists sought to build upon the gains that the 1970 law had brought, industry groups sought to limit their losses, and the EPA sought ways of easing the task of implementation. The conflict between these various groups altered significantly the matrix of benefits and costs surrounding the issue. The benefits from policy entrepreneurship became less certain as industry groups began to complain about the costs of environmental protection, and the saliency of the issue started to decline. Information costs rose as each group produced more and more evidence to support their arguments. Transaction costs increased as each group mobilized to fight their corner. The net result was the onset of a period of policy retrenchment characterized by stasis and marginal adjustments in policy.

Notes

1 Clarence Davies *The Politics of Pollution* (Indianapolis: Pegasus, 1970), p.37.
2 This is a similar process, in many respects, to that found in the Progressive Era.
3 Arthur C. Stern 'History of Air Pollution Legislation in the United States', *Journal of Air Pollution Control Association* (1982), 32:44–61; Davies *The Politics of Pollution*, pp.49–58.
4 Charles O. Jones 'Speculative-Augmentation in Federal Air Pollution Policy Making', *Journal of Politics* (1974), 36:438–64; Charles O. Jones *Clean Air* (Pittsburgh: University of Pittsburgh Press, 1975); James E. Krier and Edmund Ursin *Pollution and Policy* (Berkeley, CA: University of California Press, 1977); Helen Ingram 'The Political Rationality of Innovation: The Clean Air Act Amendments 1970' in Ann F. Friedlander (ed.), *Approaches to Controlling Air Pollution* (Cambridge, MA: MIT Press, 1978); E. Donald Elliot, Bruce A. Ackerman and John C. Millian 'Toward a Theory of Statutory Evolution: The Federalization of Environmental Law', *Journal of Law, Economics, and Organization* (1985), 1:313–40.
5 Gary C. Bryner *Blue Skies, Green Politics* (Washington, DC: Congressional Quarterly Press, 1993), p.1.
6 Henry Kenski and Helen Ingram 'The Reagan Administration and Envi-

ronmental Regulation: The Constraint of the Political Market' in Sheldon Kamieniecki, Robert O'Brien and Michael Clarke (eds), *Controversies in Environmental Policy* (Albany, NY: State University of New York Press, 1986).

7 Jones *Clean Air*, p.71.

8 An Act to Require Passenger-Carrying Motor Vehicles Purchased for Use by the Federal Government to Meet Certain Safety Standards, PL 88–515.

9 The Federal Installations, Facilities, and Equipment Pollution Control Act, S 560 (1965).

10 EO 11282 (1966).

11 US Senate, Committee on Public Works, Special Subcommittee on Air and Water Pollution, *Hearings*, 'Air Pollution Control', 88th Congress, 2nd session, 27, 29, 31 January, 17, 18, 20 February 1964. The 27 January hearing was held in Los Angeles; the 29 January hearing was held in Denver; the 31 January hearing was held in Chicago; the 17 February hearing was held in Boston; the 18 February hearing was held in New York; and the 20 February hearing was held in Tampa.

12 US Senate, Committee on Public Works, Special Subcommittee on Air and Water Pollution, *Hearing*, 'Technical Problems of Air Pollution Control', 88th Congress, 2nd session, 24, 25, 30 June, 1, 2 July 1964.

13 US Senate, Committee on Public Works, Special Subcommittee on Air and Water Pollution, *Report*, 'Steps Toward Clean Air', 88th Congress, 2nd session, October 1964.

14 US Department of Health, Education, and Welfare, Public Health Service *Automotive Air Pollution* (Washington, DC: GPO, January 1965).

15 Rep. Long introduced HR 2105 (1965). The two bills introduced by Rep. Gibbons were HR 1696 (1965) and HR 8007 (1965).

16 Davies *The Politics of Pollution*, p.67.

17 S 306 (1965).

18 See Elliot, Ackerman and Millan 'Toward a Theory of Statutory Evolution', pp.326–7, 330–1. This episode provides some support for arguments that regulations are determined by the needs of business; see George J. Stigler 'The Theory of Economic Regulation', *Bell Journal of Economics and Management Science* (1971), 2:3–21.

19 The Motor Vehicle Pollution Control Act 1960. See Krier and Ursin *Pollution and Policy*, pp.137–69.

20 Lyndon B. Johnson 'Special Message to the Congress on Conservation and Restoration of Natural Beauty', *Public Papers, 1965*, 8 February 1965, p.163.

21 US Senate, Committee on Public Works, Special Subcommittee on Air and Water Pollution, *Hearing*, 'Air Pollution Control', 89th Congress, 1st session, 6–9 April 1965, p.26.

22 See James L. Sundquist *Politics and Policy* (Washington, DC: Brookings, 1968), p.370.

23 US Senate, Committee on Public Works, Special Subcommittee on Air and Water Pollution, *Hearing*, 'Air Pollution Control', 89th Congress, 1st session, 9 April 1965, p.295.

24 Cited in *Congressional Quarterly Almanac*, 1965, p.782.

25 US House of Representatives, Committee on Interstate and Foreign Commerce, Subcommittee on Public Health and Welfare, *Hearing*, 'Clean Air Act Amendment', 89th Congress, 1st session, 10, 11, 15, 16, 29 June 1965.

26 Motor Vehicle Air Pollution Control Act, title I, PL 89–272, 79 stat. 992, 42 USC 1857f-1 to 1857f-8. Subsequently transferred to 42 USC 7401 *et seq.*

27 Lyndon B. Johnson 'Remarks in the Hospital at the Signing of the Clean Air Act Amendments and Solid Waste Disposal Bill', *Public Papers 1965*, 20 October 1965, pp.1066–7.

28 David Currie 'Motor Vehicle Air Pollution: State Authority and Federal Pre-emption', *Michigan Law Review*, (1970) 68:1083.

29 Lyndon B. Johnson 'Special Message to the Congress Proposing Measures to Preserve America's Natural Heritage', *Public Papers, 1966. Part 1* 23 February 1966, pp.195–203.

30 Cited in Hazel Erskine 'The Polls, Pollution and Its Costs', *Public Opinion Quarterly* (1972), 28:38–50.

31 Anthony Downs 'Up and Down with Ecology: The "Issue-Attention Cycle"', *Public Interest* (1972), 28:38–50.

32 HR 13199 (1966); HR 16368 (1966); HR 16876 (1966).

33 HR 13699 (1966).

34 HR 15481 (1966).

35 Krier and Ursin *Pollution and Policy*, p.193.

36 Joseph A. Pechman *Federal Tax Policy* (Washington, DC: Brookings, 1966), pp.120–1.

37 S 2857 (1966); S 3598 (1966); S 3911 (1966); S 2940 (1966); S 3210 (1966).

38 S 3112 (1966).

39 US Senate, Committee on Public Works, Subcommittee on Air and Water Pollution, *Hearing*, 'Air Pollution Control Programs, Extension', 89th Congress, 2nd session, 7–9, 14, 15 June 1966.

40 US House of Representatives, Committee on Interstate and Foreign Commerce, Subcommittee on Public Health and Welfare, *Hearing*, 'Clean Air Act Amendment 1966', 89th Congress, 2nd session, 27 September 1966.

41 The Clean Air Act Amendments 1966, PL 89–675, 80 stat. 954, 42 USC 1857c, 1857l. Some sections transferred to 42 USC 7401 *et seq.*, remaining sections repealed by the Clean Air Act Amendments 1977.

42 Derek M. Elsom *Atmospheric Pollution: A Global Problem*, 2nd edition (Oxford, Blackwell, 1992), p.201.

43 A good discussion of the role of the Johnson Administration in promoting environmentalism is Martin V. Melosi 'Lyndon Johnson and Environmental Policy' in Robert A. Divine (ed.), *The Johnson Years, Volume Two* (Lawrence, KS: University Press of Kansas, 1987), pp.113–49.

44 US Department of Health, Education, and Welfare, Public Health Service, *Proceedings, The Third National Conference on Air Pollution* 12–14 December 1966, p.8.

45 *Ibid.*, p.15.

46 Lyndon B. Johnson 'State of the Union Address', 10 January 1967, *Public Papers, 1967. Part 1*, pp.2–13.

47 Lyndon B. Johnson 'Special Message to the Congress: Protecting Our National Heritage', *Public Papers, 1967. Part 1* 30 January 1967, pp.93–102.

48 Elliot, Ackerman and Millian 'Toward a Theory of Statutory Evolution', p.332.

49 *New York Times* 14 October 1965, p.A30.

50 *New York Times* 18 December 1966, p.A41.

51 S 780 (1967).

52 US Senate, Committee on Public Works, Subcommittee on Air and Water Pollution, *Hearing*, 'Air Pollution – 1967 (Air Quality Act), part 2', 90th Congress, 1st session, 20 February 1967, p.398.

53 *Ibid.*, p.514.

54 *Ibid.*, p.781.

55 See Jones *Clean Air*, pp.79–83.

56 US Senate, Committee on Public Works, Subcommittee on Air and Water Pollution, *Hearing*, 'Air Pollution – 1967. Part 3', 90th Congress, 1st session, 19 April, 2–4, 8–10 May 1967, p.1797.

57 *Ibid.*, p.1830.

58 US Senate, Committee on Public Works, Subcommittee on Air and Water Pollution, *Hearing*, 'Air Pollution – 1967 (Air Quality Act), part 4', 90th Congress, 1st session, 17 May 1967, p.2544.

59 Elliot, Ackerman and Millian 'Toward a Theory of Statutory Evolution', pp.332–3.

60 Quoted in Congressional Quarterly, *Almanac 1967*, p. 883.

61 *Ibid.*

62 *Ibid.*

63 HR 9509 (1967).

64 See Jones *Clean Air*, pp.82–3.

65 US House of Representatives, Committee on Interstate and Foreign Commerce, *Hearing*, 'Air Quality Act 1967', 90th Congress, 1st session, 15–18, 21–24 August 1967, p.394.

66 *Ibid.*, p.506.

67 *Ibid.*, pp.477–500.

68 Quoted in Congressional Quarterly, *Almanac 1967*, p. 886.

69 *Ibid.*

70 Lyndon B. Johnson 'Remarks Upon Signing the Air Quality Act 1967', *Public Papers, 1967* 21 November 1967, p.1068.

71 The Water Quality Act 1965, PL 89–234, 79 stat. 903, 33 USC 1151 *et seq.*

72 The Air Quality Act Amendments of 1969, PL 91–137, reauthorized the research provisions for a further year.

73 The exemption for California was included because federal standards were not deemed strict enough to meet the pollution problem in that state.

74 *Congressional Record* 18 July 1967, p.S19171.

75 Paul R. Portney 'Air Pollution Policy' in Paul R. Portney (ed.), *Public Policies for Environmental Protection* (Washington DC, Resources for the Future, 1990), p.30.

76 See Krier and Ursin *Pollution and Policy*, p.201; James E. O'Fallon 'Deficiencies in the Air Quality Act 1967', *Law and Contemporary Problems* (1968), 33.

77 US House of Representatives, Committee on Science and Astronautics, Subcommittee on Science, Research, and Development, *Hearing*, 'Environmental Quality', 90th Congress, 2nd session, 12–14 March 1968.

78 US Senate, Committee on Public Works, Subcommittee on Air and Water Pollution, *Hearing*, 'Air Pollution, Part 2', 90th Congress, 2nd session, 29–31 July 1968.

79 US House of Representatives, Committee on Government Operations, Subcommittee on Research and Technical Programs, *Hearing*, 'Federal Air Pollution Research and Development on Sulphur Oxides Pollution Abatement', 90th Congress, 2nd session, 5 September 1968.

80 S 2276 (1969); HR 12085 (1969).

81 US House of Representatives, Committee on Interstate and Foreign Commerce, Subcommittee on Public Health and Welfare, *Hearing*, 'Air Pollution Control Research into Fuels and Motor Vehicles', 91st Congress, 1st session, 19 June 1969.

82 PL 91–137.

83 Quoted in Congressional Quarterly, *Almanac 1969*, p. 523.

84 *Ibid.*

85 *Ibid.*

86 *Ibid.*

87 US House of Representatives, Committee on Interstate and Foreign Commerce, Subcommittee on Public Health and Welfare, *Hearing*, 'Air Pollution Control Research into Fuels and Motor Vehicles', 91st Congress, 1st session, 19 June 1969.

88 US Congress, Joint Committee on Atomic Energy, *Hearing*, 'Environmental Effects of Producing Electric Power', 91st Congress, 1st session, 28–30 October, 4–7 November 1969.
89 US Senate, Committee on Public Works, Subcommittee on Air and Water Pollution, *Hearing*, 'Air Pollution, 1969', 91st Congress, 1st session, 27 October 1969.
90 US House of Representatives, Committee on Interstate and Foreign Commerce, Subcommittee on Public Health and Welfare, *Hearings*, 'Air Pollution Control and Recycling', 91st Congress, 1st session, 8, 9 December 1969.
91 *Ibid.*, pp.5–16.
92 Stern 'History of Air Pollution Legislation in the United States', p.44.
93 *Ibid.*
94 S 3229 (1969).
95 S 3546 (1970).
96 Riley E. Dunlap 'Public Opinion on the Environment in the Reagan Era', *Environment* (1987), 29:35.
97 Erskine, 'The Polls, Pollution and tIts Costs', pp.120–35.
98 See Charles O. Jones 'Air Pollution and Contemporary Environmental Politics', *Growth and Change* (1973) 4:22–7.
99 The Tax Reform Act 1969, PL91–172.
100 HR 13225 (1969); HR 14577 (1969).
101 HR 14534 (1969); HR 14535 (1969); HR 14578 (1969); HR 14761 (1969), S 3072 (1969), S 3276 (1969).
102 HR 640 (1969); HR 15230 (1969); HR 15335 (1969); HR 15393 (1969).
103 HJ Res 37 (1969); HJ Res 76 (1969); HJ Res 482 (1969); HJ Res 616 (1969); SJ Res 53 (1969); S 2707 (1969).
104 HR 14484 (1969); HR 14579 (1969); HR 14867 (1969); HR 15009 (1969); HR 15070 (1969), S 3229 (1969).
105 HR 17201 (1970); HR 17202 (1970); HR 17438 (1970); HR 15754 (1970); HR 16216 (1970); HR 16259 (1970); HR 16540 (1970).
106 HR 4487 (1965).
107 HR 3293 (1967).
108 HR 8772 (1969); HR 13225 (1969).
109 HR 17199 (1970); HR 17200 (1970); HR 17201 (1970); HR 17202 (1970); HR 17203 (1970); HR 17204 (1970); HR 17239 (1970); HR 17281 (1970); HR 17438 (1970); HR 17439 (1970).
110 Jones *Clean Air*, pp.178–9.
111 Davies *The Politics of Pollution*, p.67.
112 Michael E. Kraft 'Congress and Environmental Policy' in James P. Lester (ed.), *Environmental Politics and Policy* (Durham, NC: Duke University Press, 1989), p.183.

113 Jones *Clean Air*, p.179.

114 Richard M. Nixon 'State of the Union Address', *Public Papers, 1970* 22 January 1970, pp.8–15.

115 Richard M. Nixon 'Special Message to Congress on Environmental Quality', *Public Papers, 1970* 10 February 1970, pp.96–108.

116 *Ibid.*, p.103.

117 *Ibid.*

118 *Ibid.*, p.104.

119 HR 15848 (1970); S 3466 (1970). The two bills were identical.

120 See Jones *Clean Air*, p.177.

121 US House of Representatives, Committee on Interstate and Foreign Commerce, Subcommittee on Public Health and Welfare, *Hearings*, 'Air Pollution Control and Recycling', 91st Congress, 1st session, 16–21 March, 14 April 1970.

122 *Ibid.*, p.488.

123 *Ibid.*, p.515.

124 *Ibid.*, p.747.

125 *Ibid.*, p.790.

126 *Ibid.*, p.585.

127 See Jones *Clean Air*, pp.186–8.

128 House Commerce reported a bill with an amendment in the nature of a substitute (HR 17255) on 3 June 1970.

129 Quoted in Congressional Quarterly, *Almanac 1970*, p.478.

130 H. Res. 1069 (1970).

131 Quoted in Congressional Quarterly, *Almanac 1970*, p.478.

132 *Ibid.*

133 US Senate, Committee on Public Works, Subcommittee on Air and Water Pollution, *Hearing*, 'Air Pollution – 1970', 91st Congress, 2nd session, 16–20, 23–26 March, 17 April 1970.

134 *Ibid.*

135 *Ibid.*, p.473.

136 US Senate, Committee on Public Works, Subcommittee on Air and Water Pollution, *Hearing*, 'Air Pollution – 1970. Part 1', 91st Congress, 2nd session, 16–18 March 1970, p.239.

137 *Ibid.*

138 *Ibid.*

139 *Ibid.*

140 *Ibid.*

141 John C. Esposito *Vanishing Air* (New York: Grossman, 1970). For the reaction of Senator Muskie to the report see Theo Lippman and Donald C. Hansen *Muskie* (New York: Norton, 1971).

142 Jones *Clean Air*, pp.194–5.

143 Edmund S. Muskie 'The Clean Air Act: A Commitment to Public

Health' *Environmental Forum* (1990), 12:14.
144 Richard E. Cohen *Washington At Work: Back Rooms and Clean Air* (New York: Macmillan, 1992), p.15.
145 Quoted in Congressional Quarterly, *Almanac 1970*, p.482.
146 *Ibid.*
147 Jones *Clean Air*, pp.206–7.
148 Richard M. Nixon 'Remarks on Signing the Clean Air Amendments 1970', *Public Papers, 1970* 31 December 1970, p.1166.
149 James A. Henderson and Richard N. Pearson 'Implementing Federal Environmental Policies: The Limits of Aspirational Commands', *Columbia Law Review* (1978), 78:1462–3.
150 David P. Currie 'Direct Federal Regulation of Stationary Sources under the Clean Air Act', *University of Pennsylvania Law Review* (1980), 128:1469.
151 Kent E. Portney *Controversial Issues in Environmental Policy* (Newbury Park, CA, Sage, 1992), p.71.
152 Jones 'Speculative-Augmentation in Federal Air Pollution Policy Making', p.459.

6
Policy retrenchment, 1970–77

The nature of congressional interest in air pollution changed between 1970 and 1977 as the certitude that had fuelled the policy inflation of the late 1960s gave way to uncertainty and conflict. Relatively stable levels of bill introductions and committee hearings replaced the ever increasing levels of activity that had characterised the previous period. Although the purpose of much of this activity was to build upon earlier achievements, a significant proportion was dedicated to rolling back the apparatus of control established by the Clean Air Amendments 1970. A considerable number of bills were introduced to provide regulatory relief to industries adversely affected by the 1970 law. Enactments signalled a new sense of retrenchment. Minor reauthorizations were passed in 1973 and 1975. The Energy Supply and Environmental Coordination Act 1974 allowed the Environmental Protection Agency (EPA) to suspend some emission standards and postponed others.[1] The Clean Air Act Amendments 1977 contained new provisions to prevent the significant deterioration of air quality in areas with little air pollution, but also gave industry more time to comply with existing emission standards.[2]

The origins of this period of policy retrenchment can be traced to the ambition of the Clean Air Amendments 1970. The 'speculative-augmentation' of the 1970 law not only gave the newly created EPA a set of tasks that could not be achieved within the required deadlines, but also imposed costs upon major industrial groups such as the automobile, coal and steel industries. While the EPA struggled to set National Ambient Air Quality Standards (NAAQS) that would protect human health, identify and establish National Emission Standards for Hazardous Air Pollutants (NESHAPs), establish New

Source Performance Standards (NSPS) based on the 'best techno-logical system of continuous emission reduction' and approve state implementation plans (SIPs), the industrial groups complained that the requirements of the Clean Air Amendments 1970 were techno-logically and economically unfeasible. Such arguments were given particular potency by the energy crisis and growing economic prob-lems of the mid-1970s. A law which seemed to cast doubt on the continued use of coal, made motoring more expensive and imposed additional costs on industry, appeared to be a luxury that could not be afforded in a time of energy shortages and economic decline.

A new incentive structure governing legislative action on air pol-lution control was created as a result of these developments. Bene-fits became less certain and costs rose. The reduced saliency of the issue meant that the rewards that might be expected from action to strengthen air pollution control efforts were not as clear cut as had been the case in the late 1960s. Although the 1970 Amendments had given an important boost to the environmental movement, a belated but effective counter-mobilization of industrial groups posed a potential threat to members anxious to expand federal action. Environmental groups were not able to define the terms in which the debate about air pollution was conducted, and potential peril threatened legislators who were caught on the wrong side of the issue. The high saliency of energy issues and the economy meant that greater rewards might be available from action to reduce air pollution control efforts. The costs of legislative action to strengthen control of air pollution had also increased. Information costs had risen considerably as a consequence of the creation of a regulatory regime. A potential policy entrepeneur not only had to possess knowledge of the results of past action, but also be able to assess the likely effects of any changes in policy. Transaction costs had soared as a result of the greater conflict associated with the issue. Obtaining agreement for changes in the law had become much more difficult than it had been in the 1960s.

This change in the incentive structure governing legislative action is suggested in some of the literature. The studies by Charles O. Jones, and by James E. Krier and Edmund Ursin provide important material on the early implementation of the Clean Air Amendments 1970, but do not chart legislative developments in any detail.[3] A description of efforts in the Senate to amend the Clean Air Act in 1975–76 is provided by Bernard Asbell, but no explanatory framework is offered to make sense of these observations.[4] The account of legislative developments during this period provided by Arthur C. Stern also tends more to description than explanation.[5] Probably the best analysis of developments during this period is provided by Bruce A. Ackerman and William T. Hassler.[6] Although their study focuses primarily upon the debate over the use of 'scrubbers' to control emissions from power stations, their account of the way that the 1970 law generated both new problems and interest group alignments has wide pertinence. Particularly astute is their observation that: '... the Clean Air Act had tried to resolve so many disputable substantive issues in 1970 that recurrent congressional reconsideration was fundamental to the policymaking process'.[7] The main legislative result of this 'recurrent congressional reconsideration' was the Clean Air Act Amendments 1977. Testament to the difficulty of obtaining agreement on the best way forward, the 1977 law is perhaps best characterised as a 'holding operation'. It addressed many of the problems arising out of the ambition of the 1970 law by introducing greater regulatory flexibility and extending compliance deadlines. Like most 'holding operations', however, the 1977 law failed to satisfy affected interests for long. Environmentalists began to campaign for a renewed commitment to the control of air pollution, and industrialists soon started to argue that existing concessions were inadequate. A product of 'congressional reconsideration', the 1977 law prompted further 'reconsideration' almost immediately after enactment.

Problems and reaction

Demands that action be taken to reform the regulatory regime established by the Clean Air Amendments began to be articulated soon after enactment of the 1970 law. Industry groups mobilised to contest the terms in which the debate over air pollution had been conducted, sought to persuade the Nixon Administration that caution was required when implementing the law, sought to challenge regulations in the courts and campaigned to amend the law. Federal bureaucrats gave evidence to congressional committees which highlighted the difficulties they were facing in implementing the law. The newly invigorated environmental groups sought to expand the control efforts of the federal government to deal with, among other things, aircraft emissions and noise pollution. Little was unusual in this pattern of complaint and discontent. James E. Krier and Edmund Ursin note that: 'One could expect even in 1970 that there would soon be moves to amend the Clean Air Amendments. The history of federal air pollution legislation, at least since 1963, had established a trend in that direction'.[8] What was different about the complaints of the early 1970s was that they were aired against the backdrop of a worsening energy crisis. This gave added credence to the arguments of industry, engendered conflict over whether the problem of air pollution should be defined as a health or an energy issue and provided an opportunity for congressional committees with jurisdiction over energy matters to challenge the control exercised by Senator Muskie's Subcommittee on Air and Water Pollution. The result was a temporary roll-back of emission standards as energy concerns subsumed the issue of air pollution control.

Rising discontent

Discontent with the Clean Air Amendments 1970 was initially articulated by industrial groups. Undoubtedly surprised by the policy inflation of the late 1960s, the likes of the automobile, steel and coal industries rallied quickly to challenge the law in a four-pronged attack. First, they sought to disseminate information about the costs of compliance with the 1970 law in the hope of sparking an 'ecological backlash' among the general public. Stories in the press began to appear which suggested that stringent air pollution control laws were causing higher prices and unemployment.[9] Second, they sought to convince the Nixon Administration to take a pro-industry perspective when implementing the 1970 law. Nixon was persuaded to create a National Industrial Pollution Control Council in the Department of Commerce composed of business executives.[10] This provided industry with privileged access to the regulatory process. Third, they sought to challenge regulations promulgated by the EPA in the courts.[11] Finally, they sought to persuade Congress to amend the law. Sympathetic legislators such as Rep. Victor V. Veysey (R. CA) and Rep. James T. Broyhill (R. NC) began to introduce bills to weaken the Clean Air Amendments.

Concern about the feasibility and costs of establishing and meeting the standards required by the 1970 law also began to be aired by the EPA.[12] Although the EPA managed to establish NAAQS for six 'criteria pollutants' by the end of April 1971, considerable doubt surrounded both the methods that had been used to establish these health-based standards, and the ability of the states to agree effective SIPs.[13] Prohibited from taking considerations of costs into account when establishing NAAQS, the standards set by the EPA were based on a series of worse case scenarios designed to protect the most vulnerable members of the population. States were required under the law to devise SIPs within nine months of the promulgation of national standards. To help the states devise SIPs, the EPA published guidelines that stressed the need for action other than the installation of control technology. Few states were able to meet these requirements. The EPA ran into further difficulties over the question of whether states whose air quality was better than that specified by the NAAQS could allow some deterioration in the quality of their air to promote economic growth.[14] Problems with other sections of the 1970 law included defining what was meant by the 'best technological system of emission reduction' in order to establish NSPS, and identifying the air toxics that were to be the subject of NESHAPs.[15]

An inkling of the growing discontent with the Clean Air Amendments had been apparent in a number of congressional oversight hearings conducted in the early 1970s. The issue of whether states, whose air quality met the standards set by the 1970 law, should be prevented from allowing any significant deterioration in the quality of that air, was raised in hearings conducted by Senate Interior in May 1971 into problems of electrical power generation in the southwest.[16] Numerous environmental activists from southwestern states told the Committee that they had no wish to see the pristine air quality that they enjoyed damaged through the construction and operation of new power stations.

House Commerce's Subcommittee on Public Health and the Environment, chaired by Rep. Paul Rogers (D. FL), held a hearing to investigate the implementation of the Clean Air Amendments in late 1971 and early 1972.[17] Much of the evidence presented to the Subcommittee concerned the EPA's response to a air pollution episode in Birmingham, Alabama in 1971. The automobile industry used the hearing, however, to complain about the unfeasibility of the 1975 exhaust emission standards. Ford, Chrysler and the American Motor Corporation all claimed that they would be unable to meet the 1975 standards. Rep. Veysey and Rep. John H. Rousselot (R. CA) also provided the Subcommittee with a summary of a conference on motor vehicle air pollution that had been held at the western White House, San Clemente, California on 13–14 January 1972. They claimed that the conference had concluded that the

1975 exhaust emission standards were not warranted, not feasible, and costly.[18] This assessment was challenged both by Rep. Richard Hanna (D. CA) and by two witnesses from the Center for Science in the Public Interest.

The extent of the discontent with the 1970 law became clear when Senate Public Work's Subcommittee on Air and Water Pollution held a comprehensive oversight hearing in the Spring of 1972.[19] Chaired by Senator Eagleton (D. MO), as Senator Muskie was on the campaign trail seeking his party's presidential nomination, the hearings allowed a wide range of dissatisfied groups to air their grievances. A total of fifty-seven witnesses gave evidence to the Subcommittee. Fifteen witnesses represented state and local governments, fourteen represented industrial groups, eleven hailed from the executive branch, ten spoke for environmental groups and seven were academics. Among the industrial groups giving evidence were seven representatives of the automobile and petroleum industries, three representatives of the steel and copper industries and two representatives of the utility industry.

Automobile manufacturers argued that they simply could not meet the 1975 deadline for a 90 per cent reduction of exhaust emissions. Sidney L. Terry, a representative of the Chrysler Corporation, stated that: 'The automotive industry does not now have the technology to reduce emissions 90 percent from 1970 levels. While it has made substantial progress in developing even more effective emission controls, it still does not have the technology to meet the 1975 or 1976 standards'.[20] The need for more time was reiterated by Ernest S. Starkman, a representative of General Motors, who told the Subcommittee that: 'We sincerely believe that more time is required than the approximately 22 months remaining between this date and the start of the final certification testing of 1975 models'.[21] Partial support for the industry's position was provided by Edward L. Gintzon, chair of the National Academy of Science's Committee on Motor Vehicle Emissions.[22] Gintzon stated that current rates of technological progress meant that the major automobile manufacturers might be able to meet the 1975 deadline for exhaust emission reductions, but that no reduction in emission levels could be sustained without a requirement for automobile owners to have any emission control equipment serviced regularly. He estimated that the cost to the consumer would include 'an increase in sticker price of about $200, a 3 to 12 percent increase in fuel consumption, some increase in maintenance cost, and some deterioration in driveability of the car'.

The costs of meeting the requirements of the Clean Air Amendments was a common theme in almost all the evidence given by industrial groups to the Subcommittee. Charles F. Barber, chair of the American Smelting and Refining Company, stated that three of his company's plants might have to close because of the additonal costs imposed by the 1970 law.[23] Frank R. Milliken, president of the Kennecott Copper Corporation, argued that meeting the requirements of the law 'would require costs – not only to the shareholders of Kennecott but also to the communities where the company pays taxes and provides employment'.[24] William J. Young, president of the Lehigh Portland Cement Company, told the Subcommittee that: 'Attempting to meet [air pollution] standards is an enormous economic burden. Unless they are modified, they will result in further plant closing with attendant unemployment and a surge of imports.'[25] A warning that such tales of gloom and doom should be taken with a pinch of salt, however, was made by Robert J. Rauch, an economist working for Jack Faucett Associates. He counselled the Subcommittee that:

> What we are seeing is a calculated effort on the part of a number of industries to blackmail the American public. The strategy is really quite simple. An industry confronted with environmental regulations commissions an 'expert' study to show that the costs of complying with the regulations would be prohibitive. These cost estimates are then highly publicized and used to generate public demand that the standards be relaxed.[26]

Claims that industrial groups were conniving with the Nixon Administration to subvert the implementation of the Clean Air Amendments were also made at the hearing. Critics of the Administration alleged that the EPA was required to submit SIPs to the President's Office of Management and Budget (OMB) for approval. It was asserted that the OMB exercised a veto over SIPs which threatened the interests of industry. Richard E. Ayres, a representative of the National Resources Defense Council, claimed that:

> It has become painfully clear that those who are responsible for implementing the amendments are failing miserably … a substantial share [of the blame] must be placed squarely on the Nixon administration. By instituting a procedure whereby virtually every action taken by the

EPA or the states under the amendments is subjected to a final, secret revision in the Office of Management and Budget, officials of the Nixon administration have circumvented the congressional requirement for public participation and seriously weakened and delayed the implementation ... of the amendments.[27]

These charges were vigorously denied by EPA Administrator William D. Ruckelshaus. While conceding that SIPs were sent to the OMB for review, he rejected the claim that the OMB exercised a veto. 'I am the one that is going to approve those plans' he asserted.[28] As if to prove his point, Ruckelshaus announced at a press conference in May 1972 that he had denied a request from five automobile manufacturers for a year's delay in meeting the 1975 exhaust emission standards.

Relatively few bill introductions were prompted by the chorus of discontent heard in the opening years of the decade. In 1971 a total of thirty-nine air pollution control bills were introduced in the House and three in the Senate. In 1972 only nine such bills were introduced in the House and one in the Senate. All four bills introduced in the Senate sought to strengthen the air pollution control laws of the United States. The bills introduced in the House, however, fell into two broad categories. On the one hand, representatives sympathetic to the concerns of industry introduced a range of bills to amend the Clean Air Amendments or subsidize industry's pollution control efforts. A favoured option of Republicans, in particular, was to increase the tax relief available to businesses that installed air pollution control equipment. Twelve bills with that purpose in mind were introduced in 1971, eight of them by Republicans. On the other hand, representatives sympathetic to the environmental cause introduced bills to strengthen or expand the provisions of the Clean Air Amendments. An interesting development was the introduction of a few bills that sought to tax pollution. Bills to tax automobiles which failed to meet exhaust emissions standards were introduced by Rep. William F. Ryan (D. NY) and Rep. Lee H. Hamilton (D. IN); a bill to tax sulpher oxide emissions was introduced by Rep. Les Aspin (D. WI).

The relatively low level of bill introductions in the early 1970s may to a certain extent be attributed to an uncertainty about the benefits that might flow from position-taking during these years. Although the saliency of air pollution as an issue had declined from the level of 1970, the strength of public opinion remained high. As neither benefits nor harm were obvious under such circumstances, most legislators could be expected to wait for clearer cues before taking a position on the issue. The rewards that might flow from policy entrepeneurship were also not as obvious as they had been a few years earlier. Considerable barriers to entry confronted potential entrepeneurs. Not only did conflicting evaluations of the efficacy of current air pollution control policy mean higher information costs, but this lack of consensus similarly promised higher transaction costs. Potential entrepeneurs also had to confront the monopolistic position occupied by established entrepeneurs such as Senator Muskie. Preoccupied with both an effort to craft a new water pollution control law and a bid for the Democratic presidential nomination, Muskie may not have been willing to take a lead in responding to discontent about the Clean Air Amendments at this time, but he was more than willing to defend his ability to do so in the future. Other established entrepeneurs such as Rep. Paul Rogers (D. FL) appeared to view the opportunity costs of major action on air pollution at this particular time as too high.

The uncertain benefits and high costs associated with a major overhaul of the Clean Air Amendments shaped the way that Congress reauthorized the law in 1973. Efforts to amend the 1970 law were rejected by both Senator Muskie and Rep. Rogers in favour of a simple one year extension which continued funding at fiscal 1973 authorization levels. The Senate agreed to a simple reauthorization by voice vote on 26 January 1973.[29] Perfunctory hearings on companion bills introduced by Rep. Rogers and Rep. David E. Satterfield (D. VA) were held by the Subcommittee on Public Health and Environment in February 1973.[30] The only witness to give evidence was EPA Administrator Ruckelshaus who reported on the progress that was being made in implementing the 1970 law. A bill was reported out of House Commerce on 15 March 1973, and passed the House on a 387–1 roll call vote on 22 March 1973.[31] Only Rep. Earl F. Landgrebe (R. IN) voted against passage. The Senate agreed to the House-passed bill by voice vote five days later, and it was signed into law by President Nixon on 9 April 1973.[32]

A mere two days after President Nixon had signed the extension to the Clean Air Amendments, Congress was rudely reminded of the problems that still waited to be addressed when EPA Administrator Ruckelshaus announced that he had granted automobile manufacturers an additional year to meet the 90 per cent reduction in exhaust emissions required by the law.[33] Ruckelshaus told a news conference that he had granted the postponement to avoid the 'potential societal disruptions' which the industry had claimed would result from the rigid application of the law. Not all was good news for the automobile manufacturers, however, as Ruckelshaus also announced tough new interim standards for California which would effectively require emissions control devices on all new cars sold in that state. The industry claimed that the interim standards were too strict.[34] Reaction in Congress to Ruckelshaus's announcement was more circumspect. Rep. Rogers said that the decision was realistic, and Senator Muskie pronounced that they were 'nearly' consistent with the law.[35] Senator Muskie promised that his Subcommittee would hold hearings on Ruckelshaus's decision as soon as possible.

The automobile industry used the subsequent hearings conducted by the Subcommittee on Air and Water Pollution to argue for a further postponement of the exhaust emission standards.[36] Lee A. Iacocca, President of Ford, argued that the industry needed a further year's delay in order to meet the required standards. He also claimed that Ford did not know how to meet the 1976 standard for nitrogen oxide. Edward N. Cole, President of General Motors, told the Subcommittee that General Motors had prepared experimental automobiles which could meet the 1975 standards, but could not guarantee that every automobile that they manufactured would be able to do so for the required 50,000 miles or five years. He also called for a review of the nitrogen oxide standard, claiming that 'we do not yet know adequate technology for meeting all the requirements of this standard imposed by the law on the mass production of vehicles'. Both Iacocca and Cole asserted that the interim standards established by the EPA were still far too stringent and could not be met.

Claims that the automobile industry could not meet the 1976 standard for nitrogen oxide were repeated in hearings before the Subcommittee on Public Health and Environment in September 1973.[37] Witnesses from Ford and General Motors called for emission standards for nitrogen oxide to be frozen. The arguments of the industry were countered by environmentalists, and also by witnesses representing a burgeoning pollution control industry. Edward E. David, executive vice-president of Gould, Inc., and John

Quirk, president of Vortex, gave positive assessments of the technological progress that had been made regarding exhaust emission
control devices and urged the Subcommittee to reject calls for a
freeze. A growing concern about energy supplies, however, provided the automobile industry with some important allies. Russell
Train, Chairman of the Council on Environmental Quality, argued
that some environmental standards should be relaxed temporariliy
to ease the fuel shortage. John A. Love, Director of the Energy
Policy Office, argued that emission standards for sulphates needed
to be relaxed to allow more coal to be used for domestic heating.

The testimony provided by Russell Train and John A. Love signalled a change in the context of the debate over air pollution control issues. Previous claims by the automobile industry that the
exhaust emission standards required by the Clean Air Amendments
were unfeasible had not proved particularly persuasive. In the floor
debate that preceded passage of the 1970 law, Senator Muskie had
argued that his priority was to protect public health. Responding to
a comment from Senator Robert P. Griffin (R. MI) concerning the
feasibility of obtaining a 90 per cent reduction in exhaust emissions
by 1975, Senator Muskie had declared that: 'The deadline is based
not, I repeat, on economic and technological feasibility, but on considerations of public health.'[38] The imperatives that had guided
action in 1970, however, no longer seemed quite so compelling in
1973. Growing concern about the adequacy of the country's energy
supplies significantly altered the terms in which the debate about air
pollution was conducted, and began to bolster industry arguments
that the required exhaust emission standards were a luxury which
could not be afforded at that particular time.

The energy crisis
The energy crisis that flowed from the decision of the Organization
of Petroleum Exporting Countries (OPEC) in October 1973 to
quadruple oil prices and drastically reduce supplies to the United
States prompted a predictable explosion of activity in Congress.
Bills were introduced and committee hearings conducted as members scrambled either to persuade constituents that they were attentive to their problems, or to establish roles as a policy leaders on
such a major issue. Charles O. Jones and Randall Strahan, in an apt
turn of phrase, have likened this frenzy of activity to 'the Oklahoma
land rush'.[39] Legislation that gave the president authority to allocate

fuel in time of shortage and to control oil prices passed Congress in November 1973.[40]

The new imperatives generated by the energy crisis had a significant impact on the debate raging in Congress about the need to revise the Clean Air Amendments. Not only did the crisis alter the terms in which the debate was conducted, but it also made alternative venues available in which debate could take place. The terms in which the debate was conducted were altered most obviously by the imperatives to conserve energy and control prices. Past strictures about the need to protect public health regardless of cost began to appear less compelling in the face of quadrupled oil prices. Alternative venues in which to conduct debate became available as a result of the changes in the way that the issue of air pollution control was viewed. Committees with jurisdiction over energy matters began to claim parts of the air pollution brief and offered disgruntled interests new opportunities to make their case. A consequence of these developments was a transformation in the rewards and costs associated with both position-taking and policy entrepeneurship.

Much of the uncertainty that had restricted position-taking on air pollution control issues in the early 1970s was swept aside by the imperatives of the energy crisis. The overriding public concern with energy supply and prices provided legislators with a powerful incentive to stake out a position as proponents of measures to conserve energy and control prices. Increasing numbers of bills were introduced, as a result, to relax provisions of the Clean Air Amendments that were deemed to have an adverse impact on energy consumption and costs. Introduced in the House in the aftermath of the OPEC oil embargo were twelve bills to extend, suspend, or postpone the standards or deadlines required by the 1970 law, seven bills to allow the removal of air pollution control devices from cars and six bills to postpone or prohibit the promulgation of regulations governing indirect sources. The only air pollution control bill with a pro-environment flavour to be introduced in the House after October 1973 was a measure sponsored by Rep. Rogers to promote research into flurocarbons.[41] Introduced in the Senate in this period were five bills to suspend or revise emission standards mandated by the Clean Air Amendments. No bills were introduced to strengthen federal control of air pollution.

Opportunities for new policy entrepeneurs to challenge the monopolistic position of Rep. Rogers and Senator Muskie were also generated by the energy crisis. Although all the bills introduced in the House and Senate to suspend, postpone, or revise emission standards were referred to House Commerce and Senate Public Works, the intertwined nature of energy and pollution issues provided congressional venues with energy jurisdictions with an opportunity to test the strength of the 'barriers to entry' that had safeguarded the leadership roles of Rogers and Muskie over air pollution control matters. In the House, these challenges were primarily *intra*-committee as House Commerce had primary jurisdiction over energy issues.[42] Energy-oriented subcommittees of House Commerce began to contest the jurisdiction of Rogers's Subcommittee by holding hearings on matters pertinent to air pollution. The Subcommittee on Communications and Power touched upon the effect of the energy shortage on air quality standards in hearings examining the role of the Federal Power Commission in March 1973 and June 1974.[43] The Subcommittee on Energy and Power heard evidence regarding air quality standards in a hearing on middle- and long-term energy policies in March 1976.[44] In the Senate, these challenges came from other committees. Senate Commerce used its jurisdiction over transportation issues to challenge for control over matters related to automobiles and fuel economy. Senate Interior used its jurisdiction over energy issues to challenge for control over emission standards related to energy production.

The threat to Senator Muskie's position as the Senate's 'Mr Pollution' became flagrant when Senator Henry M. Jackson (D. WA), Chair of Senate Interior, introduced the National Emergency Energy Act on 18 October 1973.[45] This legislation proposed that temporary waivers of emission standards be granted to allow oil or gas-fuelled power stations to convert to coal. A hearing was conducted on the bill on 8 November 1973 and mark-up began the following day.[46] Faced with the prospect of being out-flanked by Jackson, Senator Muskie made an effort to regain some control over proceedings. On 9 November 1973, he introduced a bill which authorized the EPA to grant short-term suspensions of emission limitations until 15 May 1974, and extended final compliance with the standards mandated by the 1970 law until 1 July 1977.[47] A hearing on Muskie's bill was held just three days later in a desperate attempt to make up lost time.[48] During the hearing, Senator Muskie gave notice of just how far the energy crisis had altered the nature of the debate about air pollution when he warned that 'clean air advocates

... must accept the interim interruption' of air pollution control programmes.[49] Senate Public Works approved Muskie's bill on 14 November 1973 after extending the period in which the EPA could suspend emission limitations until 1 November 1974. The bill, however, was never formally reported. Instead, the Senate adopted its provisions waiving clean air standards as an amendment to Senator Jackson's energy bill on 15 November 1973.

A further threat to Senator Muskie's control over air pollution control policy emerged when Senator Jennings Randolph (D. WV), Chair of Senate Public Works, scheduled full committee hearings in early November 1973 on proposals to postpone automobile exhaust emission standards yet further.[50] The main focus of the hearings was the effect that the use of catalytic converters would have on energy needs. Consideration of this question was complicated by a revelation that automobiles equipped with such control devices emitted more sulphates than would otherwise have been the case. To determine whether it would be prudent to suspend the use of catalytic converters the Committee had to assess conflicting evidence not only regarding changes in fuel consumption, but also the cost and feasibility of refining low-sulphate fuel. The highly technical nature of these considerations provided Senator Muskie with an opportunity to reassert his leadership. He drafted a committee bill which proposed delaying implementation of the final automobile exhaust emission standards until 1977. An effort by Senator William L. Scott (R. VA) to postpone implementation of the interim standards announced by EPA Administrator Ruckelshaus until 1977 was rejected by the Committee, and the bill was reported on 4 December 1973.[51] The Senate passed the bill on an 85–0 roll call vote on 17 December 1973. An amendment offered by Senator Scott to postpone implementation of the final standards to 1978 was rejected 19–67.[52] Scott argued that the House had incorporated such a delay in its version of the energy emergency bill that had passed the Senate on 15 November 1973.

An energy emergency bill drafted by Rep. Harley O. Staggers (D. WV), Chair of House Commerce, had been introduced in the House on 18 October 1973.[53] Jurisdictional rivalry between various committees, however, had meant that no action had been possible. House Armed Servies Chair F. Edward Herbert (D. LA), in particular, had objected to the inclusion of provisions in the bill pertaining to the Naval Petroleum Reserve. To overcome such objections, Staggers introduced a revised bill shorn of the disputed provisions on 13 November 1973.[54] The revised bill provided the EPA with limited authority to waive Clean Air requirements. Additional authority was sought by EPA Administrator Russell E. Train during hearings on the bill.[55] Train asked that the EPA be given authorized to grant short-term variances from the Clean Air Amendments without the need for public notice or hearing, and that long-term variances be permitted as long as a plant agreed to a schedule that would bring it into compliance with the requirements of the 1970 law. Amendments to meet some of these requests were agreed during mark-up of the bill. A substitute bill introduced by Staggers at the end of mark-up included provisions which permitted both a one year suspension of automobile exhaust emission standards, and long-term suspensions of Clean Air standards until 30 June 1979 to promote the use of coal.[56] The substitute bill also prohibited the EPA from requiring surcharges on parking spaces as a means of reducing traffic in cities.[57]

House Commerce reported the substitute bill on 7 December 1973, and floor debate began five days later. The bill was passed by the House by voice vote on 14 December 1973. A number of amendments to weaken the Clean Air Amendments were offered during the three days of debate on the bill. Some of these amendments were relatively uncontroversial. Accepted by voice vote were amendments offered by Rep. John J. Murphy (D. NY) to grant the EPA authority until 15 May 1974 to suspend emission limitations, Rep. John Y. McCollister (R. NE) to exempt older coal-burning power stations from emission limitations if the costs of complaince were unreasonable, and Rep. David E. Satterfield (D. VA) to extend the right to continue burning coal until 1980 in power stations which had voluntarily begun conversion to coal. Other amendments, particularly those which effected the automobile industry, were far more controversial. Some members claimed that considerable fuel savings could be made if exhaust emission standards were relaxed; others claimed that no fuel savings would be made from such a move, and that the only result would be the emasculation of air pollution control efforts. Agreement was finally reached on an amendment offered by Rep. James F. Hastings (R. NY) to postpone implementation of the exhaust emission standards until 1977. A subsequent amendment offered by Rep. Louis C. Wyman (R. NH) to suspend all exhaust emission standards until 1 January 1977 or until the president declared that the fuel crisis was over, was defeated on a 180–210 roll call vote. A final effort by Wyman to suspend such standards until 1 January 1976 was defeated on a 170–205 roll call vote.

The House version of the energy emergency bill differed significantly from the Senate version in terms of air pollution control in three respects. First, short-term suspensions of emission limitations were permitted until 15 May 1974 in the House bill and 1 November in the Senate bill. Second, the House bill extended the date for final compliance with Clean Air Amendment standards to 30 June 1979 compared to 1 July 1977 in the Senate bill. Finally, the House bill postponed the date for implementation of automobile emission standards until 1977 and gave the Administrator of the EPA an option to delay the deadline for a further two years. Although no such provisions were contained in the Senate version, the bill which had passed the Senate on 17 December 1973 provided for a delay in implementation of the standards until 1977. The compromise bill worked out in conference was much closer to the Senate version than the House version. Short-term suspensions of emission requirements were permitted until 1 November 1974, but long-term revisions were ruled out for all industries except power stations that had converted to coal before 15 December 1973. These were given until 1 January 1979 to comply with full emission standards. Conference also limited the extension for compliance with exhaust emission standards to 1977, and permitted the EPA Administrator to allow a further year's delay if necessary.

Further progress on the bill was hamstrung by opposition in the Senate to provisions restricting the windfall profits that could be earned by energy suppliers and fuel companies. A filibuster against the conference report was launched by Senator Russell B. Long (D. LA) and Senator Paul J. Fannin (R. AZ). Long complained that the windfall profits provision was a revenue measure that should be considered by the Senate Finance Committee which he chaired. Fannin argued that the provision would inhibit the search for new sources of oil. Lacking the necessary votes to invoke cloture, Senate leaders decided upon an alternative strategy. Senator Jackson offered a compromise version of the bill without the windfall profits provisions as an amendment to a House-passed wild and scenic rivers bill.[58] The compromise measure passed the Senate on a 52–8 roll call vote, but ran into immediate trouble in the House. Reacting angrily to the Senate's rejection of the conference bill, the House rejected two substitute amendments offered by Staggers and then rejected the compromise measure on a 36–228 roll call vote. Staggers voted in favour of the bill, but refused to defend it during debate.

The fact that the House had not taken a vote on the original conference report allowed the Senate to take up the bill again in January 1974. On 29 January 1974 the Senate voted on a 57–37 roll call vote to recommit the bill to a second conference committee. The debate on the recommital motion revealed an interesting division between two of the chamber's leading environmentalists. Senator Gaylord Nelson (D. WI) viewed recommital as offering an opportunity to reconsider provisions which extended Clean Air deadlines. He argued that the five-year variance from emission standards granted to industries that converted to coal was far too long.[59] Senator Muskie viewed recommital, on the other hand, as providing an opportunity for members sympathetic to industry to attack the Clean Air Amendments. He asserted that there was 'a strong and vigorous and rising opposition' in the House 'to every piece of environmental legislation we have put on the books'.[60]

Muskie's fears that a second conference might emasculate the Clean Air Amendments even further proved goundless. The second conference report made only minor, technical, changes in the provisions pertaining to the 1970 law. A provision to place a ceiling on oil prices, however, ultimately doomed the legislation. Although the measure passed the Senate on 19 February 1974 and the House on 27 February 1974, the bill was vetoed by President Nixon on 6 March 1974. In Nixon's opinion: 'After all the hearings and speeches, all the investigations, accusations and recriminations, the Congress has succeeded only in producing legislation which solves none of the problems, threatens to undo the progress we have made, and creates a host of new problems.'[61] The Senate sustained Nixon's veto by a 58–40 roll call vote the same day.

A new energy bill, the Standby Energy Emergency Authorities Act, was introduced by Rep. Staggers in late March 1974.[62] House Commerce held hearings on the bill in early April 1974.[63] Despite being spread out over three days, the hearings were rather perfunctory as most of the issues had been well rehearsed. The only witnesses to give evidence were from the EPA, the Federal Energy Office (FEO), the Labor Department, the National Clean Air Coalition, the New York City Clean Air Campaign, the Los Angeles Air Pollution Control District, the American Federation of Labor – Congress of Industrial Organizations (AFL–CIO) and the United Automobile Workers. No witness representing industry testified. Following the hearings, the Committee decided that with the threat of a presidential veto still alive the best way to proceed would be to split the legislation into two separate bills. One bill contained proposals pertaining to air pollution control matters.[64] This bill was reported by House Commerce on 26 April 1974. The other bill contained the controversial provisions to roll back oil prices and give the president authority to ration fuel supplies. This bill was reported on 29 April 1974.

Floor action on the air pollution control bill took place on 1 May 1974. Debate focused on another amendment offered by Rep. Wyman to postpone implementation of exhaust emission controls until 30 September 1977 in areas of the United States that did not have significant air pollution problems. The amendment was supported primarily by members from rural areas who believed that catalytic converters led to reduced fuel economy. Wyman argued that:

> It seems to me ... [that] it is unwise and unnecessary for us to be so enormously wasteful of energy in this country as to insist that everyone in the country have an automobile that is equipped with expensive emission controls unless there is an honest-to-goodness, down-to-earth public necessity for this.[65]

Opposition to the amendment was led by Rep. Rogers who argued that the amendment would seriously undermine the nation's efforts to reduce air pollution. 'Now to take a step backward at this time when the automobile companies are perfecting and improving the mileage and when the energy situation has eased simply does not make sense', he declared.[66] Both arguments were similar to those aired in December 1973, and the result was much the same. The Wyman amendment was rejected on a 169–221 roll call vote. A second amendment offered by Wyman to allow 1974 exhaust emission standards to remain in effect for 1975 model automobiles was also rejected by voice vote. The House did accept an amendment offered by Rep. Broyhill to excempt the Bureau of the Census, the Internal Revenue Service and the Bureau of Labor Statistics from having to provide any information they gathered about energy usage to the Federal Energy Office, but rejected an amendment offered by Rep. Charles A. Vanik (D. OH) to conduct research into the feasibility of establishing a national fuel economy standard for all new automobiles. The bill was finally passed on a 349–43 roll call vote.

Senate Public Works met to consider the House-passed bill on 9 and 13 May 1974. Senator Muskie used the opportunity to reassert his role as a policy leader on air pollution control policy by offering a substitute amendment to the House-passed bill. This substitute added four new provisions to the legislation. First, it reauthorized the Clean Air Amendments for a further year. Second, it exempted federal agencies with an environmental protection role from having to file environmental impact statements as required under the National Environmental Policy Act (NEPA). Third, it allowed the EPA to suspend emission requirements only if the Administrator determined that such exemptions would not impair the public health standards established by the Clean Air Amendments. Fourth, it allowed the federal energy administrator to order factories to convert to coal only in areas where such a conversion would not lead to a deterioration of air quality to a level which would damage public health. Muskie's substitute deleted from the House-passed bill provisions which prohibited the EPA from using car-parking surcharges as a means of air pollution control, and a number of provisons related to studies into fuel economy, energy conservation, and public transportation. The substitute bill was adopted by Senate Public Works and passed the Senate by voice vote on 14 May 1974. No opposition to the bill was voiced.

Differences between the House and Senate versions of the bill were reconciled in conference committee. The bill that emerged from conference adopted much of the language regarding air pollution issues that had been found in the Muskie substitute. Suspension of final clean air standards would be allowed until 1 January 1979 to facilitate a greater use of coal, but only if primary NAAQS would not be violated as a result. Short-term suspensions of air pollution standards would be allowed until 30 June 1975 if 'clean' fuels were not available for use. Implementation of exhaust emission standards was delayed until 1977 and the EPA was given the option of allowing a further year's delay if requested by the automobile manufacturers. Actions taken by the EPA under the Clean Air Amendments were exempted from NEPA requirements. The Clean Air Amendments were also reauthorized for a further year. Provisions in the bill regarding energy issues tended to reflect the langauage found in the House version. Studies into energy conservation and fuel economy were authorized, and the Federal Energy Office required to gather and disseminate information about energy usage.

The compromise bill worked out in conference was adopted by voice vote in both chambers: in the House on 11 June 1974, and in the Senate on 12 June 1974. President Nixon signed the Energy Supply and Environmental Coordination Act of 1974 into law on 26 June 1974. He claimed that: 'This bill represents a first step by the Congress toward achieving a balance between our environmental requirements and our energy requirements.'[67] That the balance was still tilted towards 'environmental requirements' was testimony to the political skills of Senator Muskie. Confronted with serious challenges to his position as a policy leader, Muskie had utilized the resources at his command to protect his earlier legislative achievements. Although the timetable established by the Clean Air Amendments was abandoned, the basic philosophy that had underpinned that law was left intact. Muskie had successfully defended the position that: 'Legislation of this kind must necessarily be within the framework of existing environmental constraints, rather than outside those constraints.'[68]

Old problems, new concerns

Enactment of the Energy Supply and Environmental Coordination Act 1974 did little to assuage pressure for fundamental revision of the Clean Air Amendments. Environmentalists argued that evidence of policy failure and the discovery of new threats meant that the 1970 law needed strengthening. Not only were the goals of the law not being achieved, but new concerns about a link between air pollution and climatic change were beginning to emerge. Industry groups argued that the 1970 law imposed burdens that could not be met. The automobile industry continued to claim that exhaust emission standards were technologically unfeasible while utility companies and steel producers complained about the cost of meeting stationary source standards. Although deeply divided opinion of this sort would normally produce deadlock, the continuing energy crisis provided a powerful imperative for action. Faced with the propsect of losing control over the issue to other policy entrepreneurs, Senator Muskie and Rep. Rogers were forced to address the shortcomings of the 1970 law.

Pressure for reform

Demands that the Clean Air Amendments should be amended to address both old and new concerns began to be articulated forcefully by environmental groups in the wake of enactment of the Energy Supply and Environmental Coordination Act 1974. Concerned that the commitment to cleaning the nation's air had already been compromised by passage of the 1974 law, environmentalists argued that evidence of policy failure and the discovery of new threats required legislative action to strengthen the air pollution control laws of the nation. Not only was it clear that the targets established by the Clean Air Amendments were not going to be achieved on time, but the 1970 law did not appear capable of dealing with the problem of global climate change.

An admission that some communities and industries were experiencing difficulties in meeting required deadlines for compliance with the Clean Air Amendments was made by EPA Administrator Russell Train in a hearing conducted by the Subcommittee on Public Health and Environment on 23 September 1974.[69] Train told the Subcommittee that much had been achieved, but that problems still remained. It was a message he repeated in a press conference given on 30 May 1975. According to the timetable established by the 1970 law, most of the country was required to meet primary air quality standards by 31 May 1975. Train told the press conference, however, that 'a number of the nation's 247 air quality control regions will not meet all of the air quality standards by tomorrow's deadline'.[70] Train revealed that 188 of the regions were not in compliance with particulate standards, thirty-four with sulphur dioxide standards, seventy-nine with the standards for oxidants, sixty-nine with carbon monoxide standards and sixteen with nitrogen oxide standards.

Demands for a greater commitment to controlling air pollution were also prompted by growing evidence of new threats. Links between air pollution and climate change, in particular, began to be posited during this period. A link between chlorofluorocarbon (CFC) emissions and depletion of the ozone layer was suggested in an article published in *Nature* in June 1974 and sparked demands for controls on aerosol sprays.[71] Concern was also expressed that the ozone layer might be damaged by emissions of nitrogen oxides from supersonic stratospheric-flying aircraft (SSTs) such as Concorde.[72] Both these threats were investigated by congressional committees. Senate Aeronautical and Space Sciences Committee's Ad-hoc Subcommittee on the Upper Atmosphere held hearings on the relationship between CFCs and the ozone layer in September 1975.[73] The Subcommittee on Environment and Atmosphere of House Science conducted hearings on air pollution and climate change in November 1975.[74] Senate Commerce conducted hearings which touched upon the damage to the ozone layer caused by Concorde in February 1976.[75] An interesting feature of these hearings was that neither was conducted by House Commerce or Senate Public Works. They provide an example of how the emergence of a new dimension to an issue may be exploited by potential policy entrepeneurs to sidestep existing 'barriers to entry' to the legislative market.

A number of bills that addressed the threats posed by SSTs and CFCs were introduced in the 94th Congress (1975–76). Two bills to prohibit flights of SSTs in American air space were introduced by Rep. Lester L. Wolff (D. NY) and referred to House Public Works. No action was taken on this bill. Eight bills dealing with CFCs were introduced in the House and one in the Senate. Four of these bills were introduced by Rep. Paul Rogers, the others were introduced by Rep. Andrew Jacobs (D. IN), Rep. Thomas W. Ashley (D. OH), Rep. Richard L. Ottinger (D. NY), Senator Clifford P. Case (R. NJ) and Senator Robert W. Packwood (R. OR). All the bills, with the exception of that introduced by Ottinger, sought to promote further research into CFCs. The Ottinger bill was a concurrent resolution which simply sought to encourage the UN to promote international co-operation in the control of CFCs. Little action was taken on any of these bills. Not only was the science surrounding the issue contested, but considerable institutional rivalry also existed between House Commerce and House Science for control of the issue. Part of the reason why none of the bills made it to the floor was that all the research bills introduced in the House were referred jointly to the two committees. Similar rivalry also existed in the Senate. The bill introduced by Senator Case was jointly referred to Senate Public Works, Senate Labor, and Senate Aeronautics.

The push for greater control over air pollution was countered by a call from the power, steel, and automobile industries for a relaxation of the regulatory regime established by the Clean Air Amendments. Although much of what these groups had to say covered familiar ground, their arguments had been given additional potency by the Supreme Court's ruling in *Fri v. Sierra Club* (1973) that the EPA must reject any SIP that did not prevent the 'significant deterioration' (PSD) of air quality.[76] An early hearing into the consequences of the Court's decision had been conducted by the Subcommittee on Air and Water Pollution in July 1973.[77] The focus of this hearing had been almost entirely upon implications for the coal industry. Regulations issued by the EPA in 1974, however, opened a pandora's box of new concerns. The EPA divided the country into three categories. 'Class 1' areas would encompass parks and wilderness, where almost no change in existing air quality would be permitted. 'Class 2' areas would be permitted some increases in pollution to accomodate moderate industrial growth. 'Class 3' areas could accomodate industrial growth so long as national emission standards were not violated. The fear of many living in 'class 1' areas was that the requirement to maintain air quality would effectively freeze their standard of living at existing levels of development.

Concern about the wider impact of the Supreme Court's ruling in the *Fri* case was articulated by representatives of the National League of Cities and the National Association of Counties at an oversight hearing conducted by Muskie's renamed Subcommittee on Environmental Pollution in the spring of 1975.[78] The Subcommittee also heard evidence from a range of business and industry groups about the problems they were experiencing in meeting the standards mandated by the 1970 law. Construction groups complained about the additional costs imposed by EPA regulations that required states and local governments to review major 'indirect sources' of air pollution caused by the development of new shopping centres, roads, stadiums and airports. The power industry complained that a lack of 'clean' fuels and effective control technology meant that they were unable to meet required reductions in emission levels. The steel industry told the Subcommittee about the problems it was experiencing. Both automobile manufacturers and the United Automobile Workers (UAW) called for further delays in the implementation of exhaust emission standards. Russell Train, EPA Administrator, gave qualified support to some of the complaints aired at the hearing. He called, in particular, for the EPA to be granted authority to take account of wider considerations of cost when promulgating regulations.[79]

Complaints of unfeasibility and cost prompted the introduction of a large number of bills to weaken the Clean Air Amendments in the 94th Congress. The problem of PSD was addressed in two bills introduced in the House and one in the Senate which would prohibit the EPA from setting standards stricter than primary NAAQS. Three bills were introduced in the House and one in the Senate to require the EPA to take account of all the costs associated with controlling air pollution when promulgating regulations. Five bills were introduced, three in the House and two in the Senate, to suspend all emission controls. The majority of bills, however, addressed the perennial problem of automobile exhaust emission standards and the growing problem of emission standards for 'indirect sources'. Eleven bills were introduced in the House and two in the Senate to suspend or extend exhaust emission standards. A total of twelve bills were introduced, eleven in the House and one in the Senate, to limit the EPA's ability to regulate emissions from 'indirect sources'.

An analysis of the legislators responsible for introducing these bills reveals interesting geographical and partisan divisions. Just two of the representatives came from districts in Northeastern or Mid-Atlantic states, six hailed from districts in Midwestern or Plains states, no fewer than seventeen came from districts in the South or Border states, and just five came from Pacific Coast or Mountain states. Republicans and Southern Democrats accounted for twenty-five out of the thirty representatives. The 'conservative coalition' complexion of those wishing to roll back air pollution control laws was also apparent in the Senate. One senator came from a Northeastern or Mid-Atlantic state, five came from Southern or Border states and one came from a Pacific Coast or Mountain state. All the senators were either Republicans or Southern Democrats. Air pollution control had assumed a distinct ideological cast by the mid-1970s.

These proponents of a weaker air pollution control regime had a powerful ally in President Ford. In January 1975 the President submitted an omnibus energy bill to Congress that incorporated significant amendments to the Clean Air Amendments. Introduced by Minority Leader Senator Hugh Scott (R. PA), the Energy Independence Act, addressed many of the concerns of industry groups.[80] The bill contained provisions which would postpone final automobile exhaust emission standards until 1982, give utility companies in remote areas until 1985 to meet final emission requirements, allow traffic-congested cities until 1987 to comply with clean air standards and prevent the EPA from setting any air standards that were more stringent than primary or secondary NAAQS. Further provisions would delay the deadline for compliance with particulate standards until 1987 in regions where attainment was not possible earlier, and extend compliance deadlines until 1980 for power stations that had converted or continued to use coal under federal order. Companion legislation was introduced in the House by Rep. Staggers.[81]

Although unacceptable to environmentalists in Congress, the Energy Independence Act nevertheless sparked a serious effort to amend the 1970 law. Faced with the prospect of losing control over the issue, Senator Muskie and Rep. Rogers attempted to seize the initiative from the Administration by making revision of the Clean Air Amendments a priority. The complexity of the issues under consideration and the conflict they engendered, however, meant that progress was slow. Muskie and Rogers not only had to evaluate competing claims about policy success and failure, but also had to operate in an environment in which many other legislators viewed the costs of air pollution control as suffiently large to fight tenaciously to protect the interests of their constituents. Support for air pollution control legislation was no longer a risk free strategy.

The Clean Air Act Amendments 1977
Senator Muskie and Rep. Rogers began the process of revising the Clean Air Amendments from different starting points. Rogers was able to use the Energy Indepedence Act as a vehicle to explore the issue as the bill had been referred to House Commerce.[82] Hearings on the air pollution control provisions of the bill were conducted by the Subcommittee on Health and Environment in March 1975.[83] Muskie was not able to use the Administration's bill in the same way as it had been split between ten different committees in the Senate.[84] He decided instead upon the alternative strategy of conducting oversight hearings into the implementation of the 1970 law, and then drafting a bill based on the findings. Hearings were conducted by the Subcommittee on Environmental Pollution at various dates in the Spring of 1975.[85]

The number and range of witnesses giving evidence to both hearings was indicative of the way that the 1970 law had changed the interest group universe surrounding the issue of air pollution control. A total of sixty-nine witnesses gave evidence to the House Subcommittee and fifty-nine appeared before the Senate Subcommittee. Groups represented at both sets of hearings included administration officials and federal bureaucrats from the EPA, FEA, CEQ and Commerce Department; members of Congress; state and local government officials; environmental and health groups; academics; and a wide variety of industrial and business organizations. Among the latter were representatives of a burgeoning pollution control industry that had sprung up in the wake of the 1970 law. Putative coalitions between many of these groups had also developed. Many environmental groups were linked together in the National Clean Air Coalition, and some industry groups formed the Clear Air Coordinating Committee to advance their cause. A marriage of convenience between environmentalists and the coal lobby was also apparent on PSD.[86]

Evaluating the evidence provided by these witnesses was not easy. Not only were the two subcommittees buried under an avalanche of competing claims and opinions, but the nature of the evidence was more opaque than it had been five years previously. Senator Muskie and Rep. Rogers had been presented with testimony in 1970 that was reasonably transparent. Witnesses tended to be either for or against the legislation under consideration. Much of the testimony provided in 1975, in contrast, was less clear cut. Disagreements on the use of 'scrubbers' to control emissions from power stations, standards for exhaust emissions and efforts to prevent the degradation of air quality in states with very little pollution often revolved around disputes about the interpretation of arcane matters of science, technology or economics. The certainties that had fuelled the period of policy inflation had been swept aside and replaced by a swirling clutter of claims and counterclaims.

The complex and contentious nature of the evidence surrounding air pollution control meant that progress in revising the 1970 law was slow in both the Senate and the House. Legislation was finally approved by Senate Public Works on 5 February 1976 by a 12–1 vote after forty-eight separate subcommittee and committee markup sessions.[87] The Committee reported the bill on 29 March 1976. Objections to parts of the bill were made by most members of the Committee, but the only broad dissent came from Senator Gary Hart (D. CO) who argued that the law should be renamed 'the

Fairly Clean Air Act or Sort-of Clean Air Act'.[88] House Commerce approved legislation on 18 March 1976 by a 22–13 vote.[89] A 500-page report was filed by the Committee on 15 May 1976. The report contained a minority opinion signed by seven Republicans which stated that: 'The Clean Air Amendments of 1976 may be the most ill-advised proposal to come before the Congress in a number of years.'[90] Rep. David E. Satterfield (D. VA) described the bill as 'draconian' in his own minority opinion. Almost every issue visited by the Committees had generated partisan, ideological, or regional divisions, and both bills reflected the need to compromise.

The legislation reported by Senate Public Works endorsed the view that no 'significant deterioration' of air quality should be allowed. Clean air regions were to be divided into two classes. Class 1 areas would include all national parks, wilderness areas and memorial parks. Only small increases in air pollution would be tolerated in these areas. Class 2 areas would include all other clean air regions. Major new sources of pollution in Class 2 areas would be required to install 'best available control technology'. Buffer zones would be established between the two types of area. Senate Public Works similarly endorsed 'continuous emission controls' as 'the only acceptable basic strategy' for meeting stationary source emission limits. The EPA was also directed to promulgate regulations restricting or banning the use of CFCs as aerosol propellants if it was found that such emissions could 'reasonable be anticipated to cause or contribute to the endangerment of public health or welfare'. In most other respects, however, the Committee's bill acceded to industry arguments. Stationary sources were given until 1 January 1979 to comply with emission standards. Automobile manufacturers were given until 1979 to meet exhaust emission control standards for hydrocarbons and carbon monoxide, and the standards for nitrogen oxide were relaxed. Congested cities were given an additional five or ten years to comply with NAAQS as long as they imposed 'reasonable' transportation controls.

The bill reported out of House Commerce also endorsed the principle of no 'significant deterioration', but established a different classification scheme. All national parks and wilderness areas would be designated as Class 1 areas. No additional pollution would be allowed in these areas. Most other clean air areas would be designated as Class 2 areas and would be permitted increases in pollution up to 25 per cent of national standards. States could designate some areas as Class 3 areas, however, in which increases in pollution of up to 50 per cent of national standards would be permitted. The bill also followed that reported by Senate Public Works in mandating the use of 'continuous' methods of emission controls. It required all major new stationary sources to install the 'best technological system' that had been 'adequately demonstrated.' Also included was a provision similar to that found in the Senate bill regarding the regulation of CFCs in aerosols. Concessions to the arguments of industry mirrored those given in the bill authored by Senator Muskie. The EPA or a state could give a stationary source an extension of up to five years to comply with emission standards. Automobile manufacturers were given until 1980 to meet exhaust emission standards for hydrocarbons and carbon monoxide, and until 1981 to meet nitrogen oxide standards. Cities were given until 1 January 1985 to comply with NAAQS. Finally, limits were placed on the EPA's authority to order reviews of 'indirect sources' of air pollution.

Floor consideration of the bill reported by Senate Public Works began on 26 July 1976. Debate focused primarily on the provisions pertaining to PSD and automobile exhaust emissions. The main challenge to the non-degradation provisions of the bill came from many westerners and southerners who believed that PSD would forestall economic development in their states. As Senator Frank E. Moss (D. UT) told the chamber: 'The issue is not a clean air or dirty air issue: it is more a growth or no-growth issue.'[91] Moss offered an amendment to delete the PSD provisions from the bill, but it was defeated by a vote of 31–63. Other amendments to weaken the non-degradation provisions were also defeated. Two amendments offered by Senator William L. Scott (R. VA) and one offered by Senator James B. Allen (D. AL) to postpone nondegradation controls until proved to be justified by further studies were defeated by votes of 17–74, 20–70 and 23–59. Amendments offered by Senator Hart and Senator Mark O. Hatfield (R. OR) to stregthen the nondegradation provisions were also defeated. Hart's amendment to force states to take account of all sources of pollution when deciding whether to grant construction permits to new sources was defeated by a 26–65 vote. Hatfield's amendment to expand the definition of a Class 1 area was defeated by a 35–56 vote.

Hart's efforts to strengthen the bill reported out of Senate Public Works continued when he offered two amendments pertaining to automobile exhaust emissions. His first amendment sought to bring

forward the compliance dates in the bill by one year. Hart argued
that the automobile manufacturers had the technological capacity
to meet a tighter timetable, but needed 'the pressure of the law' to
make them act.[92] Senator James L. Buckley (R. NY), a member of
Senate Public Works, defended the committee's proposal as offering
'a reasonable accommodation of all the important factors'.[93] The
amendment was defeated by a 30–61 vote. His second amendment
sought to reverse the decision to weaken the standard for nitrogen
oxide emissions. He argued that nitrogen oxides were a known car-
cinogen, and that the automobile manufacturers had the technology
to deal with the problem. Senator Muskie indicated support for
Hart's arguments, but stated that he had no wish to undermine a
compromise worked out in committee.[94] The amendment was
defeated by a 33–58 vote.

All efforts to strengthen or weaken the bill reported by Senate
Public Works, in fact, were defeated. Central to the defence of the
bill on the floor were Republicans from the Committee like Senator
Buckley and Senator Pete V. Domenici (R. NM). Muskie had taken
considerable care during the drafting of the legislation to accommodate the views of the minority, and these efforts to create a bipartisan consensus stood him in good stead on key votes. Domenici
played a prominent role, in particular, in defusing some of the criticism of the PSD provisions. Floor passage finally occurred on 5
August 1976 when the Senate accepted the bill on a 78–13 roll call
vote.

Floor consideration of the bill reported by House Commerce
began in early August 1976 but was suspended for a month after
Rep. Rogers complained about 'ludicrous scheduling'. The bill's
provisions regarding PSD generated most debate with southerners
and westerners again to the fore in offering weakening amendments. Rep. William Chappell (D. FL) offered an amendment to
delete the nondegradation provisions from the bill and study the
matter further. He argued that the PSD provisions 'could have a
profound effect on our economy, severely limit potential jobs,
create incentives for our basic industries to locate abroad and further retard our efforts toward energy self-sufficiency'.[95] In a vote
that was much closer than that on the Moss Amendment in the
Senate, the Chappell Amendment was defeated by a 156–199 vote.
Other weakening amendments were also defeated. An amendment
offered by Rep. Satterfield to delete language that allowed local gov-

ernments to participate in classification decisions was rejected on a 32–263 vote. An amendment offered by Tim Lee Carter (R. KY) to increase the amount of pollution that would be allowed in non-degradation areas was defeated on a 100–183 vote. An amendment offered by Rep. Broyhill to delete the requirment that states include hydrocarbons, carbon monoxide, nitrogen oxides, and oxidants in nondegradation regulations was defeated by standing vote. The House accepted by voice vote, however, an amendment offered by Rep. Gunn McKay (D. UT) to allow state governors to issue variances allowing up to eleven days a year in which the sulphur dioxide increments could be violated in Class 1 areas.

Although Rep. Rogers had managed to fend off efforts to weaken significantly the nondegradation provisions of the bill, he had less success in defending the Committee's position on automobile exhaust emissions. House Commerce's decision to postpone compliance with hydrocarbon and carbon monoxide standards until 1980 and nitrogen oxides until 1981 was attacked by environmentalists who called for stricter controls, and supporters of the industry who called for longer delays. Prominent among those advocating stricter controls were two members representing district with acute air pollution problems: Rep. Henry A. Waxman (D. CA) and Rep. Andrew Maguire (D. NJ). The two offered an amendment to force compliance with all three emission standards by 1981 and imposed strict interim standards, but it was defeated on a 75–313 vote. Leading efforts to relax the standards were Rep. John D. Dingell (D. MI) and Rep. Broyhill. The two offered an amendment to postpone compliance with all three standards until 1982. No secret was made of the fact that the purpose of the amendment was to protect the automobile industry. Rep. Marvin L. Esch (R. MI) declared that: 'This amendment is designed to give predictability to the automobile industry and quite frankly, that means jobs.'[96] Such statements struck a sympathetic chord in an economy suffering from stagflation. The amendment was adopted by a 224–169 vote despite a strong statement from Rep. Rogers that: 'This issue is whether we want clean air and protection of health or whether we have no concern for that.'[97]

Adoption of the Dingell–Broyhill Amendment was the most significant change to the bill reported by House Commerce. The other amendments that were accepted made marginal changes in the bill's language. Rep. Broyhill made a final effort to recomit to bill to

committee with instructions to modify the section on nondegradation, but his motion was defeated 117–272. The House finally voted
324–68 in favour of the bill on 15 September 1976.

Differences between the bills passed by the House and Senate
were not easy to reconcile, and for a time it appeared that negotiations would end in stalemate. After a week of heated debate which
saw disputes both between and within the two delegations, a compromise version was eventually agreed by the majority of conferees.
Stationary sources were given until 1979 to meet emission standards, new sources could be built in areas violating NAAQS as long
as 'best available control technology' was installed, 'continuous
controls' were required for compliance with emission limits, cities
with acute air pollution problems were given until 1982 to meet
NAAQS, and limits were placed on the EPA's authority to require
construction permits for major 'indirect sources' of air pollution.
On the controversial issue of nondegradation, the conference committee adopted an uneasy mishmash of language from the two bills.
The conference bill divided all clean air regions into two classes, but
allowed the states to redesignate Class 2 areas as Class 3 areas to
allow larger increases in air pollution. Construction permits for new
industrial factories with the potential to emit sulphur dioxide would
be required in the clean air regions. Permits would eventually be
required to regulate nitrogen oxides, hydrocarbons, carbon monoxide and oxidants. On the equally controversial issue of automobile
exhaust emissions, the compromise adopted by the conference committee called for compliance with the hydrocarbon and carbon
monoxide standards by 1979, and compliance with the standard for
nitrogen oxides by 1981.

The conference bill was reported on 30 September 1976 but
immediately ran into difficulties. Four members of the House delegation to the conference refused to sign the report. Democrat David
Satterfield joined with Republicans James Broyhill, Tim Lee Carter,
and Samuel L. Devine (R. OH) to express dissatisfaction with the
compromise that had been fashioned in conference. They threatened to work with supporters of the Dingell–Broyhill Amendment
to defeat the conference bill. Action in the House was not required,
however, as Senator Jake Garn (R. UT) launched a filibuster against
the conference bill. Garn argued that the non-degradation provisions contained in the legislation would severely restrict economic
growth in his states. After less than a day's debate, Majority Leader

Robert Byrd (D. WV) moved a motion to adjourn. The adjournment motion was accepted by a 44–24 vote, and the bill died. Almost eighteen months of effort had come to nothing.

A fresh attempt to amend the Clean Air Act was made by Senator Muskie in January 1977 when he introduced legislation based on the conference report that Senator Garn had filibustered.[98] Hearings on the legislation were held by the Senate Subcommittee on Environmental Pollution in February 1977.[99] Little was new about the evidence presented to the Subcommittee and most of the arguments had been well rehearsed over the previous eighteen months. Obtaining a consensus on the full committee, however, took time. Disagreement flared, in particular, over what to do about the problem of 'non-attainment'. The main question that needed to be resolved was whether further industrial growth should be permitted in areas that had failed to comply with NAAQS. Senator Lloyd Bentsen (D. TX) argued that the states should be given more flexibility in allowing industrial growth. He offered an amendment to abolish strict deadlines for attainment that was initally accepted by Senate Environment and Public Works but was later removed.[100] Instead, the Committee adopted language which allowed new sources to be constructed as long as they employed best achievable emissions controls, and offset increases in air pollution with reductions from old sources. The deadline for meeting NAAQS was extended to 1982. Traffic-congested cities were permitted to request an additional five-year waiver provided they adopted reasonable transportation control measures.

The controversy surrounding the non-attainment issue delayed the reporting of a bill until 10 May 1977 as Senator Muskie was anxious to reach a consensus that would hold on the floor of the Senate.[101] These efforts eventually paid off. Although individual members of Senate Environment and Public Works did express some misgivings about the bill in the report, all voted in favour of it. Most of the reported bill's major provisions, in fact, were similar to that agreed in conference the previous year. 'With a few exceptions and only one really significant addition, it is basically the same legislation which we considered last year', Senator Jennings Randolph told the Senate when the bill came to be discussed on the floor.[102] The provisions on non-degradation, compliance, continuous emission controls and protection of the ozone layer were only marginally different from those contained in the bill that Senator Garn had vetoed. Standards and deadlines for exhaust emissions were stricter than those contained in the earlier bill. Only the provisions on non-attainment marked a departure from previous thinking.

Rep. Paul Rogers introduced companion legislation in the House in February 1977.[103] Hearings were held by the Subcommittee on Health and Environment in March and April 1977.[104] Familiar ground was covered in the hearings and rapid progress was made. A bill was reported out of House Commerce by voice vote on 12 May 1977.[105] In most respects the bill was similar to that passed by the House in 1976. The provisions on non-degradation, compliance, continuous emission controls, non-attainment and ozone protection differed little from provisions in the earlier bill. The provisions on automobile exhaust emissions, however, were different. New deadlines and standards were added to the bill after President Carter indicated that he supported a stronger effort to 'protect the environment'.[106] Although not as strict as those found in the Senate bill, the new deadlines and standards were nevertheless tougher than those found in the 1976 version of the bill.

Consensus had proved elusive during House Commerce's consideration of the bill. The report that accompanied the bill revealed deep divisions over automobile exhaust emission standards, non-degradation and continuous emission controls. Nine Democrats and nine Republicans expressed disagreement with the exhaust emission standards that had been incorporated in the bill. All favoured a proposal offered by Rep. Dingell and Rep. Broyhill that would have relaxed standards and postponed deadlines.[107] Rep. Waxman and Rep. Maguire, in contrast, called for tougher standards for nitrogen oxides. Two Democrats and six Republicans expressed opposition to the non-degradation provisions of the bill. They argued that the provisions would restrict economic growth and were not needed. The same eight members also expressed misgivings about the need for continuous emission controls. They argued that the same result could be achieved by using coal with a low sulphur content.

Rep. Roger's ability to defend the bill on the floor was compromised by the lack of unity on House Commerce as opponents were able to exploit such fissures to good effect. Amendments were adopted on the floor which weakened the bill's provisions regarding automobile exhaust emissions and non-degradation. A tough battle was also fought over the non-attainment provisions of the bill. The unity of Senate Environment and Public Works, in contrast, provided Senator Muskie with an important edge in his efforts to defend the bill on the Senate floor. Muskie was further advantaged by the fact that Senate consideration did not occur until after the House had acted. Environmental groups used the time to develop arguments to counter those that opponents had employed to good effect in the House. Although an amendment was adopted which postponed the introduction of new standards for automobile exhaust emissions, attempts to weaken the non-degradation provisions were defeated.

House consideration of the bill began on 24 May 1977 with general debate. Rep. Rogers argued that new scientific evidence had shown that tighter controls on air pollution were required than were currently in place. He insisted that: 'The committee has produced a balanced bill. We have granted waivers, we have given extensions, and we have written in flexibility to consider the economy and energy and the technology to meet goals and standards'.[108] Amendments to alter that 'balance', however, were soon to follow. Rep. John B. Breaux (D. LA) offered an amendment during the second day of debate to give state governors authority to allow increased air pollution in clean air regions for 18 days each year. the amendment was adopted on a 237–172 vote despite accusations from environmentalists that it made a mockery of the non-degradation provisions. A day later, Rep. Dingell and Rep. Broyhill offered an amendment on automobile exhaust emissions similar to that approved by the House in 1976. The amendment was approved on a 255–139 vote after heavy lobbying by industry and unions. Environmentalists enjoyed some success when the House rejected an amendment offered by Rep. Bob Gammaage (D. TX) to weaken the non-attainment provisions of the bill, but the legislation that eventually passed the House on a 326–49 vote on 26 May 1977 was undoubtedly weaker than that which had been reported out of House Commerce.

Floor consideration of the bill reported out of Senate Environment and Public Works began on 8 June 1977. Senator Muskie gave an immediate statement of his intention to pass the bill: 'I warn all of the interests affected by this bill that no more quick fixes will be forthcoming. I will not consent to splitting off any portion of this legislation should delaying tactics be used by any member of the Senate'.[109] Senator Garn again complained about the non-degradation provisions but perhaps realizing that he did not have the votes to sustain a filibuster stated that he had 'no intention of trying to gut the bill, despite what rumours may be flying around from last year'.[110] He did offer an amendment to allow some variance in emission standards in clean air regions, but agreed to support a substitute amendment offered by Senator Ted Stevens (R. AS). The Stevens Amendment was similar to the Breaux Amendment which had been adopted in the House, but it was rejected by a 33–61 vote in the Senate. Efforts to weaken the provisions on automobile exhaust emission were also less successful in the Senate than in the House. An amendment offered by Senator Donald W. Riegle (D. MI) and Senator Robert P. Griffin (R. MI) was passed, but only after it had been weakened by a substitute amendment offered by Senator Howard Baker (R. TN). The bill finally passed the Senate on a 73–7 vote on 10 June 1977.

A conference committee to iron out differences between the bills passed by the Senate and the House met at the end of July 1977. Finding a compromise between the two versions of the legislation was difficult. A dispute over automobile exhaust emission standards was particularly fractious. Eventually a bill was reported out of conference, however, on 3 August 1977. Senator Muskie called the bill 'a reasonable compromise'.[111] Others complained about particular provisions, and Rep. Dingell even refused to sign the conference report because of dissatisfaction with the final provisions on exhaust emission standards, but the overall sense was of relief that the work had been completed. Both the House and Senate approved the conference report by voice vote on 4 August 1977 and the legislation was signed into law by President Carter on 8 August 1977. Carter declared that: 'This act is the culmination of a 3-year effort by Congress to develop legislation which will continue our program toward meeting our national clean air goals in all parts of the country'.[112] In contrast to President Nixon seven years earlier, Carter also gave credit to Senator Muskie and Rep. Rogers for their work.

The Clean Air Act Amendments of 1977, as enacted, extended many of the deadlines by which compliance with the standards mandated by the 1970 Amendments would be required.[113] Automobile manufacturers were given a further two years to meet exhaust emission standards. Most industrial polluters were given a further three years to achieve the required limits on emissions. States in non-compliance with national air quality standards were given a further five years to come into compliance. Cities with particularly acute pollution problems were given a further ten years to meet the standards. The most innovative provisions of the 1977 Amendments were those which divided the country into three classes of air quality districts. No deterioration of air quality would be permitted in districts categorized as Class I, specified increments of additional pollution would be permitted in Class II districts, and no restrictions on pollution would be imposed in Class III districts as long as NAAQS were met. The 1977 Amendments also established a National Commission on Air Quality to monitor the work of the EPA, and provided funds for further research into ozone depletion and other aspects of air pollution. $200 million was authorized each year for fiscal 1978–81 to implement those provisions not authorized elsewhere.

Although the Clean Air Act Amendments of 1977 did not alter the basic structure of air pollution control that had been established at the beginning of the decade, it did represent a move away from the 'speculative-augmentation' of the 1970 law. Much of the idealism of the earlier law was forgotten as Congress struggled to address both old and new problems in a very different world. Greater flexibility was given to the EPA and the states in an effort to deal with the difficulties of non-attainment and non-deterioration; more time was given to various industries to comply with required standards; and further studies into new pollutants were authorised. The 1977 law was a triumph, in short, of the congressional art of compromise. It was an effort to meet the demands of a wide variety of affected interests, and like most such efforts it failed to satisfy many for long.

Conclusion

The incremental adjustments in air pollution control law between 1970 and 1977 marked a significant departure from the policy inflation of the late 1960s. High information and transaction costs generated by the need to evaluate complex information about the effectiveness of policy, and adjudicate between the competing claims of various interests, made radical departures from existing policy impossible. Buffeted by demands both to extend and contract the Clean Air Amendments of 1970, the response of Congress was to soften the hard edges of the 1970 law. Efforts were made to fine-tune policy, to remedy defects, and to ease the costs associated with the control of air pollution. The aspirational lawmaking of the earlier period was subdued beneath a greater concern with feasibility.

A few interests emerged as clear 'winners' or 'losers' from this period of policy retrenchment. Eastern utilities and high-sulphur coal producers were probably the greatest beneficiaries as the requirement that all power stations install 'scrubbers' enabled them to maintain their competitiveness.[114] Western utilities were probably the greatest losers. Not only did they have to install 'scrubbers' which were not needed as they burned low-sulphur coal, but new restrictions on their activites were imposed by the PSD provisions of the 1977 law. Other stationary sources, automobile manufacturers and city politicians gained temporarily from the postponement of compliance schedules. The incremental changes in the law, however, ensured that the basic 'scope of conflict' surrounding air pollution control remained little changed. The Clean Air Act Amendments of 1977 had simply deferred most arguments about the control of air pollution for future consideration.

Demands for changes to the law soon emerged in the late 1970s. Industrial groups began to demand further extensions and regulatory relief, and environmentalists began to demand action to both remedy defects in the law and address new problems. Although these demands were similar to those that had been heard since 1970, the context in which they were articulated changed considerably over the next decade. The opposition of the Reagan Administration to government regulation in general, and environmental laws in particular, meant that the transaction costs of strengthening the control of air pollution were very high. Growing public concern about the environment in the late 1980s and the election of President Bush, however, altered the matrix of benefits and costs surrounding the issue. The result was the opening of a 'policy window' which enabled an expansion of policy to occur.

Notes

1 The Energy Supply and Environmental Coordination Act (1974). PL 93–319, 88 stat. 246. Some sections subsequently transferred to 42 USC 7401 *et seq.*, remaining sections repealed by PL 95–95.
2 Clean Air Act Amendments 1977, PL 95–95, 91 stat. 685, 15 USC 7401 *et seq.*

3 Charles O. Jones *Clean Air* (Pittsburgh: University of Pittsburgh Press, 1975); James E. Krier and Edmund Ursin *Pollution and Policy* (Berkeley, CA: University of California Press, 1977).

4 Barnard Asbell *The Senate Nobody Knows* (New York: Doubleday, 1978).

5 Arthur C. Stern 'History of Air Pollution Legislation in the United States', *Journal of the Air Pollution Control Association* (1982), 32:44–61.

6 Bruce A. Ackerman and William T. Hassler *Clean Coal/Dirty Air* (New Haven, CN: Yale University Press, 1981).

7 *Ibid.*, p. 26.

8 Krier and Ursin *Pollution and Policy*, p. 238.

9 See Jones *Clean Air*, pp. 248–9.

10 See Robert A. Shanley *Presidential Influence and Environmental Policy* (Westport, CN: Greenwood Press, 1992), p. 52.

11 The best discussion of Clean Air cases during this period is R. Shep Melnick *Regulation and the Courts: The Case of the Clean Air Act* (Washington, DC: Brookings, 1983).

12 A good account of the difficulties that the EPA has experienced in implementing the Clean Air Act is Marc K. Landy, Marc J. Roberts and Stephen S. Thomas *The Environmental Protection Agency* expanded edition (New York: Oxford University Press, 1990).

13 See James E. Krier 'The Irrational National Air Quality Standards: Macro and Micro Mistakes', *UCLA Law Review* (1974), 22:323.

14 See Arthur C. Stern 'Prevention of Significant Detrioration – A Critical Review', *Journal of the Air Pollution Control Association* (1977), 27:440.

15 Twenty years after enactment of the Clean Air Amendments of 1970 the EPA had established NESHAPs for only seven chemicals: asbestos, benzene, vinl chloride, beryllium, mercury, radionuclides and arsenic. See US Environmental Protection Agency *Environmental Progress and Challenges: EPA's Update* (Washington, DC: EPA, 1988).

16 US Senate, Committee on Interior and Insular Affairs, *Hearing*, 'Problems of Electrical Power Generation in the Southwest', 92nd Congress, 1st session, 24, 25, 26, 29 May 1971.

17 US House, Committee on Interstate and Foreign Commerce, Subcommittee on Public Health and Environment, *Hearing*, 'Clean Air Oversight', 92nd Congress, 1st and 2nd sessions, 20 November 1971, 26–28 January 1972.

18 *Ibid.*, pp. 245–73.

19 US Senate, Committee on Public Works, Subcommittee on Air and Water Pollution, *Hearings*, 'Implementation of the Clean Air Act of 1970', 92nd Congress, 2nd session, 16, 17, 23, 24, 25 February, 25, 27, 28 March, 22 May 1972.

20 *Ibid.*, p. 1322.
21 *Ibid.*, p. 1272.
22 *Ibid.*, p. 1119.
23 *Ibid.*, p. 548.
24 *Ibid.*, p. 451.
25 *Ibid.*, p. 616.
26 *Ibid.*, p. 370.
27 *Ibid.*, p. 18.
28 *Ibid.*, p. 252.
29 S 498 (1973).
30 US House, Committee on Interstate and Foreign Commerce, Subcommittee on Public Health and Environment, *Hearing*, 'Clean Air Act Extension', 93rd Congress, 1st session, 28 February 1973.
31 The bill reported out of House Commerce was HR 5445 (1973).
32 Clean Air Act Extension, PL 93–15, 87 stat. 11.
33 The US Court of Appeals for the District of Columbia had ordered Ruckelshaus to reconsider an earlier decision not to grant a suspension of the exhaust emission standards. See *International Harvester Company et al. v. William D. Ruckelshaus* (1973).
34 *New York Times* 12 April 1973, p. A22. Lee Iacocca had proposed on 15 February 1973 that although standards for the rest of the country should be postponed, tough standards should be established for California in order to test pollution control devices. See *New York Times* 16 February 1973, p. A9.
35 *Ibid.*, pp. A1, A21.
36 US Senate, Committee on Public Works, Subcommittee on Air and Water Pollution, *Hearing*, 'Decision of the Administrator of the EPA Regarding Suspension of the 1975 Auto Emission Standards', 93rd Congress, 1st session, 16–18 April, 14, 21, 23, 30 May, 26, 27 June 1973.
37 US House of Representatives, Committee on Interstate and Foreign Commerce, Subcommittee on Public Health and Environment, *Hearing*, 'Clean Air Act Oversight – 1973', 93rd Congress, 1st session, 10–14, 17–21 September 1973.
38 Quoted in Congressional Quarterly, *Almanac 1970*, p. 482.
39 Charles O. Jones and Randall Strahan 'The Effects of Energy Politics on Congressional and Executive Organization in the 1970s', *Legislative Studies Quarterly* (1985), 10:153.
40 The Emergency Petroleum Allocation Act of 1973. See Alfred A. Marcus *Controversial Issues in Energy Policy* (Newbury Park, CA: Sage, 1992), pp. 39–40.
41 HR 17572 (1974).
42 In 1974 the House Select Committee on Committees, commonly known as the Bolling Committee, proposed a fundamental reorganiza-

tion of the chamber's committee system which included the creation of a Committee on Energy and Environment. Strong opposition to this proposal, however, ensured that it was dropped from the reform package that passed the House.

43 US House of Representatives, Committee on Interstate and Foreign Commerce, Subcommittee on Communications and Power, *Hearing*, 'Federal Power Commission Oversight', 93rd Congress, 1st session, 6, 7 March 1973; 93rd Congress, 2nd session, 11, 12 June 1974.

44 US House of Representatives, Committee on Interstate and Foreign Commerce, Subcommittee on Energy and Power, *Hearing*, 'Middle and Long–Term Energy Policies and Alternatives', 94th Congress, 2nd session, 25, 26 March 1976.

45 S 2589 (1973).

46 US Senate, Committee on Interior and Insular Affairs, *Hearing*, 'Energy Emergency Legislation', 93rd Congress, 1st session, 8 November 1973.

47 S 2680 (1973).

48 US Senate, Committee on Public Works, Subcommittee on Air and Water Pollution, *Hearing*, 'Fuel Shortages and the Clean Air Act', 93rd Congress, 1st session, 12 November 1973.

49 *Ibid.*, p. 3.

50 US Senate, Committee on Public Works, *Hearing*, 'Automobile Emission Controls', 93rd Congress, 1st session, 6, 7 November 1973.

51 S 2772 (1973).

52 John C. Sawhill, deputy director of the White House Federal Energy Office, had announced on 29 November 1973 that the final standards should be delayed until 1978 at the least. This position was opposed by the EPA.

53 HR 11031 (1973).

54 HR 11450 (1973).

55 US House of Representatives, Committee on Interstate and Foreign Commerce, *Hearing*, 'Emergency Energy Legislation ', 93rd Congress, 1st session, 14 November 1973.

56 HR 11882 (1973).

57 Krier and Ursin (*Pollution and Policy*, pp.229–30) provide useful background material on the controversy surrounding parking surcharges. They point out that the restriction on such surcharges 'could not possibly be related to the energy problem'.

58 S 921 (1973).

59 Quoted in *Congressional Quarterly Weekly Report*, 2 February 1974, p. 235.

60 *Ibid.*

61 Richard M. Nixon 'Veto of the Energy Emergency Bill', *Public Papers, 1974* 6 March 1974, p. 226.

62 HR 13834 (1974).
63 US House of Representatives, Committee on Interstate and Foreign Commerce, *Hearing*, 'Standby Energy Emergency Authorities Act', 93rd Congress, 2nd session, 2–4 April 1974.
64 HR 14369 (1974).
65 Quoted in Congressional Quarterly, *Almanac 1974*, p. 742.
66 *Ibid.*
67 Richard M. Nixon 'Statement About Signing the Energy Supply and Environmental Coordination Act of 1974', *Public Papers, 1974* 26 June 1974, p. 548.
68 Quoted in Congressional Quarterly, *Almanac 1974*, p. 744.
69 US House of Representatives, Committee on Interstate and Foreign Commerce, Subcommittee on Public Health and Environment, *Hearing*, 'Oversight: Clean Air Act', 93rd Congress, 2nd session, 23 September 1974, pp. 6–51.
70 *New York Times* 31 May 1975, p. A15.
71 Frank S. Rowland and Mario J. Molina 'Stratospheric Sink for Chlorofluromethanes: Chlorine Atomic-atalysed Destruction of Ozone', *Nature* 28 June 1974, pp. 810–2.
72 P. J. Crutzen 'SSTs – A Threat to the Earth's Ozone Shield', *Ambio* (1972), 1:41–51.
73 US Senate, Committee on Aeronautical and Space Sciences, Ad-hoc Subcommittee on the Upper Atmosphere, *Hearing*, 'Stratospheric Ozone Depletion', 94th Congress, 1st session, 8–9, 15, 17–19, 23 September 1975.
74 US House of Representatives, Committee on Science, Space and Technology, Subcommittee on Environment and Atmosphere, *Hearing*, 'Costs and Effects of Chronic Exposure to Low-Level Pollutants in the Environment', 94th Congress, 1st session, 7, 10–14, 17 November 1975.
75 US Senate, Committee on Commerce, Science and Transportation, *Hearing*, 'Oversight Hearings on the SST', 94th Congress, 2nd session, 20 February 1976.
76 *Fri v. Sierra Club* 412 US 541 (1973).
77 US Senate, Committee on Public Works, Subcommittee on Air and Water Pollution, *Hearing*, 'Non-degredation Policy of the Clean Air Act', 93rd Congress, 1st session, 24 July 1973.
78 US Senate, Committee on Public Works, Subcommittee on Environmental Pollution, *Hearing*, 'Implementation of the Clean Air Act – 1975', 94th Congress, 1st session, 19, 20 March, 21–23, 24, 29, 30 April, 1, 13–15 May 1975. See pp. 676–733.
79 The EPA was eventually forced to devise regulatory innovations to overcome some of the rigidities of the command-and-control approach

to pollution control contained within the Clean Air Amendments. 'Netting', which was first used in 1974, allows a factory to set up a new pollution source as long as net emissions from the factory are not increased. 'Offsets', which were first used in 1976, allow new sources of pollution to be established as long as emissions from existing sources in the same area are reduced. 'Banking', which was first used in 1979, allows sources of pollution to store up emissions reductions, beyond those required by law, to use them later as offsets. 'Bubbles', which were also introduced in 1979, allow tradeoffs among existing sources inside an imaginary bubble. For a critique of these innovations see Richard A. Liroff *Reforming Air Pollution Regulations: The Toil and Trouble of EPA's Bubble* (Washington, DC: Conservation Foundation, 1986).

80 S 594 (1975).
81 HR 2633 (1975). A virtually identical bill (HR 2650) was also introduced by House Minority Leader Rep. John J. Rhodes (R. AZ).
82 The bill was also referred to House Armed Services and House Ways and Means because it contained provisions pertaining to the naval petroleum and oil shale reserves, and taxation.
83 US House of Representatives, Committee on Interstate and Foreign Commerce, Subcommittee on Health and Environment, *Hearing*, 'Clean Air Amendment, 1975', 94th Congress, 1st session, 13–20, 26 March 1975.
84 The Committees were Armed Services, Banking, Commerce, Finance, Government Operations, Interior, Judiciary, Labor and Public Works.
85 US Senate, Committee on Public Works, Subcommittee on Environmental Pollution, *Hearing*, 'Implementation of the Clean Air Act – 1975', 94th Congress, 1st Session, 19, 20 March, 21–23, 24, 29, 30 April, 1, 13–15 May 1975.
86 See Bruce A. Ackerman and William T. Hassler *Clean Coal/Dirty Air*, pp. 31–33; Peter Navarro 'The Politics of Air Pollution', p. 36.
87 S 3219 (1976).
88 S Rept 94–717.
89 HR 10498 (1976).
90 H Rept 94–1175.
91 Quoted in Congressional Quarterly, *Almanac 1976*, p. 133.
92 *Ibid.*
93 *Ibid.*
94 *Ibid.*, p. 134.
95 *Ibid.*, p. 139.
96 *Ibid.*, p. 140.
97 *Ibid.*, p. 141.
98 S 251 (1977); S 252 (1977); S 253 (1977).

99 US Senate, Committee on Environment and Public Works, Subcommittee on Environmental Pollution, *Hearings* 'Clean Air Amendments of 1977', 95th Congress, 1st session, 9–15 February 1977.

100 The Committee on Public Works was renamed the Committee on Environment and Public Works in reforms adopted in 1977. The reforms affirmed the Committee's jurisdiction over air pollution and many other environmental programmes.

101 The Senate Environment and Public Works Committee reported S 252 (1977) on 10 May 1977.

102 Quoted in Congressional Quarterly, *Almanac 1977*, p. 641.

103 HR 4151 (1977).

104 US House of Representatives, Committee on Interstate and Foreign Commerce, Subcommittee on Health and Environment, *Hearings*, 'Clean Air Amendments of 1977', 95th Congress, 1st session, 8–11 March, 18 April 1977.

105 HR 6161 (1977).

106 Jimmy Carter 'The Energy Problem', *Public Papers, 1977* 18 April 1977, p. 659.

107 HR 4444 (1977).

108 Quoted in Congressional Quarterly, *Almanac 1977*, p. 635.

109 *Ibid.*, p. 641.

110 *Ibid.*, pp.641–2.

111 *New York Times*, 3 August 1977, p. A11.

112 Jimmy Carter, 'Clean Air Act Amendments of 1977', *Public Papers, 1977* 8 August 1977, p. 1460.

113 See David P. Currie 'Relaxation of Implementation Plans Under the 1977 Clean Air Act', *Michigan Law Review* (1979–80), 78:155–203.

114 See Ackerman and Hassler *Clean Coal/Dirty Air*; Marc J. Roberts and Susan O. Farrell 'The Political Economy of Implementation: The Clean Air Act and Stationary Sources' in Ann F. Friedlaender (ed.), *Approaches to Controlling Air Pollution* (Cambridge, MA: MIT Press, 1978), pp. 152–90.

7

Policy struggle, 1977–90

The basic pattern of congressional interest in air pollution between 1977 and 1990 was little different from that which had been evident since the early 1970s. Levels of committee activity and bill introductions remained relatively stable, but the uncertainty and conflict surrounding the issue made it impossible to obtain agreement on a major reform of the Clean Air Act until 1990. Enactments prior to passage of the Clean Air Act Amendments 1990 made minor adjustments in policy.[1] Some of the deadlines established by the Clean Air Act Amendments 1977 were postponed by the Steel Industry Compliance Extension Act 1981 and appropriation bills for fiscal years 1984 and 1988.[2] Further research was initiated by the Acid Precipitation Act 1980, the Radon Gas and Indoor Air Quality Research Act 1986, the Alternative Motor Fuels Act 1988 and the Forest Ecosystems and Atmospheric Pollution Research Act 1988.[3] Some increase in regulatory authority was provided by the Global Climate Protection Act 1987 and the Indoor Radon Abatement Act 1988.[4]

The origins of this period of policy struggle may be traced to the politics of deferral that produced the Clean Air Act Amendments 1977. Postponement of so many difficult questions about the wherewithal of air pollution control ensured a continuation of the struggle over policy between those who wished to strengthen the law and those who wished to weaken it. Environmentalists argued that evidence of poor implementation, non-compliance and the emergence of new problems meant that greater resources needed to be devoted to tackling the problem of air pollution. Many industrial groups disputed the scientific grounds for greater control, and argued that the cost of compliance with existing air pollution standards was already too high. Both sides had powerful allies in Washington, DC, in the early 1980s. Advocates of stronger controls included the Chairman of the Senate Environment and Public Works Committee Senator Robert Stafford (R. VT), Chairman of the Subcommittee on Environmental Pollution Senator John H. Chafee (R. RI), and the Chairman of the House Subcommittee on Health and Environment Rep. Henry Waxman (D. CA).[5] Opponents of stronger controls included President Ronald Reagan, the Republican leadership in the Senate, Senate Minority Leader Robert Byrd (D. WV), and the Chairman of the House Energy and Commerce Committee Rep. John Dingell (D. MI).[6]

Major reform of the Clean Air Act in the early 1980s was precluded by the balance of power that existed between these key players. Advocates of stronger controls on air pollution were able to fashion legislation because of the control they exercised over prime policy-making venues, but lacked the necessary parliamentary authority to force further action. Senator Stafford was unable to persuade the Republican leadership in the Senate to schedule floor action on major reforms reported out of Senate Environment, and Rep. Waxman was unable to overcome the opposition of Rep. Dingell to proposals reported out of his Subcommittee. Opponents of the existing air pollution control regime, on the other hand, lacked command of the prime policy-making venues that would have enabled them to fashion changes in the law. They were well positioned to block the initiatives of environmentalists, but were unable to promote their own legislative preferences. President Reagan's strategy of employing administrative means to undermine environmental regulations was also relatively ineffective when applied to air pollution. Cuts in the EPA's budget did reduce the resources dedicated to implementation, but executive orders which required cost–benefit analysis of all new regulations had little impact because of the Clean Air Act's specific prohibition on taking costs into consideration when establishing National Ambient Air Quality Standards (NAAQS).

The stalemate in Congress over reform of the Clean Air Act was finally broken at the end of the decade when the election of a new president, changes in congressional personnel and the growing saliency of environmental issues, made action possible. A critical impetus to efforts to reform the law was provided by the election of President Bush. Anxious to translate some his election rhetoric about being an environmental president into reality, Bush made enactment of a Clean Air Act a priority. The election of Senator George Mitchell (D. ME) as Senate Majority Leader in January 1989 was no less significant. Advocates of a stronger air pollution control law finally possessed the parliamentary power they needed to move beyond committee deliberations. Perhaps most important in breaking the stalemate, however, was a rise in the saliency of environmental issues at the end of the 1980s. Increased public concern about the environment generated a new interest in air pollution among many members of Congress who saw electoral benefits to be gained from portraying themselves as 'environmentally friendly'. Opponents of a stronger law were suddenly faced with the prospect of being on the wrong side of the issue.

The changed circumstances at the end of the 1980s clearly altered the matrix of costs and benefits connected with the production of air pollution control legislation. The low saliency and conflict associated with the issue in the early part of the decade meant that the benefits from action were uncertain and the transaction costs were prohibitively high. The high saliency of the issue and changes in the parliamentary position of key personnel in the later part of the decade changed this equation. Benefits were more certain and transaction costs were reduced to a certain extent. Production of the Clean Air Act Amendments 1990 was the result of these changes. The 1990 Amendments answered many of the questions that had been left unanswered in 1977, but raised a host of new concerns in the process. Demands that these new concerns be addressed emerged almost immediately after enactment.

The gridlocked years

The discontent that had greeted enactment of the Clean Air Act Amendments 1977 soon generated pressure for further action from both sides of the environmental divide. Environmentalists not only argued that existing regulations were failing to achieve all their objectives, but also maintained that new research on acid rain and stratospheric ozone depletion indicated a need for further controls. Industrial groups argued that the law was unnecessarily strict and imposed too great an economic cost. The high level of conflict associated with the issue, and uncertain public attitudes towards the environment, however, made 'consideration of anti-pollution measures an unattractive endeavour for many members of the US Senate and House of Representatives'.[7] The result was gridlock. Both sides had their champions in Congress, but none was in a position to impose a solution on a wary institution.

Unresolved problems, new concerns
Unresolved problems and new concerns shaped the debate about reform of the Clean Air Act in the late 1970s and early 1980s. Environmentalists expressed concern about levels of non-compliance, the poor record of the Environmental Protection Agency (EPA) in regulating airborne toxics and particulates and the need for stronger action to tackle the problem of acid rain and stratospheric ozone depletion. Industrial groups argued that the criteria for establishing NAAQS needed to be revised, the process for obtaining permits to build new sources of pollution needed to be simplified, and exhaust emission standards for automobiles needed to be relaxed. Each issue raised questions of considerable technical complexity and generated dispute about the quality of evidence used to support arguments.

Claims by environmentalists that the EPA was not treating the matter of non-compliance adequately were made at two hearings conducted by the Senate's Subcommittee on Environmental Pollution in early 1979. Richard Ayres from the Natural Resources Defense Council (NRDC) told the Subcommittee in February 1979 that the Carter White House was hampering the EPA's efforts to implement environmental regulations.[8] Robert Rauch from the Environmental Defense Fund (EDF) concurred in this view. Further accusations that the EPA was failing to do its job were made in a subsequent hearing in May 1979.[9] Two witnesses from the NRDC, Stephen H. Schroeder and Frances Dubrowski, criticized the EPA for delays in prosecuting industries, municipalities and federal facilities for non-compliance with Clean Air Standards. Although such charges were denied, a report published by the EPA in 1980 revealed that progress in cleaning the air had been slower than anticipated.[10] The report cited progress in reducing levels of particulates, sulphur dioxide and carbon monoxide, but noted that levels of ozone and nitrogen dioxide remained high. The EPA claimed that 93 per cent of industry was in compliance with the law. Power stations, the steel industry and the heavy metal industry were the prime industries not in compliance.

Concern about the EPA's delay in addressing the problem of air-borne toxics was raised by John R. Quarles, former Deputy Administrator of the EPA, in the hearing conducted by the Subcommittee on Environmental Pollution in February 1979.[11] Ten years after enactment of the Clean Air Amendments 1970, the EPA had only managed to establish national emission standards for hazardous air pollutants (NESHAPs) for asbestos, beryllium, mercury and vinyl chlorides. The NESHAPs for benzene, arsenic and radionuclides had been proposed, but had not been confirmed in their final form. Environmentalist also criticized the EPA for failing to establish adequate emission standards for particulates. David R. Doniger of the NRDC told House Science's Subcommittee on Natural Resources and Environment in October 1980 that the EPA's diesel emission standards failed to meet the health objectives of the Clean Air Act.[12] Truck manufacturers disputed such claims. Joseph B Bidwell of General Motors and Alfred W. Pelletier of Mack Trucks claimed that there was insufficient evidence to confirm the adverse health effects of exposure to diesel particulates.

Further disputes over evidence were generated by assertions from environmentalists that stronger action needed to be taken to address the problems of acid rain. Environmentalists claimed that evidence of increased acidity in America's lakes and soil required stricter controls on emissions of sulphur dioxide and nitrogen dioxide. Robert J. Rauch told House Commerce's Subcommittee on Oversight and Investigations in February 1980 that the EPA had contributed to the problem by approving state plans to relax sulphur dioxide emission limits.[13] The evidence that acid rain was increasing was disputed by industry groups in a hearing three months later before Senate Energy.[14] Both William N. Poundstone of the Consolidation Coal Co., and Robert W. Brocksen of the Electric Power Research Institute, questioned the accuracy of reported increases in acid rain. Regional divisions were also apparent in these hearings. Politicians from northern and northeastern states gave graphic accounts of the damage apparently caused by acid rain to rivers, lakes, and forests while those from the coal-producing states of Appalachia and the Midwest argued that there was insufficient evidence to implicate soft coal as a cause of the problem. An international dimension to the issue was revealed in a subsequent hearing conducted by the House Commerce's Subcommittee on Health and Environment when members of the Canadian Government gave evidence about acid rain.[15]

Disputes about scientific evidence were also generated by claims by environmentalists that more needed to be done to address the problem of stratospheric ozone depletion. Industry groups challenged the link between CFCs and stratospheric ozone depletion in a hearing before Senate Environment's Subcommittee on Toxic Substances and Environmental Oversight in July 1981.[16] Representatives from General Electric, E. I. du Pont de Nemours, Lenax Industries, and others contested evidence that indicted CFCs as a cause of ozone depletion. Small businesses challenged the cost-effectiveness of CFC regulations at a hearing conducted by House Small Business's Subcommittee on Antitrust and Restraint of Trade the same month.[17] Representatives of the air-conditioning industry, the foam and insulation industry, the food distribution industry, and several other small businesses argued that CFC regulations were unnecessary and threatened jobs. Notice that industry had an ally in the new Administration was provided in November 1981 when Donald Clay, Director of the EPA's Office of Toxic Substances, told House Commerce's Subcommittee on Health and Environment that the science regarding CFCs and ozone depletion was inexact.[18] The validity of ozone depletion theory was defended at the hearing by Alan S. Miller of the NRDC and Khristine L. Hall of the EDF.

A concern about costs underpinned almost all of industry's demands for reform of the Clean Air Act. General complaints about the costs of meeting environmental regulations were aired at a hearing conducted by Senate Commerce's Subcommittee on the Consumer in November 1978.[19] Roger T. Kelley of the Caterpillar Tractor Co. protested about the high cost of meeting EPA and Occupational Safety and Health Administration (OSHA) regulations. William E. Graham of the Carolina Light and Power Co. told the Subcommittee that increases in consumer electricity bills were directly attributable to environmental regulations of questionable benefit. Both statements were rejected by environmentalists who argued that the costs of compliance with environmental regulations were being exaggerated and needed to be placed in context. Further claims about the high cost of meeting Clean Air standards were made in a report published by the Business Roundtable in 1980.[20] The report asserted that the Clean Air Amendments 1970 would cost industry $400 billion by 1987.

Particular allegations were made about the cost-effectiveness of the criteria for establishing NAAQS. The 1970 Amendments required NAAQS to be set at a level to protect human health regardless of cost. Critics charged that such a requirement bordered on the 'economics of the madhouse'. Not only was it virtually impossible to protect vulnerable populations from the effects of air pollution, but the costs of the effort would probably exceed any benefits. Industry and its supporters argued that cost–benefit analysis should be used to establish NAAQS which would protect the 'general population' from 'significant risk of adverse health effects'.[21] The use of cost–benefit analysis was opposed by environmentalists and health care professionals who argued that it was extremely difficult to put a price on the benefits of cleaner air. Accusations were also made about the conflict of interest that had arisen when consultants had been employed in the past to conduct cost–benefit analyses for the EPA.[22]

A second complaint of industry concerned the process for obtaining permits to build new sources of pollution. The EPA and the states had been granted authority in the Clean Air Act Amendments 1977 to review all proposals for major new facilities to ensure that they used the best possible pollution control equipment and would not cause a significant deterioration in air quality. In areas with relatively clean air, a company had to obtain a permit from the state air pollution board which specified the control equipment that would be used for every emission source at the new factory. In areas that were not in compliance with clean air standards, a company had to obtain a permit from both the state air pollution board and the EPA which not only specified use of control equipment, but also indicated how emissions from existing factories owned by that company in the area would be reduced. Industry groups argued that these requirements were time-consuming and expensive. Representatives of the steel and oil industries complained about delays in obtaining permits at a hearing conducted by House Commerce's Subcommittee on Health and Environment in November 1979.[23] A study commissioned by the Business Roundtable in 1980 claimed that the process for obtaining permits took approximately three years and cost $250–300 million per factory.[24]

Complaints about the cost of compliance with automobile exhaust emission standards were also made in the aftermath of the 1977 Amendments. Representatives of General Motors, Ford and Chrysler expressed concern about the cost-effectiveness of existing regulations at a hearing conducted by House Government Operations' Subcommittee on Government Activities and Transportation in May 1981.[25] The automobile industry argued that the standards for Carbon Monoxide and Nitrogen Oxides should be relaxed both to make it easier for the industry to meet mandated fuel economy figures and to allow more diesels to be produced.[26] Opposition to such arguments came not only from environmentalists, but also from the burgeoning pollution control industry. John R. Blizzard, executive director of the Manufacturers of Emissions Controls Association, told the Subcommittee that standards needed to be maintained at their existing levels.

The disputes over unresolved problems and new concerns that raged in the aftermath of the passage of the Clean Air Act Amendments 1977 provide clear evidence of the complex and 'unbounded' nature of air pollution issues.[27] Not only were the causes and consequences of the various problems a matter of argument, but in the words of Barry Commoner 'everything connected to everything else'.[28] Such attributes made law-making particularly difficult. Complexity and 'unboundedness' produced uncertainty, conflict and confusion. Debate was usually couched in difficult technical language, large numbers of groups were involved in the issue and legislative structures were ill-adapted to cope with a problem that was difficult to contain within discrete analytic 'boxes'. The potential for legislative production was further reduced by the low public saliency of the issue in the late 1970s and early 1980s. A powerful incentive for legislative entrepreneurship and compromise disappeared when 'pollution' vanished from the Gallup Poll's 'Most Important Problem' public opinion survey in 1978.[29]

Legislative stalemate
The number of air pollution control bills introduced in Congress in the late 1970s remained reasonably high as legislators responded to the various demands articulated by environmental and industry groups. A total of seventy-nine air pollution control bills were introduced in the House of Representatives in the 96th Congress (1979–80). Twenty of these bills addressed the concerns of industry directly: ten sought to postpone compliance deadlines or delay penalties for non-compliance, four to weaken standards, three to change the regulations governing PSD and three to force the EPA to employ cost–benefit analysis when setting standards. A further twelve bills proposed to increase the tax relief on pollution control

equipment. Only seven bills unambiguously sought to strengthen aspects of the Clean Air Act. A further bill called for the EPA to study the effectiveness of fees and rebates as a means of achieving NAAQS. The remainder of the bills touched on a variety of issues from airport development to the promotion of new energy sources. Fewer air pollution control bills were introduced in the Senate, but the basic pattern was similar to the House. Five of the twenty-six bills introduced in the Senate addressed the concerns of industry. Four bills called for an increase in tax relief, and four sought to strengthen the air pollution control regime in one way or another. The rest of the bills addressed miscellaneous issues. No bill introduced in either the House or the Senate in the 96th Congress sought a comprehensive reform of the Clean Air Act.

Little interest was paid to most of these bills. Not only were the concerns they addressed complex and of limited public saliency, but the retirement of Rep. Rogers in 1978 and the departure of Senator Muskie to become Secretary of State in 1980 left Congress bereft of leadership on the issue. Efforts to enact the Comprehensive Environmental Response, Compensation, and Liability Act 1980 (CERCLA) and to reauthorize the Solid Waste Disposal Act also distracted the attention of environmentalists away from air pollution and consumed valuable parliamentary resources. Growing concern about acid rain, however, did prompt Congress to enact the Acid Precipitation Act 1980 which established a Federal Interagency Task Force to conduct research into the causes and consequences of acid rain.[30]

The prospect of significant action to strengthen efforts to control air pollution diminished in the wake of the 1980 elections. Not only did industry groups gain an important new ally in the White House, but the Republican capture of the Senate and gains in the House promised a sympathetic audience for pro-business arguments in Congress. Although Senate Environment and Public Works retained its pro-environment bias under the leadership of Senator Stafford, and the staunchly pro-environment Rep. Waxman remained as Chair of the House Subcommittee on Health and Environment, the majority in both chambers had a pro-business slant.[31] A report published by the National Commission on Air Quality in 1981 further compounded matters by offering support for most of the arguments advanced by industrial groups.[32] The Commission recommended that compliance deadlines be extended, that exhaust emission standards be lowered, and that the regulations governing deterioration of clean air be simplified. Joint hearings on the Commission's report were conducted by Senate Environment and Public Works and the House Subcommittee on Health and Environment in March 1981.[33]

Fundamental revision of the Clean Air Act was advocated by the Reagan Administration as part of a general assault on federal involvement in controlling air pollution.[34] The Administration not only sought to provide regulatory relief to the states and cut federal funding for air pollution control, but also planned to submit a detailed package of reforms to Congress which would have weakened the Clean Air Act. A change of tactics became necessary, however, when the strength of public support for the law became apparent.[35] On 5 August 1981 President Reagan sent Congress a set of eleven principles to guide reform of the Clean Air Act rather than a set of specific legislative recommendations.[36] The principles included a call for more research on acid rain, adjustment of the deadlines for achieving NAAQS 'to reflect realities', adjustment of automobile emission standards 'to more reasonable levels', and the restoration of state responsibility for controlling air pollution with the federal government reduced to a monitoring role. The principles were greeted with enthusiasm by industrial groups, but with caution by environmentalists. Kent E. Portney has argued that they constituted a 'call for the federal role in air pollution to revert to its earlier position – one of conducting research'.[37]

The failure of the Reagan Administration to offer draft legislation left advocates of reform in Congress lacking a focus for action. A total of seventy-seven air pollution control bills were introduced in the House during the 97th Congress (1981–82). Twenty-five of these bills had a clear pro-business focus, twenty had a clear pro-environment focus and seven sought to increase the level of tax relief on air pollution control equipment. The remainder of the bills touched on a variety of different issues pertinent to air pollution control. A total of thirty-five air pollution control bills were introduced in the Senate. Thirteen of these bills had a clear pro-environment focus, ten had a clear pro-business focus and four were concerned with tax relief. The rest of the bills touched upon matters tangential to air pollution control.

Little action was taken on the vast majority of these bills. The House Subcommittee on Health and Environment held hearings on bills to postpone the regulation of CFCs until further research had been conducted into stratospheric ozone depletion and to provide regulatory relief to the automobile industry.[38] No further action was taken, however, on either of these bills. Greater attention was paid to a bill introduced by Rep. Thomas A. Luken (D. OH) in December 1981 to overhaul the entire Clean Air Act.[39] The bill was supported by industry and the Reagan Administration which regarded it as reflecting the eleven principles, but was opposed by environmental groups who argued that it would lead to more pollution. In a press conference held on 23 December 1981 the NRDC and the National Audubon Society suggested that the bill was a 'sweetheart deal' for industries that want to weaken the Clean Air Act.[40] This pattern of industry support and environmental group opposition for the bill was repeated in hearings conducted by the Subcommittee on Health and Environment in February 1982.[41]

Although Rep. Waxman did not believe that a comprehensive overhaul of the Clean Air Act was necessary, he lacked sufficient votes on the Subcommittee on Health and Environment to block the Luken bill. Subcommittee Democrats Dingell, Luken, Phil Gramm (D. TX) and Richard C. Shelby (D. TX) voted with the Republicans to provide a 12–8 majority in favour of the bill. Reported out of the Subcommittee in March 1982 the bill had a distinct pro-industry tint. It relaxed emission standards for both stationary and mobile sources, permitted more industrial growth in western states, and eliminated the existing ban on industrial growth in areas of non-attainment. The scope of conflict surrounding air pollution control issues, however, frustrated the efforts of Rep. Dingell to construct a winning bipartisan coalition in favour of the bill in the full Committee. A series of votes on range of issues from non-attainment to PSD revealed divisions so deep among the forty-six members of House Energy that no compromise could be fashioned. The bill died when Congress recessed in December 1982.

Efforts to reform the Clean Air Act took a different form in the Senate. Senator Stafford (R. VT), Chair of the Environment and Public Works Committee, believed that 'fine-tuning' rather than comprehensive reform of the law was needed. Rejecting the conventional method of holding hearings and mark-ups on a fresh bill to reauthorize the 1977 Act, Stafford decided to conduct a series of oversight hearings in the Spring 1981, and then hold 'seminars' on clean air in November 1981 which reviewed the law on a section-by-section basis.[42] Early in the new year, Stafford decided that the Committee needed a clearer focus for its deliberations and introduced a package of reforms. Although the reform package included provisions to postpone some standards and deadlines, it also proposed to tighten controls on acid rain and other forms of inter-state air pollution. The Committee conducted a series of mark-up sessions on Stafford's proposals, and eventually reported a bill in August 1982 by a 15–1 vote.[43] Senator Steven D. Symms (R. ID) was the only dissenting voice.

The reported bill reflected the pro-environment bias of the Environment and Public Works Committee. It retained existing prevention of significant deterioration (PSD), provisions and automobile exhaust emission standards, required the EPA to take more urgent action to regulate hazardous air pollutants, and mandated reductions in emissions of sulphur dioxide standards to curb acid rain. Some standards and deadlines were relaxed, but they were relatively minor. The deadline for states to meet NAAQS was extended for two years, and states suffering from automobile pollution were given an additional five years to meet standards provided they employed all reasonable available control technologies. The clear pro-environment bias of the reported bill, however, meant that it was received with little enthusiasm by Senate leaders. No effort was made to schedule floor action on the bill as neither Majority Leader Senator Howard Baker (R. TN) nor Minority Leader Senator Robert Byrd (D. WV) wished to see such a controversial bill consuming what time remained before recess.

Comprehensive reform of the Clean Air Act foundered in the 97th Congress because the conflict associated with the issue proved impossible to reconcile within the prevailing balance of political forces. Funding to enforce the 1977 Act was provided through the fiscal 1983 appropriations bill for the Department of Housing and Urban Affairs. Action did prove possible, however, on legislation of more limited ambition. Calls for the steel industry to be given relief from emission standards had grown during the late 1970s and a federal advisory board in the autumn 1980 had concurred with such demands. Bills to provide relief to the steel industry were introduced in the House by Democrats and Republicans from steel producing areas: Rep. George M. O'Brien (R. IL), Rep. Joseph M. Gaydos (D. PA), Rep. Doug Walgren (D. PA), Rep. Ralph S. Regula (R. OH) and Rep. Clarence J. Brown (R. OH). Companion legislation was introduced in the Senate by Senator Jennings Randolph (D. WV). Hearings in both the House and Senate revealed a consensus about the need for such legislation and progress was rapid.[44] The House passed the measure on 28 May 1981 by a vote of 322–3; the Senate passed its version on 11 June 1981. Both chambers agreed to a compromise version produced by conference two weeks later, and President Reagan signed the bill into law on 17 July 1981.[45] Reagan claimed at the signing ceremony that: 'This act, affecting one of America's most vital industries, is a symbol of the administration's commitment – a commitment to cast aside the over-zealous and unnecessary regulation that has shackled the most productive forces in our economy.'[46]

Congress's failure to address the basic concerns of industry and environment groups ensured continued agitation for reform in the 98th Congress. Sixty-two air pollution control bills were introduced in the House during the 98th Congress (1983–84). Thirty-two of these bills had a clear pro-environment bias and sixteen had a clear pro-industry bias. Evidence of a pro-environment bias was even more palpable in the Senate. No fewer than twenty of the twenty-eight air pollution control bills that were introduced in the Senate during the 98th Congress had a clear pro-environment bias. Only two of the bills had a pro-industry bias. Interest in alternative regulatory methods of controlling air pollution remained apparent in both chambers. Five bills introduced in the House and one in the Senate contained provisions to introduce a variety of environmental taxes and fees. Two bills introduced in the Senate proposed to increase the tax relief available on the purchase of pollution control equipment.

New urgency was added to reform efforts by the prospect that economic sanctions would be imposed on communities that had failed to meet required clean air standards. On 3 February 1983 EPA Administrator Anne M. Burford published a list of 218 communities that had failed to meet the 31 December 1982 deadline for achieving NAAQS established in the 1977 Amendments. Burford stated that these communities faced bans on new construction and a reduction of federal grants for highways and clean air programmes. Although environmentalists charged that the Reagan Administration was using the threat of sanctions to pressure Congress to reauthorize the Clean Air Act on terms favourable to industry, a majority of members proved unwilling to call Burford's bluff. On 2 June 1983 the House adopted an amendment offered by Rep. William E. Dannemeyer (R. CA) to the Fiscal 1984 Housing and

Urban Development Appropriation Act which prohibited the EPA from imposing sanctions for one year.[47] The Senate Appropriations Committee adopted the amendment during mark-up and it provoked little opposition during floor debate.

Efforts to enact major reform of the Clean Air Act revealed the same conflict and divisions that had been apparent previously. Early in 1983 Senator Robert T. Stafford reintroduced the clean air bill that had been reported in 1982 with similar consequences.[48] Hearings on the bill were conducted in November 1983 and February 1984, and the bill was reported out of Committee in May 1984 on a 16–2 vote.[49] Voting against the motion to report the bill were Senators Steven D. Symms (R. ID) and Jennings Randolph (D. WV). The latter opposed the bill because its provisions on acid rain would have threatened coal-mining operations in Appalachia and penalized utilities in the Midwest. Fear of strong opposition to the acid rain provisions from senators representing midwestern states persuaded the Senate's leadership not to schedule floor action in the 98th Congress.

The lines of conflict over acid rain had earlier been revealed in an oversight hearing conducted by the Senate's Committee on Energy and Natural Resources.[50] Support for more stringent controls on emissions of sulphur dioxide came from those members who represented states in the northeast which suffered most from acid rain. Senator George Mitchell (D. ME) told the Committee that there was a clear justification for reductions in sulphur dioxide. Representatives of the Canadian government also called for stricter controls on the precursors of acid rain. Opposition to greater controls came primarily from members who represented states in Appalachia and the Midwest which produced and used coal with a high sulphur content. Minority Leader Robert Byrd (D. WV) told the Committee that the findings of research into acid rain were too inconclusive to warrant regulatory controls. The reason for Byrd's position on the issue was made plain when representatives of the coal and electricity industries claimed that greater controls on sulphur dioxide emissions would lead to job losses in the mines of Appalachia and the Ohio Valley and higher electricity prices throughout the Midwest.

Regional differences over the best way to control acid rain similarly undermined efforts in the House to revise the Clean Air Act. Evidence presented during hearings conducted by the Subcommittee on Health and Environment in March 1984 on a reauthorization measure drafted by Rep. Waxman revealed the same regional split that had been apparent in the Senate.[51] Waxman's proposal that annual emissions of sulphur dioxide be reduced by 12 million tons was supported by Rep. Norman E. D'Amours (D. NH), Rep. James M. Jeffords (R. VT) and Rep. Silvio O. Conte (R. MA), but was opposed by Rep. Nick Joe Rahall (D. WV), Rep. Harley O. Staggers (D. WV) and Rep. Alan B. Mullohan (D. WV). Waxman eventually decided to postpone consideration of a clean air bill in May 1984 when the Subcommittee voted 10–9 to remove acid rain provisions from the bill.[52] Joining the Subcommittee's six Republicans in the motion to strike the acid rain provisions were Rep. Richard C. Shelby (D. AL) and three midwestern Democrats: Rep. Dennis E. Eckart (D. OH), Rep. John D. Dingell (D. MI) and Rep. Thomas A. Luken (D. OH).

The problem of acid rain dominated efforts to amend the Clean Air Act in the 99th Congress (1985–86).[53] Thirteen of the fifty-three air pollution control bills introduced in the House and ten of the twenty-four bills introduced in the Senate specifically addressed the problem of acid rain. Eleven of the acid rain bills were introduced by representatives or senators from states in New England. Nine of the forty-three hearings conducted by congressional committees into air pollution focused on acid rain. Hearings were conducted not only by the House Subcommittee on Health and Environment and the Senate Environment and Public Works Committee, but also by subcommittees of House Interior and House Agriculture. The latter two panels seized upon the damage caused to forests by acid rain to claim some jurisdiction over the issue as public concern about the problem increased.[54]

Little progress was made on finding an acceptable solution to acid rain despite the increased attention to the issue in the 99th Congress. In 1986 Rep. Waxman introduced legislation that provided for a phased reduction in the emissions that caused acid rain and sought to reduce the financial burden on the Midwest by imposing a national tax on electricity.[55] Hearings on the bill, however, revealed the same basic fault lines that had hindered progress in the 98th Congress.[56] EPA Administrator Lee M. Thomas told Waxman's Subcommittee that there was insufficient scientific evidence to warrant acid rain regulation, and Energy Secretary John S. Herrington warned of the adverse economic impact of tighter sulphur dioxide emissions. The Governor of West Virginia and representatives of mining interests in Illinois and Ohio further warned the Subcommittee about the likely adverse impact of tighter regulations in coal-producing areas. The Subcommittee reported the bill by a 16–9 vote but further action was blocked by Rep. Dingell who refused to schedule full committee action on the measure. Companion legislation was introduced in the Senate by Senator Stafford.[57] Hearings were conducted on the measure but no further action took place in the 99th Congress.[58]

Although the 99th Congress failed to find a solution to the problem of acid rain, a measure to address the problem of radon and indoor air pollution was enacted in 1986.[59] Interest in indoor air pollution had grown during the 1980s. Rep. Claudine C. Schneider (R. RI) introduced the first bill to conduct research into indoor air pollution in the 97th Congress (1981–82).[60] The problem of radon and indoor air pollution was investigated in hearings conducted by a subcommittee of the House Committee on Science, Space and Technology in 1983.[61] The so-called Watras incident in which the clothes and skin of a worker at a nuclear power station in Pennsylvania were found to be contaminated with isotopes of natural background radiation, however, sparked considerable interest in radon in 1985. Seven bills dealing with radon were introduced in the House during the 99th Congress and five were introduced in the Senate. Nine of these bills sought to promote research into radon while the other three sought to provide tax relief on equipment to detect radon. A 1986 report issued by the EPA which concluded that as many as 10 per cent of the nation's homes could be contaminated by radon provided the stimulus that was needed for further action. Legislation was rapidly enacted which authorized further federal research into the problem.[62]

Advocates of further action to address the problem of radon received a boost when the Democrats recaptured control of the Senate following the 1986 mid-term elections. Democratic control meant that Senator Frank Lautenberg (D. NJ), the Senate's 'Mr Radon', became Chairman of the Superfund and Environmental Oversight Subcommittee of Senate Environment and Public Works.[63] Lautenberg used his position to push for new legislation. His Subcommittee held joint hearings with the Subcommittee on Environmental Protection in April 1987 on a bill introduced by Senator Chafee to assess the problem of radon in schools.[64] Working closely with Senator Mitchell, Chairman of the renamed Subcommittee on Environmental Protection, he drafted a compromise bill that was approved by the full committee on 17 June 1987 and passed the Senate by voice vote on 8 July 1987.[65] The bill passed by the Senate authorized $10 million annually during fiscal 1988–90 for federal grants to help states develop and implement programmes to control radon in homes and schools. Companion legislation introduced by Rep. Luken was reported out of House Energy's Subcommittee on Transportation, Tourism, and Hazardous Materials on 1 July 1987 following an earlier hearing.[66] No further legislative action took place in 1987.

Anxious to maintain some momentum on the radon issue, Senator Lautenberg commissioned a General Accounting Office (GAO) Report into radon and held hearings on its findings in May 1988.[67] The report heavily criticized federal efforts to deal with radon and provided evidence of the need for further legislation. Prompted into action the House Energy and Commerce Committee finally reported the bill that had been cleared the previous year by the Subcommittee on Transportation on 4 October 1988. The House passed the bill the next day and the Senate adopted the House's version on the 7 October 1988. President Reagan signed the Indoor Radon Abatement Act into law on 28 October 1988.[68] The law authorized $45 million to study and control radon contamination in homes, schools and federal buildings over three years. Perhaps most significant, the ambition of earlier air pollution control statutes had reappeared. The stated long-term aim of the Indoor Radon Abatement Act was to ensure that 'the air within buildings should be as free of radon as ambient air outside of buildings'. Many doubted that such a goal was technically feasible.[69]

The ambition of the Indoor Radon Abatement Act was a sign that the matrix of costs and benefits surrounding air pollution control was beginning to change. Not only did improved scientific evidence about the health and environmental damage caused by air pollution begin to reduce some of the uncertainty that had plagued efforts to address the problem since the early 1970s, but increased public appreciation that the problem had not been resolved by enactment of earlier legislation also held out a promise of electoral benefits to those who advocated tougher action. The likelihood of action was further enhanced by partisan change in the Senate provided a new generation of legislative entrepreneurs with enhanced parliamentary resources to shape events. Several proponents of stronger air pollution control laws emerged as subcommittee chairmen in the wake of the 1986 elections.

The most important 'change of the guard' in the 100th Congress occurred when Senator Mitchell, a protege of Senator Muskie, became Chairman of the Subcommittee on Environmental Protection. Although Mitchell's voting record on environmental issues was similar in many respects to that of his immediate predecessor, Senator Chafee, he was far more able and willing than the Rhode Island Republican to use the parliamentary resources available to him as a subcommittee chairman to address the problem of air pollution. Whereas Chafee had been forced to cede leadership on air pollution control issues to Senator Stafford, the new octogenarian Chairman of Environment and Public Works, Senator Quentin Burdick (D. ND), had little interest in environmental issues and left control over clean air legislation to Mitchell.[70] Not only did Mitchell seize the opportunity he had been given by introducing more air pollution control bills in the 100th Congress than Chafee had introduced in the previous three Congresses, he also used the Subcommittee to promote his agenda in a way which had not been seen since the days of Senator Muskie.

An early hearing on acid rain provided a clear indication of Senator Mitchell's determination to use the Subcommittee on Environmental Protection to set the agenda. Acid rain had long been a particular concern of Mitchell because of the damage that acidification had caused to Maine's rivers, lakes and forests. In a change of tactics, however, he used his subcommittee chairmanship to shift the focus of the debate away from environmental damage to adverse health effects. At a hearing conducted in February 1987 a long line of medical experts provided testimony about the dangers to human health posed by acid rain precursors.[71] No other witnesses gave evidence to the Subcommittee. Two months later Mitchell scheduled another hearing in which EPA Administrator Lee Thomas was grilled about the EPA's acid rain control programmes.[72] The clear bias revealed in these hearings contrasted markedly with hearings in the House. In a hearing conducted by the House Subcommittee on Health and the Environment in July 1987 representatives of the National Coal Association, Ohio Edison Company and the American Public Power Association continued to maintain that more knowledge was needed about the extent and effect of acid rain to justify additional emission controls.[73]

Little dispute about evidence was apparent in hearings conducted by either panel into the problem of stratospheric ozone depletion. Hearings on the discovery of a hole in the ozone layer over Antarctica by the National Ozone Expedition in 1986 conducted by the two subcommittees in Spring 1987 revealed widespread acceptance of the scientific evidence.[74] What was disputed was whether the problem was best tackled by unilateral or multilateral action. Industry groups and the EPA argued that global action was needed to deal with the problem while environmental groups called for a ban on the production of CFCs in the United States. Substantial media coverage of the discovery of a hole in the ozone layer also prompted other panels to seek a slice of the action on an issue of growing public saliency. Not only did House Science's Subcommittee on Natural Resources, Agricultural Research, and Environment also review the findings of the 1986 National Ozone Expedition, but the Subcommittee on Human Rights and International Organizations of House Foreign Affairs conducted a hearing on American participation in international negotiations on a ozone protocol.[75]

Concern about acid rain and stratospheric ozone depletion was reflected in the number of bills introduced in the 100th Congress that focused on the two issues. Of the total of seventy-six air pollution control bills introduced in the House, seven addressed the problem of acid rain and five the problem of stratospheric ozone depletion. Of the total of eighty-seven air pollution control bills introduced in the Senate, five focused on acid rain and no fewer than thirteen dealt with the problem of the disappearing ozone layer. Both issues were rapidly subsumed, however, by the efforts of Mitchell and Waxman to engineer more general revision of the Clean Air Act. Sufficient evidence had accumulated by the mid-1980s to suggest that the framework of laws governing air pollution in the United States was not only incapable of dealing with new issues such as stratospheric ozone depletion, but was also failing to deal with old problems adequately. Hearings conducted by the Subcommittee on Health and the Environment and the Subcommittee on Environmental Protection in 1987 revealed that non-attainment of clean air standards was widespread.[76]

The effort to overhaul the Clean Air Act made good initial progress in the Senate. Mitchell's Subcommittee held hearings on legislation to revise the law in June and July 1987 and reported a bill before the summer recess.[77] Senator Burdick's lack of engagement with the issue allowed Mitchell to dominate proceedings when the full committee met to mark-up the bill. A compromise bill which tightened controls on acid rain precursors and toxic air pollutants, but gave major cities more time to meet air pollution standards, was reported by the Committee on 22 October 1987.[78] No floor action was scheduled, however, as Majority Leader Robert C Byrd (D. WV) feared that provisions in the bill providing for tighter controls on sulphur dioxide emissions would reduce the market for the high-sulphur coal mined in West Virginia. Mitchell sought to allay the fears of Byrd and senators from the midwest by proposing that the capital cost of installing 'scrubbers' on smokestacks be subsidized by the federal government, but such a proposal was opposed by some senators from western states.[79] Most utilities in the west used low-sulphur coal and had already installed 'scrubbers' at their own expense. After a year of obstruction and delay, Mitchell finally conceded defeat in October 1988.

Two bills to tighten controls on ozone, carbon monoxide, and acid rain precursors were introduced in the House by Rep. Waxman in 1987.[80] Progress was even slower than in the Senate, however, as opposition from Rep. Dingell and ranking subcommittee member Rep. Edward R. Madigan (R. IL) led to delay and prevarication. Although the Subcommittee on Health and the Environment held hearings on the two measures, Rep. Waxman was unable to secure a majority on the panel to report either of the measures.[81] Rep. Dingell also used his position as chairman of the Subcommittee on Oversight and Investigations to conduct hearings that appeared to question the need for further controls on acid rain.[82] The hearings highlighted a report by the National Acid Precipitation Program (NAPAP) which concluded that acid rain was unlikely to make northeastern lakes any more acidic during the next few decades. Rep. Waxman made a further effort to produce a clean air bill in 1988, but was no more successful than in previous years. Deep divisions within the Subcommittee on Health and the Environment ensured that no bill was reported.

Efforts to reauthorize the Clean Air Act in the 100th Congress ground to a halt because the conflict generated by the issue could not be resolved within the existing balance of political forces. Increased public concern and personnel changes following the 1988 elections, however, changed the dynamics surrounding the issue sufficiently to create a 'window of opportunity' for policy change to

Kingdon

occur.[83] Improved benefits and lower costs allowed the gridlock that had existed for a decade to be broken.

Breaking the gridlock

Regional divisions over acid rain, disputes between environmental and business groups, the anti-regulation ethos of the Reagan Administration and the distribution of power within Congress contributed to the gridlock on clean air during the 1980s. The dynamics surrounding the issue began to change, however, as the decade came to a close. First, the saliency of air pollution increased as a series of dire warnings about the fate of the planet, and catastrophic events like the *Exxon Valdez* disaster when millions of gallons of oil were spilled along Alaska's coastline, combined to propel environmental matters to the public's attention. Second, Senator Mitchell replaced Senator Byrd as Majority Leader in January 1989 and made reauthorization of the Clean Air Act his main priority. The new Majority Leader promised to schedule floor action for any clean air measure reported out of committee. Third, President Bush saw environmental issues as a means both of courting public approval and of distancing himself from the Reagan Administration.

The environmental impulse

Public concern about environmental issues had begun to resurface in the early years of the Reagan Administration as environmental groups mobilized support to counter the Administration's efforts to undermine environmental laws. Fearful that the gains of the 'environmental decade' would be swept away in a bout of deregulation, Americans began both to express increased support for environmental objectives and to join environmental groups. The percentage of respondents who believed that more should be done to protect the environment regardless of cost increased from 45 to 58 per cent between 1981 and 1983.[84] Membership of environmental groups rose rapidly. Between 1980 and 1983 membership of the Sierra Club, for example, rose from 180,000 to 346,000.[85] This rise in public concern about the environment slowed during the mid-1980s as the Administration softened its anti-environment rhetoric and retreated from a full-scale effort to emasculate environmental laws, but was rekindled during the late 1980s as the media began to devote attention to issues such as global warming and the

Exxon Valdez ran aground in Alaska. The percentage of respondents who believed that more should be done to protect the environment rose to 65 per cent in 1988 and reached 80 per cent a year later.[86] Membership of environment groups rose accordingly. The Sierra Club alone gained 200,000 new members between 1987 and 1990.[87]

policy entrepreneurship

Evidence of growing public concern about the state of the environment provoked a flurry of activity in Congress as members began to appreciate the benefits that could be obtained from 'position-taking' and 'entrepreneurship' on air pollution control issues. Public alarm about global warming and urban smog prompted a competition among various committees for a 'slice of the action' that was similar to the scramble for jurisdiction over energy issues that had occurred in the mid-1970s. Oversight hearings on global warming were conducted in 1989 by the Senate Committee on Commerce, Science and Transportation, the Senate Committee on Foreign Relations, the House Committee on Energy and Commerce and the House Committee on Foreign Affairs.[88] Oversight hearings on urban smog were conducted by various subcommittees of the Senate Committee on Energy and Natural Resources, the House Committee on Public Works, as well as by House Energy and Commerce.[89] Bill introductions in the 101st Congress (1989–90) rose slightly in the House where eighty-three air pollution control bills were introduced, but fell in the Senate where only forty-eight bills were introduced.

The prospects for action on air pollution were boosted at the beginning of the 101st Congress when Senator Mitchell was elected as Majority Leader. Mitchell promised to schedule floor action on any air pollution bill reported out of committee. Hearings on a range of bills in the early months 1989, however, revealed a familiar pattern of conflict. Legislation to regulate the manufacture and use of CFCs was considered by both Senate Environment's Subcommittee on Environmental Protection, chaired by Senator Baucus, and Senate Commerce's Subcommittee on the Consumer, chaired by Senator Richard H. Bryan (D. NV).[90] Witnesses from industry acknowledged the problems caused by CFCs but claimed that they needed more time to develop alternative products. Legislation introduced by Rep. Sikorski to control acid rain was considered by the House Subcommittee on Health and the Environment where a representative from the National Coal Association repeated the familiar mantra that more research was needed before stricter emissions controls were introduced.[91] Perhaps most significantly, hearings on legislation to overhaul the Clean Air Act conducted by the House Subcommittee on Health and the Environment revealed the same problems that had plagued efforts to revise the law for over a decade.[92]

Resolving the problems surrounding the issue of air pollution proved difficult despite increased public concern about the environment. In the House, the conflict between Rep. Dingell and Rep. Waxman made it difficult to reconcile conflicting views about reform. Efforts by an informal 'Group of Nine' of moderate Democrats and Republicans to find common ground between the two failed to overcome disagreements on automobile emission standards and acid rain.[93] In the Senate, Senator Mitchell's elevation to Majority Leader and Senator Stafford's retirement in 1988 had left the Subcommittee on Environmental Protection bereft of experience on air pollution issues. Although Senator Baucus had a good environmental record, he lacked detailed knowledge about the problems of air pollution, and had other commitments which impinged upon the time he could devote to the Subcommittee on Environmental Protection.[94] Not until President Bush provided needed leadership on the issue did it prove possible to overcome these institutional road-blocks.

The shock waves of the environmental impulse resonated loudly in the presidential election 1988. Anxious to attract the votes of environmentalists Vice-President Bush gave a speech at the Detroit Metropark on 31 August 1988 in which he declared that he was an environmentalist in the Teddy Roosevelt tradition.[95] He promised action on a wide range of environmental issues that included a plan to 'cut millions of tons of sulphur dioxide emissions by the year 2000'. In a clear break with the Reagan Administration's position on acid rain, Bush asserted that 'the time for study alone has passed'. The following day he took to the waters of Boston Harbor to launch an attack on Governor Dukakis's record as an environmentalist. 'Two hundred years ago, tea was spilled into this harbor in the name of liberty' Bush stated, 'Now it's something else. We've got to do better'.[96] Dukakis eventually responded to these attacks by offering his own proposals in September and October to protect the environment. Among other things he promised to cut emissions of sulphur dioxide by 12 million tons and nitrogen oxide emissions by

4 million tons by 2000. Developed late in the campaign these proposals received little attention despite being more specific than
those offered by Bush. Good timing had allowed Bush to seize the
initiative on environmental issues.

   Although exit polls suggest that the stands of the two candidates
on the environment made little difference to the outcome of the
election, President Bush chose to interpret his victory as a mandate
for his environmental policies.[97] Believing that the environment
offered him a good opportunity to break free of Reagan's shadow,
Bush decided to devote considerable attention to environmental
issues. 'I hope that it is plain to everyone in this room and around
the country that among my first items on my personal agenda is the
protection of America's environment' he remarked at the swearing-
in ceremony for the new EPA Administrator William K. Reilly.[98] Particularly high on Bush's agenda, perhaps because of the importance
of California in the 1992 election, was a desire to overhaul the
Clean Air Act.[99] In his first formal message to Congress he stated
that: 'I will send you shortly legislation for a new, more effective
Clean Air Act. It will include a plan to reduce the emissions which
cause acid rain because the time for study alone has passed, and the
time for action is now'.[100]

The Clean Air Act Amendments 1990
President Bush revealed the general outline of his proposals to
reform the Clean Air Act on 12 June 1989.[101] The proposals had
three main goals. First, the problem of acid rain was to be addressed
by cutting emissions of sulphur dioxide and nitrogen oxides. Emissions of sulphur dioxide were to be cut by 10 million tons and those
of nitrogen oxides by 2 million tons by 2000. Bush claimed that
these reductions would ensure that 'the degradation caused by acid
rain will stop by the end of the century'. Second, the problem of
urban smog was to be addressed through tighter exhaust emission
controls and sponsorship of alternative fuels and clean cars. Bush
proposed 'to put up to a million clean-fuelled vehicles a year on the
road by 1997'. Third, the problem of air toxics was to be addressed
by mandating the use of control technology. Bush claimed that the
proposals would 'cut all categories of airborne toxic chemicals by
three-quarters within this decade'.

   The most innovative aspect of the proposals was a strong emphasis on 'marketplace' solutions to air pollution. Bush proposed that a

system of tradable permits be established to control emissions of sulphur dioxide. 'We've set an ambitious reduction target, and applying market forces will be the fastest, most cost-effective way to achieve it', he stated, 'So, we're allowing utilities to trade credits among themselves for reductions they make, to let them decide how to bring aggregate emissions down as cost-effectively as possible'. Bush also announced that he was 'asking the EPA to develop rules like those we're employing on acid rain to allow auto and fuel companies to trade required reductions in order to meet the standard in the most cost-effective way'.

Interest in the use of market mechanisms to control pollution had increased during the 1980s as environmentalists such as Fred Krupp and Dan Dudek of the EDF and Jay Hair of the National Wildlife Federation began to advocate market-based incentives as more cost-effective than traditional command-and-control regulatory techniques.[102] Senator John Heinz (R. PA) and Senator Timothy Wirth (D. CO) sponsored a study into market–based incentives called *Project 88*.[103] These sentiments proved popular with the Bush Administration, and Dudek was consulted widely during the drafting of the President's clean air proposals. Air pollution control legislation incorporating forms of market incentives had been introduced sporadically in Congress, but had not aroused much interest until the late 1980s. The Administration's proposals for a system of tradable permits for sulphur dioxide were welcomed, however, as a means to overcome the deadlock on acid rain that had frustrated progress on clean air revision for the better part of a decade.

Although Bush had declared that 'it's time to clear the air' when announcing his proposed legislation, another six weeks were to pass before the Administration's proposals were submitted to Congress. Introduced by Senator Chafee and Rep. Dingell, the legislation signalled a slight retreat from the pro-environment position that Bush had taken in June.[104] Although the main thrust of the provisions on acid rain, non-attainment, and toxic air pollutants remained the same, the details of the legislation revealed that some concessions had been made to industry. Automobile exhaust emission reductions were to be made on a fleet rather than an individual car basis, and a greater number of cities were to be granted extensions in meeting clean air standards.[105]

This softening in the Administration's position was attacked by environmentalists and their supporters in Congress. Both Senator Mitchell and Senator Baucus publically criticized the move. Representative Waxman held a hastily organized hearing on the Administration's proposals on 24 July 1989 in which he attacked the legislation as 'riddled with exemptions and relaxations that were never mentioned in the president's statement and are wholly inconsistent with many of his stated objectives'.[106]

Opposition from Senators Baucus and Mitchell meant that the Administration's proposals were effectively 'dead on arrival' in the Senate. The Administration's bill was given only marginal consideration in a series of hearings on Clean Air Act amendments that were conducted by the Subcommittee on Environmental Protection in September 1989, and was not reported by the panel.[107] Pointedly snubbing the President, the Subcommittee reported three separate bills on acid rain, air toxics, and smog that were significantly stronger than the provisions contained in the Administration Bill.[108] These three bills were subsequently combined into one package when the Environment and Public Works Committee held its mark-up on 16 November 1989.[109] The Committee approved the marked-up bill by a 15–1 vote. Only Senator Steve Symms (R. ID) voted against the measure.

The bill reported by the Environment and Public Works Committee was similar in some respects to that submitted by the Administration. The urban smog provisions of the two bills were practically the same. Cities were divided into four categories based on the severity of their pollution, and given between five and fifteen years to meet ozone standards. Los Angeles was given twenty years. The acid rain provisions of the Committee bill were also similar to those found in the Administration's bill. Both bills mandated reductions in emissions of acid rain precursors, and established a marketable permit system for controlling sulphur dioxide. Provisions on toxic air pollutants and automobile exhaust emissions, however, were much tougher in the Committee bill. The Committee bill required all sources of toxic air pollution to install 'maximum achievable control technology' (MACT), and directed the EPA to establish health-based standards to remove any remaining threat to human health. These health-based standards had to reduce the risk of cancer from carcinogenic air pollutants to less than one in a million. The automobile exhaust emission provisions contained in the Committee bill were particularly tough. Administration proposals

that a major programme be established to develop clean automobiles and fuels were rejected on a rare partisan vote in the Committee in favour of a two-stage reduction in exhaust emissions.

Senator Mitchell kept his promise to schedule floor action, but
was forced to withdraw the bill from the floor in early February
1990 after less than two weeks' consideration when it became evident that more negotiation was required on issues such as acid rain,
toxic air pollutants, and automobile exhaust emissions. Minority
Whip Senator Alan Simpson (R. WY) had warned Mitchell that the
floor debate would be a 'riotous occasion' full of 'anguish and
horror', and his prediction proved accurate.[110] The speed with
which the Environment and Public Works Committee had
processed the bill meant that a number of major issues had not been
resolved properly. Looming large among these issues was the vexed
question of how to reduce the economic dislocation that would be
caused in the Midwest by increased controls on acid rain precursors.
The overall cost of the bill was also a matter of dispute. Critics
charged that the Environment and Public Works Committee had
produced a bill with such a pro-environment bias that costs had
escalated dramatically. The EPA estimated that the Committee bill
would cost $41.9 billion per year whereas the Administration bill
would cost $18.9 billion per year. President Bush promised to veto
any bill whose costs exceeded those of his proposals by more than
10 percent.[111]

Although Mitchell and Baucus believed that a majority of senators would vote for the Committee bill, they did not believe that
they had sufficient votes either to invoke cloture if someone like
Senator Byrd decided to filibuster the measure or to override a
potential presidential veto. They decided, as a result, to work with
the Administration to produce a compromise. A month of negotiations followed in which Mitchell and Minority Leader Dole, a few
members of the Environment and Public Works Committee, EPA
officials, and White House officials led by Roger B. Porter met
behind closed door to fashion legislation acceptable to both sides.[112]
The result was a substitute bill that steered a middle line between
the original Committee and Administration bills. It phased in automobile exhaust emission reductions, mandated a study of the best
way to assess the health risk of air toxics after MACT had been
installed, provided midwestern utilities with extra sulphur dioxide
'allowances' which could be sold to defray the cost of installing

'scrubbers', and restored the Administration's alternative fuel programme.

Support from the White House enabled Mitchell, Baucus, Dole,
and Chafee to fend off a series of 'deal-buster' amendments that
were offered by environmentalists and conservatives when the substitute bill was brought up for floor debate on 5 March 1990. In a
speech at a power station belonging to the Potomac Electric Power
Co. President Bush urged senators to support the compromise bill:
'The Dole–Mitchell compromise substitute is now under consideration, and my appeal again would be to urge all members to move
forward on it within the parameters hammered out in compromise
by Senator Mitchell and Senator Dole'.[113] The most important challenge to the White House–Senate compromise came from Senator
Byrd who offered an amendment to compensate miners who lost
their jobs as a result of stricter controls on sulphur dioxide. With a
price tag of approximately $1.4 billion, the Administration warned
that adoption of the amendment would push the bill through the
cost ceiling established by President Bush and lead to a veto.[114]
Byrd's position as Chairman of the Appropriations Committee
made him a powerful adversary and the vote on the amendment was
very close as senators were reluctant to antagonize the person who
controlled access to the 'pork barrel'. Heavy lobbying by the White
House made the difference. Byrd's amendment was defeated on 26
March 1990 on a 49–50 vote.

Defeat of the Byrd Amendment ended the last significant chal-
lenge to the bill. The Senate passed the bill by a margin of 89–11 on
3 April 1990. Voting against the bill were six conservative Republi-
cans and five midwestern Democrats: Jake Garn (R. UT), Jesse
Helms (R. NC), James McClure (R. ID), Don Nickles (R. OK),
Steve Symms (R. ID), Malcolm Wallop (R. WY), Robert Byrd (D.
WV), John Rockefeller (D. WV), John Glenn (D. OH), Alan Dixon
(D. IL) and Paul Simon (D. IL).

Progress in the House was initially much slower than in the
Senate. Unlike Senator Baucus, Rep. Waxman was forced to negotiate with proponents of a more cautious approach from the outset,
and found his freedom to act circumscribed by an alliance between
Energy Committee Chairman Rep. Dingell and Ranking Minority
Member Rep. Norman F. Lent (R. NY). Dingell and Lent offered a
substitute version of the Administration's bill when the Subcommittee on Health and the Environment began marking up the bill in

September 1989. Intended to address some of the criticism that environmentalists had levelled at Bush's proposals, the Dingell–Lent substitute strengthened the bill's provisions on the control of toxic air pollutants. Waxman welcomed the changes but argued that more needed to be done to address the problem of urban smog in particular. After offering a series of amendments to tighten controls on automobile emissions which were defeated in the Subcommittee, Waxman eventually negotiated a compromise agreement with Dingell that both agreed to support until the bill reached President Bush's desk. Adopted by the Subcommittee on a 22–0 vote, the Waxman–Dingell agreement proposed to phase in Californian exhaust emission standards across the nation from 1994 and impose even tougher standards from 2003.

Similar agreements proved impossible to fashion on the highly contentious issues of toxic air pollutants and acid rain. Amendments to tighten the bill's provisions on air toxics were offered by Rep. Bill Richardson (D. NM) and Rep. Gerry Sikorski (D. MN), but all were defeated by a coalition of Republicans and conservative Democrats marshalled by Dingell and Lent. An amendment offered by Sikorski to double the reduction in nitrogen oxide emissions specified in the bill's acid rain provisions was defeated by voice vote. The Subcommittee also voted 12–10 to weaken the Administration's proposal to mandate a new generation of clean cars and fuels. The definition of a 'clean fuel' was loosened, and automanufacturers were required only to 'certify' that they could produce automobiles that could run on such fuels.

The amended Dingell–Lent substitute was reported by the Subcommittee on Health and the Environment on 11 October 1989, and was sent to the Subcommittee on Energy and Power which had jurisdiction over certain of the acid rain and alternative fuel provisions in the bill. Hearings conducted by the latter panel had revealed considerable disquiet among midwestern members about the economic costs of the proposed acid rain controls, and Subcommittee Chairman Philip R. Sharp (D. IN) refused to schedule a mark-up session until he had negotiated a cost-sharing plan to help defray these costs.[115] Sharp produced a cost-sharing plan on 28 February 1990 that proposed to levy a fee on large industrial sources of sulphur dioxide emissions and use the money raised to help midwestern utilities meet the costs of installing 'scrubbers'. Agreement proved impossible to obtain on the Subcommittee, however, and

Dingell finally decided to remove the bill from the Sharp's control by bringing it before the full committee on 14 March 1990. Dingell declared that he wanted to report the measure before the Easter recess began on 6 April 1990.

To speed progress much of the negotiations during mark-up proceeded behind closed doors. On 22 March 1990 members emerged to report that a compromise had been agreed on urban smog which divided the worst polluted areas of the country into categories based on the severity of their pollution and established methods to bring them into compliance with health standards. The compromise included some provisions that had been stripped from the Senate version of the bill. Closed-door negotiations failed to reconcile differences over alternative fuels, however, and after several close votes the Committee agreed on 29 March 1990 to retain a modified version of the Subcommittee's language on the issue. A compromise was achieved on air toxics when pro-environment members agreed to moderate the second round health standards in return for more extensive first round technological controls. Agreement on acid rain was finally reached when Sharp dropped his insistence that midwestern utilities receive cash to help them defray costs and accepted a modified trading system which gave Midwest states additional sulphur dioxide allowances. The Committee finally voted 42–1 to report the bill on 5 April 1990. Only Rep. William E. Dannemeyer voted no.

The compromises that had been reached during Subcommittee and Committee mark-up allowed the House to deal with the measure after only two days of debate. Waxman made a final effort to tighten the provision on 'clean cars' and won a slight concession from Dingell who agreed to a pilot programme which would require automanufacturers to produce 150,000 clean-fuelled automobiles for the Californian market from 1994 and 300,000 such cars from 1997. The House adopted the compromise on a 405–15 vote. More controversial was a 274–146 vote to approve a $250 million five year compensation package for workers who lost their jobs as a result of the new law. President Bush stated that he was opposed to the amendment but did not issue an explicit veto threat. The House finally passed the bill on 23 May 1990 on a 401–21 vote.

Although the House and Senate versions of the bill had similar structures, it proved difficult to smooth out the hundreds of differences, some significant, in their language. Agreement was not finally

great support

reached until late October 1990. The House voted 401–25 to approve the conference report on 26 October 1990. Voting against the report were 20 Republicans and five Democrats. A day later the Senate voted 89–10 to approve the report. The same five Democrats who opposed the bill in April voted against it again, but Republican Senators Nickles and Wallop changed their vote to support the measure while Senator Orrin Hatch (R. UT) switched his vote to a 'nay'. President Bush signed the bill into law on 15 November 1990. 'This legislation isn't just the centerpiece of our environmental agenda', stated Bush, 'It is simply the most significant air pollution legislation in our nation's history, and it restores America's place as the global leader in environmental protection'.[116]

The Clean Air Act Amendments 1990, as finally enacted, was divided into four main titles.[117] Title I provided the states with the regulatory authority necessary to meet NAAQS. Six categories of 'ozone non-attainment' areas were established and deadlines set for them to meet federal standards. Title II imposed new controls on mobile sources of pollution. Automobile manufacturers were not only required to reduce exhaust emissions, but also produce experimental cars for sale in southern California. Oil companies were required to produce alternative formulations of fuel that produced fewer pollutants. Title III required industry to reduce emissions of 189 toxic substances to the average level of the twelve cleanest similar facilities. Title IV required utilities to reduce emissions of sulphur dioxide. In an important innovation, the 1990 Amendments established a system of tradable emission allowances. Other titles of the Act phased out the production of CFCs, provided compensation for those made unemployed as a consequence of compliance with the law, provided funds for research, and outlined permit and enforcement provisions.

Conclusion

The complexity and 'unbounded' nature of air pollution control issues in the 1980s generated a policy struggle in Congress that took a decade to resolve. Disputes over scientific evidence and cost-effectiveness that spilled over into different policy domains, and a distribution of parliamentary power that placed opponents of reform in positions of authority, made it impossible to reconcile differences. Resolution only became possible when the saliency of the issue rose, key congressional personnel changed parliamentary positions and President Bush committed the resources of the executive branch to breaking the 'gridlock'. Presidential initiative was the catalyst that facilitated enactment of the Clean Air Act Amendments 1990.

The 1990 Amendments addressed many of the questions that had been left unanswered in 1977 and dealt with some of the new issues that had emerged in the 1980s.[118] New efforts were made to deal with the persistent problem of urban air pollution, the failure of the EPA to regulate toxic air pollutants, and the problem of acid rain. Each effort was shaped by political realities and policy learning. Extended deadlines and stricter controls were used to deal with urban air pollution. Technological controls were mandated to control specified air toxics as the risk assessment procedure required by the Clean Air Act Amendments 1970 had proved unworkable. Market mechanism were used to overcome the political conflict surrounding acid rain. The compromises that had to be made to obtain agreement on each section of the law ensured that no group ended up as a clear 'winner or loser' when the dust of negotiation settled. Both environmental and industry groups could claim some successes and setbacks.

Demands for changes in the law began to emerge in the early 1990s as growing evidence about global warming and other problems prompted environmentalists to argue for new controls while industry groups began to campaign for regulatory relief as the cost of the law became apparent. The Republican capture of Congress following the 1994 elections changed the context in which these demands were processed. Greater credence was given to advocates of regulatory relief as a period of policy reaction was ushered in.

Notes

1 The Clean Air Act Amendments 1990, PL 101–549, 104 stat. 2399.
2 The Steel Industry Compliance Extension Act 1981, PL 97–23, 95 stat. 139, 42 USC 7401.
3 The Acid Precipitation Act 1980, title VII, PL 96–294, 94 stat. 770, 42 USC 8901–8905; Radon Gas and Indoor Air Quality Research Act 1986, title IV, PL 99–499, 100 stat. 1758; Alternative Motor Fuels Act 1988, PL 100–494, 102 stat. 2441, 42 USC 6374–6374d; Forest Ecosystems and Atmospheric Pollution Research Act 1988, PL 100–521, 102 stat. 2601, 16 USC 1642.

4 Global Climate Protection Act 1987, title XI, PL 100–204, 101 stat. 1407, 15 USC 2901; Indoor Radon Abatement, PL 100–551, 102 stat. 2755, 15 USC 2661–2671.

5 See Richard E. Cohen *Washington At Work: Back Rooms and Clean Air* (New York: Macmillan, 1992), pp.31–3, 36.

6 *Ibid.*, pp.26, 29–30, 38.

7 Mary Etta Cook and Roger H. Davidson 'Deferral Politics: Congressional Decision Making on Environmental Issues in the 1980s' in Helen M. Ingram and R. Kenneth Godwin (eds), *Public Policy and the Natural Environment* (New York: JAI Press, 1985), p.50.

8 US Senate, Committee on Environment and Public Works, Subcommittee on Environmental Pollution, *Hearing*, 'Executive Branch Review of Environmental Regulations', 96th Congress, 1st session, 26–27 February 1979.

9 US Senate, Committee on Environment and Public Works, Subcommittee on Environmental Pollution, *Hearing*, 'Enforcement of Environmental Regulations', 96th Congress, 1st session, 23–24 May 1979.

10 US Environmental Protection Agency *National Accomplishments in Pollution Control: 1970–1980* (Washington, DC: EPA, December 1980), p.82.

11 US Senate, Committee on Environment and Public Works, Subcommittee on Environmental Pollution, *Hearing*, 'Executive Branch Review of Environmental Regulation', 96th Congress, 1st session, 26–27 February 1979, p.20.

12 US House of Representatives, Committee on Science, Space and Technology, Subcommittee on Natural Resources and Environment, *Hearing*, 'EPA Diesel Particulate Standards', 96th Congress, 2nd session, 1–2 October 1980, pp.35–88.

13 US House of Representatives, Committee on Interstate and Foreign Commerce, Subcommittee on Oversight and Investigations, *Hearing*, 'Acid Rain', 96th Congress, 2nd session, 26–27 February 1980.

14 US Senate, Committee on Energy and Natural Resources, *Hearing*, 'Effects of Acid Rain', 96th Congress, 2nd session, 28 May 1980.

15 US House of Representatives, Committee on Energy and Commerce, Subcommittee on Health and Environment, *Hearing*, 'Acid Precipitation', 97th Congress, 1st session, 1–2 October 1981.

16 US Senate, Committee on Environment and Public Works, Subcommittee on Toxic Substances and Environmental Oversight', *Hearing*, 'Effect of Chloroflurocarbons on the Ozone Layer' 97th Congress, 1st session, 23 July 1981.

17 US House of Representatives, Committee on Small Business, Subcommittee on Antitrust and Restraint of Trade Activities Affecting Small Business, *Hearing*, 'EPA Proposed Rulemaking on Chloroflurocarbons

(CFCs) and Its Impact on Small Business', 97th Congress, 1st session, 15 July 1981.

18 US House of Representatives, Committee on Energy and Commerce, Subcommittee on Health and Environment, *Hearing*, 'Clean Air Act. Part 1', 97th Congress, 1st session, 22, 28 October, 5, 10 November 1981.

19 US Senate, Committee on Commerce, Science and Transportation, Subcommittee on the Consumer, *Hearing*, 'Cost of Government Regulations to Consumer', 95th Congress, 2nd session, 21–22 November 1978.

20 See Congressional Quarterly (CQ) *Almanac 1981*, p.505.

21 See US House of Representatives, Committee on Energy and Commerce, Subcommittee on Health and Environment, *Hearing*, 'Health Standards for Air Pollutants', 97th Congress, 1st session, 14–15 October 1981.

22 US House of Representatives, Committee on Interstate and Foreign Commerce, Subcommittee on Oversight and Investigations, *Hearing*, 'Cost–Benefit Analysis: The Potential for Conflict of Interest', 96th Congress, 2nd session, 17 April, 17 June, 22 August, 29–30 September 1980.

23 US House of Representatives, Committee on Interstate and Foreign Commerce, Subcommittee on Health and Environment, *Hearing*, 'Oversight – Clean Air Act Amendments 1977', 96th Congress, 1st session, 30 July 30, 27–28 November 1979.

24 See CQ *Almanac 1981*, p.506.

25 US House of Representatives, Committee on Government Operations, Subcommittee on Government Activities and Transportation, *Hearing*, 'Administration's Proposals to Help the US Automobile Industry', 97th Congress, 1st session, 13–14 May 1981.

26 Corporate Average Fuel Economy (CAFE) figures were mandated by the Energy Policy and Conservation Act 1975.

27 See John S. Dryzek *Discursive Democracy* (Cambridge: Cambridge University Press, 1990), chapter 3.

28 Barry Commoner *The Closing Circle* (New York: Bantam, 1972), p.33.

29 See Cook and Davidson 'Deferral Politics', pp.50–2.

30 Acid Precipitation Act 1980, title VII, PL 96–294, 94 stat. 770, 42 USC 8901–8905, 8911, 8912.

31 The leadership role of Senator Stafford is examined in C. Lawrence Evans *Leadership in Committees* (Ann Arbor, MI: Unversity of Michigan Press, 1991).

32 National Commission on Air Quality *To Breathe Clean Air* (Washington DC, Government Printing Office, 1981).

33 US Senate, Committee on Environment and Public Works, US House of

Representatives, Committee on Energy and Commerce, Subcommittee on Health and Environment, *Hearing*, 'Report of the National Commission on Air Quality and the National Academy of Science', 97th Congress, 1st session, 2 March 1981.

34 See Robert A. Shanley *Presidential Influence and Environmental Policy* (Westport, CN: Greenwood Press, 1992), especially chapter 5.

35 See Richard J. Tobin 'Revising the Clean Air Act: Legislative Failure and Administrative Success' in Norman J. Vig and Michael E. Kraft (eds), *Environmental Policy in the 1980s* (Washington, DC: Congressional Quarterly Press, 1984), p.232.

36 See *New York Times* 6 April 1981, p.A11.

37 Kent R. Portney *Controversial Issues in Environmental Policy* (Newbury Park, CA: Sage, 1992), p.73.

38 US House of Representatives, Committee on Energy and Commerce, Subcommittee on Health and Environment, *Hearings*, 'Clean Air Act (Part 1)' 97th Congress. 1st session, 22, 28 October, 5, 10 November 1981; US House of Representatives, Committee on Energy and Commerce, Subcommittee on Health and Environment, *Hearings*, 'Mobile Source Provisions', 97th Congress, 1st and 2nd sessions, 21–23 September, 7 December 1981, 21 January 1982.

39 HR 5252 (1981).

40 *New York Times* 23 December 1981, p.A18.

41 US House of Representatives, Committee on Energy and Commerce, Subcommittee on Health and Environment, *Hearing*, 'Clean Air Act (Part 3)', 97th Congress, 2nd session, 10, 17–18, 22–23 February 1982.

42 US Senate, Committee on Environment and Public Works, *Hearing*, 'Clean Air Oversight, Part 1', 97th Congress, 1st session, 8–9 April, 20 May, 2 June 1981; 'Clean Air Oversight, Part 2', 97th Congress, 1st session, 3–4 June 1981; 'Clean Air Oversight, Part 3', 97th Congress, 1st session, 5, 9, 11, 22 June 1981.

43 S 3041 (1982).

44 US Senate, Committee on Environment and Public Works, *Hearing*, 'Steel Industry Compliance Extension Act 1981', 97th Congress, 1st session, 3 March 1981; US House of Representatives, Committee on Energy and Commerce, Subcommittee on Health and Environment, *Hearing*, 'Health and the Environment Miscellaneous, Part 5', 97th Congress, 1st session, 25 March, 1, 19–20 May 1981.

45 Steel Industry Compliance Extension Act 1981, PL 97–23, 95 stat. 139, 42 USC 7401.

46 Ronald Reagan 'Remarks on Signing the Steel Industry Compliance Extension Act 1981', *Public Papers, 1981* 17 July 1981, p.632.

47 Department of Housing and Urban Development; Selected Independent Agencies; Appropriation Fiscal Year 1984. PL 98–45.

48 S 768 (1983).

49 US Senate, Committee on Environment and Public Works, *Hearing*, 'Clean Air Act Amendments 1983', 98th Congress, 1st session, 15, 17 November 1983; US Senate, Committee on Environment and Public Works, *Hearing*, 'Clean Air Act Amendments 1983, Part 2', 98th Congress, 2nd session, 24 February 1984.

50 US Senate, Committee on Energy and Natural Resources, *Hearing*, 'Implementation of the Acid Precipitation Act 1980', 98th Congress, 2nd session, 30 April 1984.

51 US House of Representatives, Committee on Energy and Commerce, Subcommittee on Health and Environment, *Hearing*, 'Clean Air Act Reauthorization (Part 1)', 98th Congress, 2nd session, 20 March 1984; US House of Representatives, Committee on Energy and Commerce, Subcommittee on Health and Environment, *Hearing*, 'Clean Air Act Reauthorization (Part 2)', 98th Congress, 2nd session, 23 March 1984; US House of Representatives, Committee on Energy and Commerce, Subcommittee on Health and Environment, *Hearing*, 'Clean Air Act Reauthorization (Part 3)', 98th Congress, 2nd session, 29, 30 March 1984.

52 HR 5314 (1983).

53 See Bryner, Gary C. *Blue Skies, Green Politics* (Washington, DC: Congressional Quarterly Press, 1993), p.91.

54 US House of Representatives, Committee on Interior and Insular Affairs, Subcommittee on General Oversight, Northwest Power, and Forest Management, *Hearing*, 'Effect of Atmospheric Pollution on Forest Ecosystems', 99th Congress, 1st and 2nd sessions, 16 July 1985, 6 December 1986; US House of Representatives, Committee on Agriculture, Subcommittee on Forests, Family Farms, and Energy, *Hearing*, 'Review the Effect of Acid Deposition and other Air Pollutants on Forest Productivity', 99th Congress, 2nd session, 13 May 1986.

55 HR 4567 (1986).

56 US House of Representatives, Committee on Energy and Commerce, Subcommittee on Health and Environment, *Hearing*, 'Acid Deposition Control Act 1986 (Part 1)', 99th Congress, 2nd session, 29–30 April 1986; US House of Representatives, Committee on Energy and Commerce, Subcommittee on Health and Environment, *Hearing*, 'Acid Deposition Control Act 1986 (Part 2)', 99th Congress, 2nd session, 1 May 1986; US House of Representatives, Committee on Energy and Commerce, Subcommittee on Health and Environment, *Hearing*, 'Acid Deposition Control Act 1986 (Part 3)', 99th Congress, 2nd session, 7 May 1986.

57 S 2203 (1986).

58 US Senate, Committee on Environment and Public Works, *Hearing*,

'New Clean Air Act', 99th Congress, 2nd session, 25–26, 30 September, 2 October 1986.

59 The radon issue is examined comprehensively in Leonard A. Cole *Element of Risk: The Politics of Radon* (New York: Oxford University Press, 1993).

60 HR 6289 (1982)

61 US House of Representatives, Committee on Science, Space, and Technology, Subcommittee on Energy Development and Application, *Hearing*, 'Indoor Air Quality Research', 98th Congress, 1st session, 2–3 August 1983.

62 Radon Gas and Indoor Air Quality Research Act 1986, Title IV, PL 99–499, 100 stat. 1758.

63 See Cole *Element orf Risk*, pp.96–9.

64 US Senate, Committee on Environment and Public Works, Subcommittee on Environmental Protection and Subcommittee on Superfund and Environmental Oversight, *Hearing* 'Radon Gas Issues', 100th Congress, 1st session, 2 April 1987. The bill introduced by Chafee was S 743 (1987).

65 S 744 (1987).

66 US House of Representatives, Committee on Energy and Commerce, Subcommittee on Transportation, Tourism, and Hazardous Materials, *Hearing*, 'Radon Pollution Control Act 1987', 100th Congress, 1st session, 23 April 1987. The reported bill was HR 2837 (1987).

67 US Senate, Committee on Environment and Public Works, Subcommittee on Superfund and Environmental Oversight, *Hearing*, 'Radon Contamination: How Federal Agencies Deal With It', 100th Congress, 2nd session, 18 May 1988.

68 Indoor Radon Abatement Act (PL 100–521, 102 stat. 2755, 15 USC 2661–2671).

69 Cole *Element of Risk*, p.14.

70 Cohen *Washington at Work*, p.37.

71 US Senate, Committee on Environment and Public Works, Subcommittee on Environmental Protection, *Hearing*, 'Health Effects of Acid Rain Precursors', 100th Congress, 1st session, 3 February 1987.

72 US Senate, Committee on Environment and Public Works, Subcommittee on Environmental Protection, *Hearing*, 'Acid Rain and Non-attainment Issues', 100th Congress, 1st session, 22 April 1987.

73 US House of Representatives, Committee on Energy and Commerce, Subcommittee on Health and the Environment, *Hearing*, 'Acid Deposition Control Act 1987', 100th Congress, 1st session, 9–10 July 1987.

74 US House of Representatives, Committee on Energy and Commerce, Subcommittee on Health and the Environment, *Hearing*, 'Ozone Layer Depletion', 100th Congress, 1st session, 9 March 1987; US Senate, Committee on Environment and Public Works, Subcommittee on Envi-

ronmental Protection and Subcommittee on Hazardous Wastes and Toxic Substances, *Hearing*, 'Stratospheric Ozone Depletion and Chlorofluorocarbons', 100th Congress, 1st session, 12–14 May 1987.

75 US House of Representatives, Committee on Science, Space and Technology, Subcommittee on Natural Resources, Agricultural Research, and Environment, *Hearing*, 'Stratospheric Ozone Depletion', 100th Congress, 1st session, 10, 12 March 1987; US House of Representatives, Committee on Foreign Affairs, Subcommittee on Human Rights and International Organizations, *Hearing*, 'US Participation in International Negotiations on Ozone Protocol', 100th Congress, 1st session, 5 March 1987.

76 US House of Representatives, Committee on Energy and Commerce, Subcommittee on Health and the Environment, *Hearing*, 'Clean Air Standards', 100th Congress, 1st session, 19 February 1987; US Senate, Committee on Environment and Public Works, Subcommittee on Environmental Protection, *Hearing*, 'Ozone and Carbon Monoxide Standards: Nonattainment Issues', 100th Congress, 1st session, 26, 31 March, 9 April 1987; US Senate, Committee on Environment and Public Works, Subcommittee on Environmental Protection, *Hearing*, 'Environmental Protection Agency: Post-1987 Ozone and Carbon Monoxide Attainment Strategies', 100th Congress, 1st session, 2 December 1987. See also US House of Representatives, Committee on Energy and Commerce, Subcommittee on Oversight and Investigation, *Hearing*, 'EPA: Ozone and the Clean Air Act' 100th Congress, 1st session, 27 April 1987.

77 US Senate, Committee on Environment and Public Works, Subcommittee on Environmental Protection, *Hearing*, 'Clean Air Act Amendments 1987', 100th Congress, 1st session, 16–17 June 1987; US Senate, Committee on Environment and Public Works, Subcommittee on Environmental Protection, *Hearing*, 'Clean Air Act Amendments 1987, Part 2', 100th Congress, 1st session, 19 June, 22–23 July 1987.

78 S 1894 (1987).

79 Senator Alan K. Simpson (R. WY) and Senator Steve Symms (R. ID) threatened to filibuster any measure that contained federal subsidies for high-sulphur coal.

80 HR 3054 (1987); HR 2666 (1987).

81 US House of Representatives, Committee on Energy and Commerce, Subcommittee on Health and the Environment, *Hearing*, 'Ozone and Carbon Monoxide Problems', 100th Congress, 1st session, 3 August 1987; US House of Representatives, Committee on Energy and Commerce, Subcommittee on Health and the Environment, *Hearing*, 'Acid Deposition Act 1987', 100th Congress, 1st session, 9, 10 July 1987.

82 US House of Representatives, Committee on Energy and Commerce,

Subcommittee on Oversight and Investigation, *Hearing*, 'US/Canadian Air Quality Efforts' 100th Congress, 1st session, 2 October 1987.

83 See John Kingdon *Agendas, Alternatives, and Public Policy* (Boston: Little, Brown, 1984).

84 See Robert Cameron Mitchell 'Public Opinion and the Green Lobby: Poised for the 1990s?' in Norman J. Vig and Michael E. Kraft (eds), *Environmental Policy in the 1990s* (Washington, DC: Congressional Quarterly Press, 1990), pp.85–6.

85 Helen M. Ingram, David H. Colnic and Dean E. Mann 'Interest Groups and Environmental Policy' in James P. Lester (ed.), *Environmental Politics and Policy* 2nd edition (Durham, NC: Duke University Press, 1995), p.122; Robert Cameron Mitchell 'From Conservation to Environmental Movement: The Development of Modern Environmental Lobbies' in Michael J. Lacey (ed.), *Government and Environmental Politics* (Washington, DC: Woodrow Wilson Center Press, 1991), p.99.

86 See Mitchell 'Public Opinion and the Green Lobby', pp.85–6.

87 Ingram, Colnic and Mann 'Interest Groups and Environmental Policy', p.123.

88 US Senate, Committee on Commerce, Science and Transportation, Subcommittee on Science, Technology and Space, *Hearing*, 'Arctic and Antarctic Ozone Depletion', 101st Congress, 1st session, 23 February 1989; US Senate, Committee on Foreign Relations, *Hearing*, 'International Environmental Agenda for the 101st Congress', 101st Congress, 1st session, 20 April 1989; US House of Representatives, Committee on Energy and Commerce, Subcommittee on Oversight and Investigations, *Hearing*, 'Ozone Layer Depletion', 101st Congress, 1st session, 15 May 1989; US House of Representatives, Committee on Foreign Affairs, Subcommittee on Human Rights and International Organizations', *Hearing*, 'Update on Recent International Environmental Meetings', 101st Congress, 1st session, 6 April 1989.

89 US Senate, Committee on Energy and Natural Resources, Subcommittee on Energy Regulation and Conservation, *Hearing*, 'Automobile Fuel Efficiency Standards', 101st Congress, 1st session, 4 April 1989; US Senate, Committee on Energy and Natural Resources, Subcommittee on Mineral Resources Development and Products, *Hearing*, 'Availability, Production and Distribution of Clean-Burning Fuels', 101st Congress, 1st session, 25 May 1989; US House of Representatives, Committee on Public Works and Transportation, Subcommittee on Investigations and Oversight, *Hearing*, 'Impact of Air Quality Regulation on Federal Highway and Transit Programs, and on Fuel Tax Collections', 101st Congress, 1st session, 9 November 1989; US House of Representatives, Committee on Energy and Commerce, *Hearing*, 'Air Pollution and Alternative Fuels', 101st Congress, 11 January 1989.

90 US Senate, Committee on Environment and Public Works, Subcommittee on Environmental Protection, *Hearing*, 'Proposals to Control the Manufacture, Use and Disposal of Ozone-Depleting Substances', 101st Congress, 1st session, 19 May 1989; US Senate, Committee on Commerce, Science and Transportation, Subcommittee on the Consumer, *Hearing*, 'Consumer Ozone Protection Act 1989', 101st Congress, 1st session, 19 October 1989.

91 US House of Representatives, Subcommittee on Health and the Environment, *Hearing*, 'Acid Rain Control', 101st Congress, 1st session, 6 April 1989.

92 US House of Representatives, Committee on Energy and Commerce, Subcommittee on Health and the Environment, *Hearing*, 'Clean Air Act Amendments (Part 1)', 101st Congress, 1st session, 23 May 1989; US House of Representatives, Committee on Energy and Commerce, Subcommittee on Health and the Environment, *Hearing*, 'Clean Air Act Amendments (Part 2)', 101st Congress, 1st session, 24 May 1989; US House of Representatives, Committee on Energy and Commerce, Subcommittee on Health and the Environment, *Hearing*, 'Clean Air Act Amendments (Part 3)', 101st Congress, 1st session, 22 June, 24 July 1989.

93 Cohen *Washington at Work*, p.73.

94 *Ibid.*, p.79.

95 See Norman J. Vig 'Presidential Leadership: From the Reagan to the Bush Administration' in Norman J. Vig and Michael E. Kraft (eds), *Environmental Policy in the 1990s* (Washington, DC: Congressional Quarterly Press, 1990), p.46.

96 See *New York Times* 1 September 1988, p.A1.

97 *Ibid.*, p.47.

98 George Bush 'Remarks at the Swearing-in Ceremony for William K. Reilly as Administrator of the Environmental Protection Agency', *Public Papers, 1989* 8 February 1989, p.68.

99 See Cohen *Washington at Work*, p.50.

100 George Bush 'Address on Administration Goals before a Joint Session of Congress', *Public Papers, 1989* 9 February 1989, p.77.

101 George Bush 'Remarks Announcing Legislation To Amend the Clean Air Act', *Public Papers, 1989* 12 June 1989, pp.706–8.

102 See Mark Dowie *Losing Ground* (Cambridge, MA: MIT Press, 1995), p.107.

103 Robert N. Stavins (ed.) *Project 88: Harnessing Market Forces to Protect Our Environment – Initiatives for the New President*. A Public Policy Study sponsored by Senator Timothy E. Wirth and Senator John Heinz (Washington, DC: December 1988).

104 S 1490 (1989); HR 3030 (1989).

105 See Cohen *Washington at Work*, p.61.
106 US House of Representatives, Subcommittee on Health and the Environment, *Hearing*, 'Clean Air Act Amendments (Part 3)',101st Congress, 1st session, 22 June, 24 July 1989.
107 US Senate, Committee on Environment and Public Works, Subcommittee on Environmental Protection, *Hearing*, 'Clean Air Act Amendments 1989, Part 1', 101st Congress, 1st session, 21 September 1989; US Senate, Committee on Environment and Public Works, Subcommittee on Environmental Protection, *Hearing*, 'Clean Air Act Amendments 1989, Part 2', 101st Congress, 1st session, 26 September 1989; US Senate, Committee on Environment and Public Works, Subcommittee on Environmental Protection, *Hearing*, 'Clean Air Act Amendments 1989, Part 3', 101st Congress, 1st session, 27 September 1989; US Senate, Committee on Environment and Public Works, Subcommittee on Environmental Protection, *Hearing*, 'Clean Air Act Amendments 1989, Part 4', 101st Congress, 1st session, 28 September 1989; US Senate, Committee on Environment and Public Works, Subcommittee on Environmental Protection, *Hearing*, 'Clean Air Act Amendments 1989, Part 5', 101st Congress, 1st session, 3–4, 9 October 1989.
108 S 816 (1989) dealt with air toxics; S 1630 (1989) dealt with smog; the acid rain measure was unnumbered.
109 The omnibus clean air package was designated as S 1630 (1989).
110 Bryner, *Blue Skies, Green Politics*, p.100.
111 See *New York Times* 20 January 1990, p.A26.
112 This example figures prominently in many discussions of new legislative procedures. See Barbara Sinclair *Unorthodox Lawmaking* (Washington, DC: Congressional Quarterly Press, 1997).
113 George Bush 'Remarks Following a Tour of the Potomac Electric Power Company Generating Station at Chalk Point, Maryland', *Public Papers, 1990* 14 March 1990, p.365.
114 See *New York Times* 30 March 1990, p.A11.
115 US House of Representatives, Committee on Energy and Commerce, Subcommittee on Energy and Power, *Hearing*, 'Clean Air Act Reauthorization (Part 1)', 101st Congress, 1st session, 7 September 1989; US House of Representatives, Committee on Energy and Commerce, Subcommittee on Energy and Power, *Hearing*, 'Clean Air Act Reauthorization (Part 2)', 101st Congress, 1st session, 12 September, 4, 11 October 1989; US House of Representatives, Committee on Energy and Commerce, Subcommittee on Energy and Power, *Hearing*, 'Clean Air Act Reauthorization (Part 3)', 101st Congress, 1st session, 18–19 October 1989.
116 George Bush 'Remarks on Signing the Bill Amending the Clean Air Act', *Public Papers, 1990* 15 November 1990, p.1601.

117 The Clean Air Act Amendments 1990, PL 101–549, 104 stat. 2399 42 USC 7401–671q.
118 See Marc K. Landy, Marc J. Roberts and Stephen R. Thomas *The Environmental Protection Agency* expanded edition (New York: Oxford University Press, 1994), pp.288–91.

8
From policy fatigue to policy reaction, 1990–96

The intensity of congressional interest in air pollution control during the first four years of the 1990s was notably lower than in the last years of the previous decade. Although the number of bill introductions and committee hearings remained high, the purpose of almost all of this activity was to engineer marginal adjustments in policy. Debates were low key, no major reform of the law was advocated, and congressional attention turned to other issues. The only changes to policy came in provisions of the National Energy Security Act 1992 which dealt with clean fuels and clean automobiles.[1] The Republican takeover of Congress following the mid-term elections of 1994, however, changed this pattern of interest. Bill introductions rose as Republicans sought to weaken the regulatory structures that controlled air pollution in the United States. No laws amending the Clean Air Act were passed, but a number of riders were attached to appropriation bills which weakened the Environmental Protection Agency's (EPA's) ability to enforce the law.[2]

The muted interest in air pollution control evident in Congress during the early years of the decade was a natural consequence of passage of the Clean Air Act Amendments of 1990. Although criticisms of the 1990 Amendments were soon aired by both environmentalists and industry groups, a general weariness with the issue meant that most members were unwilling to revisit old battles at a time when the Gulf War and health care were increasing in public saliency. Even efforts to promote marginal reform came to nothing in this period of policy fatigue. Legislative entrepeneurs such as Senator Max Baucus (D. MT), who became Chairman of the Senate's Environment and Public Works Committee in the 103rd Congress, Senator Joseph Lieberman (D. CT), who became Chairman of a reorganized Subcommittee on Clean Air and Nuclear Regulation, and Rep. Henry Waxman (D. CA), the long-time Chairman of House Energy's Subcommittee on Health and the Environment, found it impossible to mobilize support behind new air pollution control initiatives. The only policy change came when new energy legislation containing a few provisions pertinent to air pollution control was enacted in the aftermath of the Gulf War.

Republican victories in the 1994 elections ended this period of policy fatigue in dramatic fashion. Anxious to act upon campaign promises to reduce the size of the federal government, the new Republican majorities in the House and the Senate launched a number of deregulation intiatives that threatened to weaken the air pollution control regime. Not only did Republicans attempt to reform the general regulatory process by making it more difficult for federal agencies to promulgate new regulations and giving industry greater protection against government action, but specific efforts to reform the Clean Air Act threatened to weaken key provisions of the law. Despite the fact that control of many of the key policy-making venues on air pollution had passed to proponents of regulatory reform, evidence of continued public commitment to environmental protection made it difficult to mobilize support for frontal attacks on the Clean Air Act. Efforts to weaken the law through the backdoor of the appropriations process were a result of this resistance to direct regulatory reform. Divisions between the House and the Senate, however, limited even the sucess of this strategy.

The period of policy reaction ushered in by Speaker Gingrich and colleagues may have changed the context in which the discussion of air pollution control took place, but the 'unbounded' and multidimensional nature of the issue made it difficult to engineer change. Continued high transaction costs produced a familiar picture of gridlock and marginal change.

Policy fatique

The fatique surrounding Clean Air in the early 1990s was shown more in the purpose of air pollution control bills introduced in the 102nd Congress (1991–92) and the 103rd Congress (1993–94) than in their number. Bill introductions continued at a level that was consistent with the late 1980s. The number of air pollution control bills introduced in the House rose from fifty-five in the 102nd Con-

gress to eighty-six in the 103rd Congress while the number introduced in the Senate fell from fifty-five to forty-five over the same
period. The basic pattern of subjects addressed by these bills was
similar in both chambers. Although the Gulf War forced a reconsideration of policy towards clean cars and clean fuels, and public concern about global climate change prompted some action on
international environmental issues, the problem of indoor air pollution consumed most attention during the early 1990s. This pattern began to change in the 103rd Congress as oversight hearings
began to provide evidence about the successes and failures of the
1990 law. The context in which that evidence would be evaluated
changed dramatically when the Republicans gained control of Congress following the 1994 elections. A period of policy reaction soon
replaced the policy fatigue of the early years of the decade.

Cleaning the great American indoors
Efforts to address the problem of indoor air pollution were boosted
in the 102nd Congress by the publication of reports that such pollution caused more than 14,000 deaths from cancer each year, and
cost the nation more than $4 billion in lost productivity.[3] Legislation
introduced by Senator Mitchell to create an office within the EPA
which would co-ordinate national efforts to control indoor air pollution was reported out of Senate Environment and Public Works
on 1 August 1991.[4] The measure passed the Senate on a 88–7 vote
on 6 November 1991 despite opposition from the Bush Administration. Companion legislation introduced in the House by Rep.
Joseph P. Kennedy (D. MA) failed to reach the floor in the 102nd
Congress because of jurisdictional disputes between three committees.[5] Separate hearings on the bill were conducted by the Environment Subcommittee of House Science, Space and Technology, the
Subcommittee on Health and Safety of House Education and Labor,
and the Subcommittee on Health and Environment of House
Energy and Commerce.[6] The bill was reported out of House Science
on 1 August 1991, but no further action was taken by the other
committees. Contested science and economic concerns meant that
no consensus could be reached on how best to proceed.

Senator Mitchell and Rep. Kennedy introduced further legislation in the 103rd Congress to address the problem of indoor air pollution.[7] Mitchell was able to use his institutional authority to ensure
that his bill progressed rapidly. Hearings on Mitchell's bill were

conducted by the Subcommittee on Clean Air and Nuclear Regulation, chaired by Senator Lieberman, in May 1993.[8] Senate Environment and Public Works reported the bill at the end of July and it
passed the Senate by voice vote on 29 October 1993. The bill
required the EPA to draw up a list of indoor air contaminants and
to issue health advisories for those pollutants. Progress in the House
was less certain as Rep. Kennedy lacked the parliamentary authority possessed by Senator Mitchell. The Health and Environment
Subcommittee conducted hearings on Kennedy's bill in November
1993, but it was not until Rep. Waxman drafted a compromise version of the legislation in August 1994 that weakened many of its
provisions that Republicans on the Subcommittee could be persuaded to report the bill.[9] The House passed the bill by voice vote
on 3 October 1994, but insufficient time was available for the
Senate to consider the House's version of the bill.

The need to reauthorize the Indoor Radon Abatement Act of
1988 prompted the introduction of six bills in the Senate and five in
the House in the 102nd Congress which focused on this particular
form of indoor air pollution. Policy leadership on the issue was provided by Senator Lautenberg who authored a bill which expanded
the scope of the 1988 law to include certification of contractors
who tested for radon, mandated regular radon checks in schools,
required radon testing in federally owned housing, extended financial support for state radon abatement programmes and established
a presidential commision to educate the public about the dangers
from radon.[10] The legislation passed the Senate on 10 March 1992
on a 82–6 vote. Companion legislation was introduced in the House
by Rep. Edward J. Markey (D. MA) and was reported out of House
Energy and Commerce on 17 September 1992. Although the House
approved the bill on 29 September 1992, insufficient time to reconcile differences in the language of the House and Senate versions
meant that the legislation did not reach President Bush's desk.

Further efforts to enact radon legislation in the 103rd Congress
were similarly frustrated by bicameral politics. Legislation introduced by Rep. Markey in 1993 which required real estate agents
and house sellers to inform prospective buyers of the risk of radon
in a house was reported by House Energy and Commerce in May
1994, and cleared the House on a 255–164 vote on 28 July 1994.[11]
The Senate failed to act upon the bill, however, and it died at the
end of the session. Legislation introduced by Senator Lautenberg to

reauthorize the Indoor Radon Abatement Act of 1988 was reported by the Senate Environment and Public Works Committee, but the measure did not come to a vote on the Senate floor.[12]

Part of the problem facing those who wished to expand the federal government's role in controlling indoor air pollution was the wide 'scope of conflict' associated with the issue. Efforts to address the problem of indoor air pollution brought legislators into conflict with a variety of different interests. Allegations that carpets were a source of indoor air pollution, for example, generated opposition from the carpet industry.[13] Moves by Rep. Waxman to address the problem of environmental tobacco smoke created even more powerful opposition to efforts to control indoor air pollution. The fact that much indoor air pollution occurred in private property also made it difficult to mobilize a majority in favour of legislation. Opponents were easily able to categorize efforts to expand the role of the federal government as an attack on private property. The information and transaction costs associated with the issue, in other words, were too high to be overcome. No legislative entrepeneur had the means to resolve the problems caused by disputed science, high levels of conflict, and perceptions of an attack on private property.

Discontent about the Clean Air Act Amendments 1990
The major controversies that had surrounded air pollution control in Congress in the 1980s subsided following enactment of the Clean Air Act Amendments 1990 as few members had the energy to reopen old arguments so soon after the battles of the period of policy struggle. Bills to amend the 1990 law were few and far between in the 102nd Congress. Marginal changes in the regulatory regime that had been established in the previous Congress were sought in seven of the air pollution control bills introduced in the House and nine of those introduced in the Senate. Bills were introduced, for example, to prohibit the burning of hazardous wastes in cement kilns, to improve the reporting of compliance with clean air deadlines and to establish standards for clean-fuel vehicle refuelling facilities. Proposals from Rep. Jim Cooper (D. TN), Senator Lieberman and Senator Gore to establish a tradeable permit system for carbon dioxide were the most radical changes suggested. No action occurred on any of these bills. The only amendment to the Clean Air Act that passed in the 102nd Congress was a 'house-keeping'

resolution introduced by Senator Mitchell to remove one substance from the list of hazardous air pollutants contained in the 1990 law.[14]

Clean air issues received most attention in the 102nd Congress during consideration of energy legislation. Concern that the Iraqi invasion of Kuwait in August 1990 would lead to an energy crisis comparable to that of the mid-1970s prompted the introduction of a number of energy bills with implications for the control of air pollution. Bills were introduced to impose a carbon tax, promote the use of alternative fuels, sponsor the production of clean automobiles and conduct research into clean coal technologies. Although no legislative action was taken on any of these measures, some of the provisions contained in these bills were incorporated in an omnibus energy bill that finally passed Congress on 8 October 1992. The Energy Policy Act of 1992 contained provisions which required federal and state governments to begin purchasing alternative fuel vehicles, mandated a study into methods of reducing emissions of 'greenhouse' gases, increased taxes on some ozone-depleting chemicals, and capped existing benefits for employer-provided car parking.[15] Efforts to mandate stricter Corporate Average Fuel Economy (CAFE) standards were rejected during mark-up by the Senate Energy and Natural Resources Committee much to the chagrin of environmentalists who argued that fuel-efficient cars were the best way to cut America's dependency on foreign oil.

The provisions on 'greenhouse' gases and ozone-depleting chemicals in the Energy Policy Act 1992 were a response to growing concern about global climate change in the early 1990s. Public alarm at reports of global warming and the destruction of the stratospheric ozone layer prompted a burst of legislative activity in the 102nd Congress. Oversight hearings on global climate change were conducted by no less than four different committees in the Senate.[16] Bills were introduced both to hasten the phase-out of chlorofluorocarbons (CFCs) and limit emissions of carbon dioxide. Agitation for action on these bills stopped when the Senate adopted an amendment to the Energy Policy Act offered by Senator Al Gore (D. TN) which accelerated the phase-out of CFCs required under the Clean Air Act Amendments 1990. Growing appreciation of the wider international dimension to air pollution issues was further reflected in the introduction of two bills which sought to increase overseas environmental aid and make the General Agreement on Trade and Tariffs (GATT) compatible with environmental laws. Both bills made substantial progress but were not enacted. The bill to increase overseas environmental aid, introduced by Rep. Dante B. Fascell (D. FL), passed both chambers but died when the House rejected the conference report.[17] The bill to bring GATT into line with environmental laws, introduced by Rep. Waxman, passed the House but died when the Senate took no action.[18]

Clean air issues began to command greater attention in the 103rd Congress as evidence of discontent with the Clean Air Act Amendments 1990 started to emerge. Seventeen bills to amend the law were introduced in the House as members began to respond to complaints from constituents and industry about the costs of compliance. 'If you think our constituents are upset about free congressional carparking lots, wait until they hear they may not be allowed to drive their own cars to work', Rep. Donald Manzullo (R. IL) told the House, after criticizing provisions in the 1990 law which required certain businesses to establish compulsory car pools.[19] Hearings conducted by House Small Business's Subcommittee on Development of Rural Enterprises, Exports, and the Environment into employee commute options found considerable opposition to such provisions among managers and workers alike.[20] Employee commute options were supported by environmentalists and health care workers.

Although the purpose of most of the bills introduced in the 103rd Congress was to secure increased flexibility in the implementation of the law, Rep. Thomas D. DeLay (R. TX) introduced seven bills to repeal either individual titles of the 1990 law or the law as a whole. Three bills to extend compliance deadlines or grant waivers were introduced in the Senate. No action was taken on any of these bills, however, as advocates of strong action to combat air pollution remained in control of the prime policy-making venues in both the House and the Senate. Not only was Rep. Waxman still the Chairman of the House Subcommittee on Health and the Environment, but Senator Burdick's death in September 1992, and Senator Daniel P. Moynihan's (D. NY) decision several months later to assume the Chairmanship of the Finance Committee rather than Environment and Public Works, had allowed proponents of a rigorous approach to air pollution control to consolidate their institutional power in the Senate. Senator Baucus, the author of the 1990 law, became Chairman of the Environment and Public Works Committee, and Senator Lieberman, who had established a strong pro-environment record, became Chairman of a reorganized Subcommittee on Clean Air and Nuclear Regulation.

Discontent with aspects of the Clean Air Act was investigated in oversight hearings into the effectiveness of the law. In the early 1990s oversight hearings conducted by the House Subcommittee on Health and the Environment had focused primarily on White House interference in the implementation of the 1990 law. Particular complaints were aired about the activities of Vice-President Quayle's Council on Competitiveness.[21] A more widespread investigation of the effectiveness of the law was initiated in the 103rd Congress, however, by Senators Baucus and Lieberman. Hearings conducted by the Subcommittee on Clean Air and Nuclear Regulation in the spring of 1993 revealed mixed results and prompted Baucus to investigate matters further.[22] Announcing plans for a thorough investigation of the law, Baucus told the Senate in August 1993 that: 'it is time to get to the bottom of what is working and what is broken in the process of implementing the Clean Air Act amendments, and figure out how to fix that break'.[23] Extensive hearings on the implementation of the law were conducted by both the Environment and Public Works Committee and Lieberman's Subcommittee in the late summer of 1993.[24]

The findings of these hearings were summarized in a report released by Senators Baucus, Chafee and Lieberman in November 1993.[25] Senator Lieberman told the Senate that: 'The report raises serious questions about whether the law's promise to provide healthy air as expeditiously as practicable will be fulfilled'.[26] 'The principle problem areas', he continued, 'are in the timely adoption, review and approval of State Implementation Plans, the advancement of the low emission vehicle, and the abatement of air toxics'. The report gave the EPA 'Ds' for its work on SIPs and air toxics. Progress was deemed to be slow and indaequate. Not all was bad news, however. The report gave the EPA 'As' for both the Acid Rain Allowance Trading Program and the Stratospheric Ozone Protection Program. It claimed that emissions of sulphur dioxide were falling faster than expected and that the phaseout of CFCs was progressing smoothly. Overall, the report gave the EPA a B minus for its implementation of the 1990 law.

'After closely examining EPA's progress', Senator Baucus informed the Senate, 'we concluded that despite some progress, something is clearly wrong'.[27] Baucus conceded that inadequate resources might partially explain this poor performance and urged the Clinton administration to 'remember that most Americans still breathe dirty air the next time they sit down with the OMB bud-getmakers', but claimed that the 'EPA's bloated bureaucratic process' was the main culprit. Notably lacking in his diagnosis of the causes of the EPA's problems was any criticism of the law itself. Such reticence may have been understandable given Baucus's role in authoring the Clean Air Act Amendments 1990, but this was not something that would trouble most Republicans as they swept to power a year after the report was published. The new Republican majority, particularly in the House, viewed the law as the main problem.

Republican reaction

The Republican victory in the 1994 elections dramatically altered the context in which clean air issues were considered. Not only did the elections return a large number of Republicans to Congress who had little commitment to existing regulatory arrangements, but majority status also elevated some opponents of the Clean Air Act to positions of parliamentary power. The result was the introduc-tion of a flood of bills designed to undermine the air pollution con-trol regime that had been established over four decades. Republicans leaders also tried to use the appropriations process to disguise their attack on the Clean Air Act. Attempts were made to attach riders to appropriation bills which both reduced funds for implementing the law and 'micro-managed' the EPA's rule-making procedures. Evidence of strong public support for clean air, how-ever, forced the Republicans to retreat from overt attacks on envi-ronmental laws like the Clean Air Act in the 2nd session of the 104th Congress. Anxious not to be branded as anti-environment, Speaker Gingrich created a task force to redefine Republican atti-tudes towards the environment.

Rolling back the clock
The 104th Congress that assembled in January 1995 was markedly different from those that had gradually created a complex frame-work of air pollution control laws over the previous four decades. Not only was the new Republican majority less sympathetic to the arguments of environmental groups, but the switch in partisan con-

trol had allowed opponents of environmental protection to assume positions of parliamentary authority. In the House, Rep. DeLay became Majority Whip, Rep. Thomas Bliley (R. VA) replaced Rep. Dingell as Chairman of a reorganized House Commerce Committee and Rep. Michael Bilirakis (R. FL) replaced Rep. Waxman as Chairman of the Subcommittee on Health and Environment. DeLay was well known for his efforts to repeal the Clean Air Act, and Bliley and Bilirakis had League of Conservation Voters (LCV) scores approximately fifty points lower than Dingell and seventy points lower than Waxman. Changes in key personnel in the Senate were not as profound as in the House. Senator Chafee replaced Baucus as Chairman of the Senate Environment and Public Works Committee, and Senator McLauchlin Fairchild (R. NC) replaced Senator Lieberman as Chairman of a reorganized Subcommittee on Clean Air, Wetlands, Private Property and Nuclear Safety. Chafee and Baucus differed little in their support for environmental issues, but Fairchild had a LCV score over eighty points lower than Lieberman.

Republican control of Congress gave industry groups privileged access to policy-making venues. Political Action Committees (PACs) associated with two coalitions campaigning for weaker environmental standards, the Alliance for Reasonable Regulations and Project Relief, secured unprecedented access to committees as a reward for the millions of dollars that they had contributed to Republican 'war chests'.[28] Rep. Bliley was a particularly notable example of a member who received sizeable campaign contributions from PACs representing industries with clear interests in the deliberations of the Commerce Committee.[29] Industry lobbyists were often invited to draft legislation and on a few occasions were even given permission to sit with committee members in hearings.[30] A flood of bills to reduce the regulatory burden on industry was the result.

Republican disquiet with the Clean Air Act was reflected in the large number of bills to weaken the law that were introduced in the 104th Congress (1995–96). No fewer than thirty-two bills to extend deadlines, exempt particular industries, introduce greater flexibility, or repeal the law were introduced in the House. Majority Whip DeLay alone introduced eight bills to repeal either sections of the law or the law in its entirety. Only two bills were introduced in the House to strengthen the law. Bill introductions in the Senate were less numerous but covered similar ground. Twelve bills were introduced to amend the Clean Air Act. All proposed to weaken the law in one way or another, but none went as far as to recommend repeal. Senator Fairchild introduced a bill, for example, to weaken several sections of the Clean Air Act. The bill proposed to undermine the EPA's efforts to control hazardous air pollutants, allow states to opt out of the federal permit system which required all pollution sources to keep information about emission levels and compliance records in one document, and eliminate automobile emissions and mainentance programmes.

Little action took place on any of these bills as Contract With America legislation dominated the congressional agenda. Two amendments to the Clean Air Act were enacted but both were relatively minor. A bill introduced by Rep. Manzullo to prohibit the EPA from requiring a reduction in work-related trips in ozone nonattainment areas gained bipartisan support and was signed into law by President Clinton.[31] During a brief debate in the Senate on the measure, Senator Baucus expressed his support for what he described as 'a short, simple bill that seeks to maintain our clean air standards while giving States greater flexibility in how they achieve them'.[32] Senator Chafee told the Senate that the bill 'makes amendments to the Clean Air Act to fix a provision that has not worked'.[33] Both were adament that the bill did not undermine the Clean Air Act in any way as cities still had to meet established ozone standards. The other bill that was enacted prohibited the EPA from interfering with the synchronization of traffic lights to control the air pollution from automobiles.[34] Introduced by Rep Howard McKeon (R. CA) the bill encountered little opposition.

A more serious threat to the air pollution control regime established by the Clean Air Act than any of the bills introduced to amend the law came from the deregulation legislation promised in the Contract With America.[35] Rep. David Skaggs (D. CO) claimed that 'the Republican Contract on America is a public health accident waiting to happen', and counselled, 'those who are not already gagging on the Republicans' so-called Contract With America, hold your breath'.[36] In March 1995 the House passed a regulatory reform bill which would have required to EPA to conduct a cost-benefit analysis of any proposed regulations.[37] Language in the Clean Air Act which prohibited the EPA from taking costs into consideration when establshing National Ambient Air Quality Standards (NAAQS) would have been pre-empted under the proposed legislation. Action in the Senate was much slower than in the House.

Companion legislation was introduced by Majority Leader Dole and Senator Bennett Johnston (D. LA).[38] The bill required federal agencies to perform cost-benefit analysis for all major new regulations. Where a statute like the Clean Air Act prohibited the use of such criteria the agency had to show that a proposed rule imposed lower costs than any reasonable alteranative. Heated opposition meant that the Johnston–Dole Bill was filibustered on the floor, and Dole eventually withdraw the bill after three unsuccessful cloture attempts. Frustrated with this lack of progress, Republican leaders in the House attached their version of the bill to a debt limit extension bill. President Clinton vetoed the bill in November 1995. Clinton claimed that the bill would 'reverse a 30-year bi-partisan commitment to environmental protection and public health'.[39]

Other proposed regulatory reforms that would have weakened the Clean Air Act included bills which gave states and local governments more autonomy to formulate and implement policies, allowed regulated industries greater involvement in the rule-making process, established a moratorium on new regulations, and created 'correction days' when Congress could eliminate federal regulations. Many of these bills passed the House but encountered strong opposition in the Senate where the sway of party was less strong. An Unfunded Mandates law was enacted in March 1995 which made it more difficult for the federal government to impose new regulatory responsibilites on the states without appropriating adequate funds, but the new requirement did not apply to laws already on the statute book.

Republican leaders also sought to eviscorate environmental statutes like the Clean Air Act through the annual appropriations process. Budget cuts and riders which waived environmental standards were added to various appropriation bills in an effort to bypass the authorization process. Often hidden in lengthy appropriation bills, these budget cuts and riders had the advantage of being far less visible than traditional methods of engineering legislative change. In a speech on the House floor given in July 1995 Rep. Skaggs charged the Republican leadership were

> following the unfortunate example of James Watt, they are distorting the normal legislative process around here, acting against House rules by using the appropriations process to rewrite laws and reshape policy, so that they can achieve by stealth, objectives that lack real public support.[40]

Republican leaders simply shrugged off such attacks. Minority Whip DeLay stated: 'We are going to fund only those programs we want to fund. We're in charge. We don't have to negotiate with the Senate. We don't have to negotiate with the Democrats'.[41]

An early indication of the Republicans' intention to use the appropriations process to attack environmental programmes was given in a hearing on 'Downsizing Government' conducted by the House Appropriations Committee in January 1995.[42] Republicans listened appreciatively as David Gibbons, a former Office of Management and Budget (OMB) Deputy Associate Director, and Fred Smith, President of the Competitive Enterprise Institute, told the Committee that various EPA functions could be transfered to non-federal programmes. Counter views offered by Mary D. Nicholls, an Assistant Administrator of the EPA, Jim Strock, Secretary of the Californian EPA, and Ralp De Gennaro of Friends of the Earth, were largely ignored.

The fiscal 1996 appropriations bill reported by the House VA-HUD (Veterans Affairs – Housing and Urban Development) Appropriations Subcommittee on 10 July 1995 was the main vehicle for attacking environmental programmes.[43] Chaired by Rep. Jerry Lewis (R. CA) the panel approved a bill which not only proposed to reduce the EPA's budget by 33 percent, but also contained seventeen riders that restricted the EPA's authority to implement a variety of environmental laws. Rep. Louis Stokes (D. OH), the ranking minority member of the Subcommittee, criticised the bill but lacked the votes to do anything about the riders during full committee deliberations. The House Appropriations Committee approved the bill on 18 July 1995. An amendment offered by Stokes to strip the seventeen riders from the bill was adopted by the House on 28 July 1995 when moderate Republicans joined with Democrats to provide a 212–206 margin of victory. The House reversed itself three days later, however, when Republican leaders seized an opportunity to schedule a revote at a time when several pro-environment members were absent. The bill was then approved by a 228–193 vote the same day.

The Senate's version of the fiscal 1996 VA-HUD Appropriations Bill passed the chamber on 26 September 1995. Slightly less extreme than the House-passed bill, the bill nonetheless proposed to cut the EPA's budget by 22 percent and contained seven riders which reduced the EPA's authority. A compromise version worked out in conference committee proposed cuts of 25 percent in the EPA's budget and included eleven environmental riders. Four of these riders specifically limited the EPA's authority to enforce sections of the Clean Air Act 1990. The EPA was encouraged to exempt natural gas processors from the law's risk management requirements, was required to include site-specific calculations of risk in the regulation of hazardous emissions from cement kilns, was urged to delay implementation of the permit programme for one year, and prohibited from expanding the Toxic Release Inventory. President Clinton vetoed the final version of the bill on 18 December 1995. Clinton claimed that the bill 'would threaten public health and the environment'.[44]

Searching for a 'new environmentalism'

Republican efforts to undermine environmental laws diminished as opponents successfully mobilized public opinion against what was portrayed as an anti-environment agenda. Opinion polls conducted in 1995 revealed strong public support for existing environmental laws.[45] Particularly important was a poll conducted by Republican pollster Linda DiVall. DiVall found that while a majority of Americans believed that there was too much government regulation only 21 percent believed that there was too much environmental regulation. Perhaps most striking, she found that not even a majority of Republicans 'trust the GOP most on environmental matters'.

Democrats used such poll findings to put the Republicans on the defensive on environmental issues. In February 1996 Rep. Frank Pallone (D. NJ) argued that the Republican leadership had become aware

> that this was not a popular agenda, that destroying environmental laws and turning back the clock was not something the public was responding to in a favorable way. What we see now is an effort in some ways by the Republican leadership to suggest to their Members that perhaps they should go slow on this agenda.[46]

He referred to a memo written by Majority Whip DeLay in September 1995 which told Republicans to 'sponsor tree planting programs in their districts or participate in ongoing tree planting programs' to re-establish their environmental credentials. The attack was continued a month later by Rep. David E. Bonior (D. MI) who informed the House that 'Speaker Gingrich is advising his colleagues to do photo-ops at local zoos to counter the image that the Republicans are extremists on the environment'.[47]

Relentless Democratic attacks forced Speaker Gingrich to appoint a task force on the environment in March 1996 to redefine Republican positions. Co-chaired by moderate Rep. Sherwood Boehlert (R. NY) and conservative Rep. Richard W. Pombo (R. CA), the task force sought to bridge the ideological and regional differences that increasingly divided Republicans on environmental issues. While many easterners like Boehlert believed that the broad Republican attacks on environmental laws had been a mistake, many westerners and southerners articulated a strong defence of deregulation and support for private property rights. Finding common ground between these two positions was not easy and the task force simply published a general one-page 'vision statement and principles' on 15 May 1996 containing few specific proposals. The document called for policy to be developed which meshed conservative Republican philosophy with environmental protection, but gave little idea of how that would be achieved.

Recognizing the difficulties of developing a policy that would unite Republicans, Speaker Gingrich decided that the best tactic in an election year was to avoid initiatives that undermined environmental statutes. Attempts to use the appropriations process to reduce the effectiveness of the EPA were largely abandoned. The fiscal 1997 VA-HUD Appropriations Bill increased the budget of the EPA and contained no riders that limited the EPA's enforcement powers.[48] Stripped of such controversial provisions the bill enjoyed bipartisan support and was signed into law on 26 September 1996. Efforts to enact deregulation legislation were also put on hold. None of the bills that had stalled in the 1st session of the 104th Congress were resurrected for consideration as the Republican leadership toned down its rhetoric in advance of the 1996 elections.

Little effort was made to launch a new deregulation onslaught in the 1st session of 105th Congress (1997–98). A reduction in the size of the Republican majority in the House, the ethical problems of Speaker Gingrich and Republican in-fighting diminished the de-regulation impulse to a large extent. Direct attacks on environmental statutes faded in this post-election climate. Few bills were introduced to weaken the Clean Air Act as Republicans tried to present a more pro-environment face. In the first session of the 105th Congress only nine bills to weaken the law were introduced in the

House. For the first time since 1992 Majority Whip DeLay failed to introduce his plethora of bills to repeal the law. In the Senate, only four bills to amend the Clean Air Act were introduced. Two of these bills even sought to strengthen the law. No action was taken on any of these bills.

Prospects of renewed battles over the Clean Air Act were resurrected, however, when the EPA gave notice that it planned to issue more stringent NAAQS for ozone and particulates in June 1997. Familiar themes began to emerge as supporters and opponents of the new rules squared up in Congress. Supporters claimed that new standards were needed to take account of advances in scientific knowledge. Opponents disputed the science upon which the new standards were based and questioned the costs. As emotive commercials began to be aired on television the hope that Speaker Gingrich had entertained in 1996 of repositioning the Republicans on environmental issues seemed forlorn. Old divisions and arguments within the Republican Party began to re-emerge as congressional committees started to schedule hearings on the new NAAQS.

Conclusion

The fate of Republican efforts to undermine the Clean Air Act during the 104th Congress provides a good illustration of the limits of partisan initiatives on environmental issues. Strong public concern for the environment, contested science and rising marginal costs of control, have made air pollution control policy such a sensitive issue that a bipartisan consensus is needed to bring about change. The party government that Speaker Gingrich managed to create at the beginning of the 104th Congress was sufficient to force partisan reform efforts through the House, but lack of bipartisan support meant that they floundered either in the Senate or in the White House. It is instructive to note that both the air pollution control laws that were enacted in the 104th Congress enjoyed strong bipartisan support.

Failure to reform the Clean Air Act meant that legislators were faced with familiar problems as the 105th Congress assembled. On the one hand, pro-environment groups seized upon new scientific evidence to claim that tougher standards were needed to meet the law's requirement that NAAQS should protect human health without reference to costs. On the other hand, pro-industry groups argued that stricter standards would impose considerable costs upon business but bring only marginal benefits in health. With both sides able to count upon support in Congress, the politics surrounding air pollution control in the late 1990s had a similar cast to that of earlier decades.

Notes

1 The National Energy Security Act (1992).
2 Gary Bryner 'Reforming the Regulatory Process: Congress and the Next Generation of Environmental Laws'. Paper presented at the annual meeting of the Western Political Science Association, 1996.
3 US EPA *Environmental Investments: The Cost of a Clean Environment* (Washington, DC: EPA, 1990).
4 S 455 (1991).
5 HR 1066 (1991).
6 US House of Representatives, Committee on Energy and Commerce, Subcommittee on Health and the Environment, *Hearing*, 'Indoor Air Pollution', 102nd Congress, 1st session, 10 April 1991; US House of Representatives, Committee on Science, Space and Technology, Subcommittee on Environment, *Hearing*, 'The Indoor Air Quality Act of 1991', 102nd Congress, 1st session, 9 May 1991; US House of Representatives, Committee on Education and Labor, Subcommittee on Health and Safety, *Hearing*, 'Legislative *Hearings* on HR 1066, the Indoor Air Quality Act of 1991', 102nd Congress, 1st session, 26 June, 10, 17, 24, 31 July 1991.
7 S 656 (1993); HR 2919 (1993).
8 US Senate, Committee on Environment and Public Works, Subcommittee on Clean Air and Nuclear Regulation, *Hearing*, 'Pending Indoor Air Quality and Radon Abatement Legislation', 103rd Congress, 1st session, 23 May 1993.
9 US House of Representatives, Committee on Energy and Commerce, Subcommittee on Health and the Environment, *Hearing*, 'Indoor Air Pollution', 103rd Congress, 1st session, 1 November 1993.
10 S 792 (1991).
11 HR 2448 (1993).
12 S 657 (1993).
13 US Senate, Committee on Governmental Affairs, Ad-hoc Subcommittee on Consumer and Environmental Affairs' *Hearing*, 'New Research on the Potential Risks of Carpets', 102nd Congress, 2nd session, 1 October, 1992.
14 SJ Res 187 (1991) 'An Act to Designate the Week of October 13, 1991

through October 19, 1991, as "National Radon Action Week"', PL 102–128.

15 The Energy Policy Act of 1992, PL 102–486.

16 US Senate, Committee on Commerce, Science and Transportation, Sub-committee on Science, Technology and Space, *Hearing*, 'New Data on the Depletion of the Ozone Layer', 102nd Congress, 1st session, 16 April 1991; US Senate, Committee on Environment and Public Works, Subcommittee on Environmental Protection, *Hearing*, 'Preventing Ozone Depletion', 102nd Congress, 1st session, 11 June 1991; US Senate, Committee on Environment and Public Works, Subcommittee on Environmental Protection, *Hearing*, 'Global Climate Change and Stratospheric Ozone Depletion', 102nd Congress, 1st session, 30 July 1991; US Senate, Committee on Commerce, Science and Transportation, *Hearing*, 'Global Change Research: Ozone Depletion and Its Impact', 102nd Congress, 1st session, 15 November 1991; US Senate, Committee on Governmental Affairs, Ad-hoc Subcommittee on Consumer and Environmental Affairs, *Hearing*, 'Stratospheric Ozone Depletion', 102nd Congress, 1st session, 2nd session, 17 December 1991, 15 May 1992; US Senate, Committee on Energy and Natural Resources, *Hearing*, 'Global Climate Change', 102nd Congress, 2nd session, 6, 12 May 1992.

17 HR 2508 (1991).

18 H Con Res 241 (1991).

19 *Congressional Record*, June 16, 1994, p. H4556.

20 US House of Representatives, Committee on Small Business, Subcommittee on Development of Rural Enterprises, Exports, and the Environment, *Hearing* 'Environmental Benefits and Impact on Moderate-Sized Businesses of Employee Commute Options Required by the Clean Air Act Amendments of 1990', 103rd Congress, 2nd session, 6 September 1994.

21 US House of Representatives, Subcommittee on Health and the Environment, *Hearings*, 'Clean Air Act Implementation (Part 1)', 102nd Congress, 1st session, March 21, 1 May, 22 July 1991; US House of Representatives, Subcommittee on Health and the Environment, *Hearings*, 'Clean Air Act Implementation (Part 2)', 102nd Congress, 1st and 2nd sessions, 14 November, 10 December 1991, 7 February 1992.

22 US Senate, Committee on Environment and Public Works, Subcommittee on Clean Air and Nuclear Regulation, *Hearing*, 'Implementation of Section 507 of the Clean Air Act', 103rd Congress, 1st session, 10 March 1993; US Senate, Committee on Environment and Public Works, Subcommittee on Clean Air and Nuclear Regulation, *Hearing*, 'Status of Efforts to Develop a Clean Car', 103rd Congress, 1st session, 27 April 1993.

23 *Congressional Record* 2 August 1993, p. S10026.
24 US Senate, Committee on Environment and Public Works, Subcommittee on Clean Air and Nuclear Regulation, *Hearing*, 'State and Local Compliance with Title 1 of the Clean Air Act', 103rd Congress, 1st session, 3 August 1993; US Senate, Committee on Environment and Public Works, *Hearing*, 'Implementation of the Clean Air Act Amendments of 1990', 103rd Congress, 1st session, 23 September 1993.
25 Environment and Public Works Committee Leadership – Interim Report Card on EPA's Implementation of CAAA of 1990. Printed in *Congressional Record* 20 November 1993.
26 *Congressional Record* 16 November 1993, p. S15780.
27 *Congressional Record* 20 November 1993, p. S16845.
28 See *New York Times* 7 July 1996, VI p. 28.
29 *Wall Street Journal* 23 December 1994, p. A14.
30 *New York Times* 31 March 1995, p. A1.
31 HR 325 (1995) PL 104–70.
32 *Congressional Record* 13 December 1995, p. S18574.
33 *Ibid.*
34 HR 2988 (1995) PL 104–260.
35 See Gary Bryner 'Reforming the Regulatory Process'.
36 *Congressional Record*, 15 March 1995, p. H3160.
37 HR 9 (1995).
38 S 343 (1995).
39 William J. Clinton 'Remarks on Vetoing Temporary Public Debt Limit Increase Legislation and an Exchange With Reporters', *Public Papers, 1995* 13 November 1995, p. 1739.
40 *Congressional Record* 17 July 1995, p. H7016.
41 Quoted in *Wall Street Journal* 6 March 1995, p. A16.
42 US House of Representatives, Committee on Appropriations, *Hearing*, 'Downsizing Government and Setting Priorities of Federal Programs, Part 3', 104th Congress, 1st session, 11, 18–19, 24 January, 1–2, 9 February 1995.
43 HR 2099 (1995).
44 William J. Clinton 'Message to the House of Representatives Returning Without Approval the Departments of Veterans Affairs and Housing and Urban Development and Independent Agencies Appropriations Act, 1996' *Public Papers, 1995* 18 December 1995, p. 1901.
45 See Bryner 'Reforming the Regulatory Process', pp. 30–1.
46 *Congressional Record* 27 February 1996, p. H1290.
47 *Congressional Record* 27 March 1996, p. H2890.
48 HR 3666 (1996).

9

Congress and air pollution

Few Americans believe that Congress does a good job.[1] Books, essays and op-ed pieces in newspapers frequently denigrate congressional mores and performance.[2] Members often campaign by 'running against Congress'. Opinion polls consistently reveal that fewer than 20 per cent of Americans approve of the way that Congress goes about its business. Nearly 60 per cent of respondents in these polls believe that members of Congress are more interested in serving themselves than their constituents. The message that comes across is familiar and unambiguous. Americans believe that Congress is peopled by self-seeking politicians who are incapable of responding to their nation's myriad problems.[3]

The problem with this message is that it does not accord particularly well with congressional efforts to control air pollution. Since the 1950s Congress has initiated and enacted a framework of laws designed to control air pollution that stands favourable comparison with the efforts of most other countries.[4] Some of the laws may have taken years to produce, they may often posit unobtainable goals and they may employ a bewildering variety of regulatory means, but they undoubtedly address a national problem in a meaningful way. Americans would be breathing much dirtier air if the Clean Air Act did not exist. Whether sufficient incentives exist to do more, however, is a moot point. The air pollution problems that plague the United States at the end of the twentieth century seem particularly intractable. It may even be beyond the capacity of a single country, regardless of its economic power, to deal with global problems.

Congressional incapacity reconsidered

Critiques of congressional capacity have been well rehearsed and do not require detailed exposition. Two claims lie at the heart of most critiques. The first is that members of Congress are not concerned with the national interest. Extreme versions of this view tar all legislators with the brush of corruption. They suggest that senators and representatives are simply interested in personal gain. Less extreme versions tar all legislators with the brush of parochialism. Members are deemed to be incapable of seeing beyond the scope of their constituency and the next election. 'Two years and one Congressional District is the scope of [a representative's] horizon', David Stockman has argued.[5] The second criticism is that Congress lacks the institutional structures to process the complex information associated with problems in modern society. It is condemned as a creation of the horse age that has failed to come to terms with the rocket age.[6]

The problem for 'Congress bashers' is that the history of congressional efforts to control air pollution vitiates both of these claims. Since the 1950s a small group of legislators have devoted considerable resources to acquire policy expertise, fashion solutions and negotiate compromises. The high opportunity cost associated with such action suggests that a few legislators, at least, are motivated by a desire to address major national problems. Not all are simply 'position-takers'. Institutional venues have also evolved during this period to process the highly technical information needed to fashion laws. House Commerce's Subcommittee on Health and the Environment and Senate Environment and Public Work's Subcommittee on Clean Air, Wetlands, Private Property, and Nuclear Safety have become repositories of considerable policy expertise.

Legislative entrepreneurs have used this policy expertise to initiate and design air pollution control laws in a way that undermines the conventional wisdom that Congress relies upon and reacts to presidential initiative. The initiative to do something about air pollution has, with rare exceptions, come primarily from the legislative branch. This does not mean that presidents have not had an important role to play in the construction of the statutory framework that controls air pollution. Presidential engagement has been necessary to secure the enactment of every major air pollution control law of

the last four decades. But this role has been primarily that of a 'catalyst to pull together all the supporting forces in Congress', rather
than that of agenda-setter.[7] Presidents Nixon and Bush apart, few
presidents have displayed much interest in the issue of air pollution.

The shape of the air pollution control laws produced by Congress
has been determined by knowledge levels and political expediency.
On the one hand, legislators have responded to improved scientific
evidence and the feedback provided by policy learning to expand
the remit of the law and adjust regulatory means. Congress has
proved capable of reacting to new concerns and learning from past
mistakes. On the other hand, the choice of what and how to regulate has been tempered by political realities. Strong efforts have
been made to ensure that the costs of controlling air pollution do
not exceed what the American public have been willing to pay. Technological solutions have been chosen to deal with automobile
exhaust emissions, for example, rather than higher taxes on petrol
or controls on automobile usage.[8] Americans may want cleaner air
but not at the expense of their unwritten constitutional right to
drive a car.

The production of air pollution control laws has undoubtedly
become more difficult and time-consuming over time as the com-
plexities of the issue have become more apparent and its associated
scope of conflict has widened. Acquiring information and reconcil-
ing differences has become correspondingly harder as a result. The
struggle to produce the Clean Air Act Amendments of 1990, for
example, took the best part of a decade. Delays of such length have
led some observers to talk about 'environmental gridlock' or the
practice of 'deferral politics'.[9] The accusation is that environmental
degradation has continued while legislators have bickered and
obfuscated. Rapidly produced laws, however, are not necessarily
good laws. Although speed may be a virtue on the sports field, it is
not always a blessing in the legislative arena. Numerous examples
could be produced, from around the world, of laws passed in haste
and regretted at leisure. Legislators may be better advised to take
time and find a workable solution to a problem than choose an inap-
propriate or incomplete answer in the rush to do something.

The wonder, given conventional wisdom about the inadequacies
of Congress, is that laws have been produced at all. Critics would
suggest that the technical complexity of air pollution control issues
places it within the domain of technocrats rather than legislators.[10]

But Congress has produced Clean Air Acts that reveal a considerable grasp of pertinent information. Critics would also suggest that the regional and ideological cleavages that divide legislators create an insurmountable barrier on a multi-dimensional issue like air pollution. But compromises have been fashioned which have gained the support of overwhelming majorities in both the House of Representatives and the Senate. The laws that have resulted are clearly the product of politicians rather than scientists or economists. 'Our environmental laws illustrate that we are governed by legislatures, not by markets', Mark Sagoff has observed.[11] The air pollution control laws that have been produced by Congress may be overly ambitious, often inconsistent and lack a internal logic, but their legitimacy is widely accepted and they have brought results.

Future challenges

Congressional interest in controlling air pollution has broadened since the 1950s. The horizons of those seeking to clean the air have expanded from an initial concern about automobile pollution in the urban centres of southern California to cover a wide variety of pollution forms across the nation. In recent years concern has spread to global problems as scientists have provided growing evidence about climate change and stratospheric ozone depletion. Viewed as a local problem in the early 1950s, as a national problem in the late 1960s and early 1970s, air pollution has increasingly been viewed as an international problem.

Each stage of this broadening of interest has generated new challenges for those in Congress who are anxious to control air pollution. Legislative entrepreneurs have had to collect and interpret contested information, design new solutions when old ones have failed and persuade colleagues that action would bring both political and environmental benefits. All three tasks have become increasingly difficult as time has passed. Information has become more copious, complex and contentious. Solutions have become more difficult to devise as the unbounded and multi-dimensional nature of air pollution has become clear. And persuading colleagues of the need for new laws has become more difficult as the marginal costs of new regulations have often seemed to exceed the marginal benefits. Laws have become harder to produce as a result.

The challenges confronting legislators wishing to respond to the global problems of air pollution are even more formidable. First, Congress lacks the necessary tools to force multilateral or even bilateral action to tackle air pollution. Some impact can be made by using foreign aid or trade policy to promote environmental objectives, but neither method has proved particularly useful in achieving America's aims in other policy areas. Second, Congress lacks the incentive to take unilateral action. The American public has proved willing to pay a price for improved domestic air quality, but has not been willing to accept further emission controls when other countries continue to pollute the skies at will. Unless the public mood changes in a way which makes unilateral action palatable, the internationalization of air pollution control will inevitably enhance the role of the President at the expense of Congress. The President simply holds most of the cards in the foreign policy arena.

Conclusion

Congress has responded well to the problem of air pollution. It has adjusted to changes in public concern, been able to assimilate complex information, proved willing to employ innovative regulatory methods and actually made a difference to the quality of most people's lives. Whether it will be able to continue doing such things in the future is a matter of great debate. The intractable nature of contemporary air pollution and the acute international dimension of global climate change will create conditions that make legislative entrepreneurship unlikely. International organizations may well offer the best means to control air pollution in the future. The prime of Congress has probably passed.

Notes

1 See Christopher J. Bailey 'Congress and the Crisis of Legitimacy' in Philip John Davies and Fredric A. Waldstein (eds), *Political Issues in America Today* (Manchester: Manchester University Press, 1996).
2 Examples include Hendrick Smith *The Power Game* (London: Fontana, 1988); Philip M. Stern *The Best Congress Money Can Buy* (New York: Pantheon, 1988); Alan Ehrenhalt *The United States of Ambition* (New York: Times Books, 1991).
3 See John R. Hibbing and Elizabeth Theiss-Morse *Congress as Public Enemy* (Cambridge: Cambridge University Press, 1995).

4 See Susan Rose-Ackerman *Controlling Environmental Policy* (New Haven, CN: Yale University Press, 1995).

5 David Stockman *The Triumph of Politics* (London: Coronet, 1986), p.15.

6 See Alvin Toffler 'Congress in the Year 2000', *GAO Review* (1980), Fall: 38–48.

7 Erwin C. Hargrove *The Power of the Modern Presidency* (New York: Knopf, 1974), p.232.

8 See Sudhir Chella Rajan *The Enigma of Automobility* (Pittsburgh: University of Pittsburgh Press, 1996).

9 See Michael E. Kraft 'Environmental Gridlock: Searching for Consensus in Congress' in Norman J. Vig and Michael E. Kraft (ed.), *Environmental Policy in the 1990s* (Washington, DC: Congressional Quarterly Press, 1990); Mary Etta Cook and Roger H. Davidson 'Deferral Politics: Congressional Decision Making on Environmental Issues in the 1980s' in Helen M. Ingram and R. Kenneth Godwin (eds), *Public Policy and the Natural Environment* (New York: JAI Press, 1985).

10 Theodore Lowi 'Decision Making vs Policy Making: Toward An Antidote for Technocracy', *Public Administration Review* (1970), 30:314–25.

11 Mark Sagoff 'Economic Theory and Environmental Law', *Michigan Law Review* (1980–81), 79:1399.

Bibliography

References to congressional committee hearings cited can be found in the notes at the end of each chapter.

Ackerman, Bruce A. and Hassler, William T. *Clean Coal/Dirty Air* (New Haven, CN: Yale University Press, 1981).

Arnold, R. Douglas *The Logic of Congressional Action* (New Haven, CN: Yale University Press: 1990).

Asbell, Bernard *The Senate Nobody Knows* (New York: Doubleday, 1978).

Bailey, Christopher J. *The Republican Party in the US Senate, 1974–1984* (Manchester: Manchester University Press, 1988).

———— 'Explaining the Choice of Air-Pollution Control Strategies in the United States: Some Evidence of Institutional Bias', *Environmental Politics* (1996), 5:74–92.

———— 'Congress and the Crisis of Legitimacy' in Philip John Davies and Frederic A. Waldstein (eds), *Political Issues in America Today* (Manchester: Manchester University Press, 1996).

Baumgartner, Frank R. and Jones, Bryan D. *Agendas and Instability in American Politics* (Chicago: University of Chicago Press, 1993).

Baumol, William J. and Oates, Wallace E. *Economics, Environmental Policy, and the Quality of Life* (Englewood Cliffs, NJ: Prentice-Hall, 1979).

Becker, Gary 'Competition Among Interest Groups for Political Influence' *Quarterly Journal of Economics* (1983), 98:371–98.

Bimber, Bruce 'Information as a Factor in Congressional Politics', *Legislative Studies Quarterly* (1991), 16:585–606.

Bosso, Christopher J. *Pesticides and Politics* (Pittsburgh, PA: University of Pittsburgh Press, 1987).

———— 'Environmental Values and Democratic Institutions' in John Martin Gilroy (ed), *Environmental Risk, Environmental Values, and Political Choice* (Boulder, CO: Westview Press, 1993).

Bregman, Jack and Lenormond, Sergei *The Pollution Paradox* (New York: Spartan Books, 1966).

Brimblecombe, Peter *The Big Smoke* (London: Methuen, 1987).

Bryner, Gary C. *Blue Skies, Green Politics* (Washington, DC: Congressional Quarterly Press, 1993).

—— 'Reforming the Regulatory Process: Congress and the Next Generation of Environmental Laws'. Paper presented at the annual meeting of the Western Political Science Association, 1996.

Bush, George *Public Papers*.

Carson, Rachel *Silent Spring* (Boston: Houghton Mifflin, 1962).

Carter, Jimmy *Public Papers*.

Casson, Mark *The Entrepreneur: An Economic Theory* (Oxford: Robertson, 1982).

Clinton, William J. *Public Papers*.

Cohen, Richard E. *Washington At Work: Back Rooms and Clean Air* (New York: Macmillan, 1992).

Cole, Leonard A. *Element of Risk: The Politics of Radon* (New York: Oxford University Press, 1993).

Commoner, Barry *The Closing Circle* (New York: Bantam, 1972).

Connelly, William F. and Pitney, John J. *Congress's Permanent Minority?* (Lanham, MD: Rowman and Littlefield, 1994).

Cook, Mary Etta and Davidson, Roger H. 'Deferral Politics: Congressional Decision Making on Environmental Issues in the 1980s' in Helen M. Ingram and R. Kenneth Godwin (eds), *Public Policy and the Natural Environment* (New York: JAI Press, 1985).

Council on Environmental Quality *Environmental Quality 1990* (Washington, DC: CEQ, 1990).

Crandall, Robert *Controlling Industrial Air Pollution* (Washington, DC, Brookings, 1983).

Crenson, Matthew *The Un-politics of Air Pollution: A Study of Non-decisionmaking in the Cities* (Baltimore: Johns Hopkins University Press, 1971).

Crutzen, P. J. 'SSTs – A Threat to the Earth's Ozone Shield', *Ambio* (1972), 1:41–51.

Currie, David 'Motor Vehicle Air Pollution: State Authority and Federal Pre-emption', *Michigan Law Review* (1970), 68:1083–1102.

—— 'Relaxation of Implementation Plans Under the 1977 Clean Air Act', *Michigan Law Review* (1979–80), 79:155–203.

—— 'Direct Federal Regulation of Stationary Sources under the Clean Air Act', *University of Pennsylvania Law Review* (1980), 128:1442–1773.

Davidson, Roger H. and Olescek, Walter J. 'Adaptation and Consolidation: Structural Innovation in the US House of Representatives', *Legislative Studies Quarterly* (1976), 1:37–66.

—— *Congress and its Members* 2nd edition (Washington, DC: Congressional Quarterly Press, 1985).

Davies, J. Clarence *The Politics of Pollution* (Indianapolis: Pegasus, 1970).

Denzau, Arthur T. and Munger, Michael C. 'Legislators and Interest Groups: How Unorganized Groups Get Represented', *American Political Science Review* (1986), 80:89–106.

Dion, Douglas 'The Robustness of Structure-Induced Equilibrium', *American Journal of Political Science* (1992), 36:462–82.

Dodd, Lawrence C. 'Congress and the Quest for Power' in Lawrence C. Dodd and Bruce I. Oppenheimer (eds), *Congress Reconsidered* (New York: Praeger, 1977).

—— Review of *The Logic of Congressional Action, American Political Science Review* (1992), 86:1052–3.

Dowding, Keith 'Model or Metaphor? A Critical Review of the Policy Network Approach', *Political Studies* (1995), 43:136–58.

Dowie, Mark *Losing Ground* (Cambridge, MA: MIT Press, 1995).

Downs, Anthony 'Up and Down with Ecology: The "Issue-Attention Cycle"', *Public Interest* (1972), 28:38–50.

Dryzek, John S. *Discursive Democracy* (Cambridge: Cambridge University Press, 1990).

Dunlap, Riley E. 'Public Opinion on the Environment in the Reagan Era', *Environment* (1987), 29:6–11, 32–7.

—— 'Public Opinion and Environmental Policy' in James P. Lester (ed), *Environmental Politics and Policy* (Durham, NC: Duke University Press, 1995).

Eckstein, H. 'Case Study and Theory in Political Science' in Fred I. Greenstein and Nelson W. Polsby (eds), *Handbook of Political Science* vol. 7 (Reading, MA: Addison-Wesley, 1975).

Ehrenhalt, Alan, *The United States of Ambition* (New York: Times Books, 1991).

Eisenhower, Dwight D. *Public Papers*.

Elliot, Donald E., Ackerman, Bruce A. and Millian, John C. 'Toward a Theory of Statutory Evolution: The Federalization of Environmental Law', *Journal of Law, Economics, and Organization* (1985), 1:313–40.

Elmore, Richard F. 'Instruments and Strategy in Public Policy', *Policy Studies Review* (1987), 7:174–86.

Elsom, Derek M. *Atmospheric Pollution: A Global Problem* 2nd edition (Oxford: Blackwell, 1992).

Erskine, Hazel 'The Polls, Pollution and Its Costs', *Public Opinion Quarterly* (1972), 28:38–50.

Esposito, John C. *Vanishing Air* (New York: Grossman, 1970).

Evans, C. Lawrence *Leadership in Committees* (Ann Arbor, MI: University of Michigan Press, 1991).

Fenno, Richard F. *Congressmen in Committees* (Boston: Little, Brown, 1973).
—— *Home Style* (Boston: Little, Brown, 1978).
—— 'Observation, Context, and Sequence in the Study of Politics', *American Political Science Review* (1986), 80:3–16.
Fiorina, Morris P. *Representatives, Roll Calls, and Constituencies* (Boston: Heath, 1974).
—— 'Legislative Choice of Regulatory Form', *Public Choice* (1982), 39:33–66.
Fiorino, Daniel J. *Making Environmental Policy* (Berkeley, CA: University of California Press, 1995).
Francis, John *The Politics of Regulation* (Oxford: Blackwell, 1993).
Freeman, A. Myrick *Air and Water Pollution Control: A Benefit-Cost Assessment* (New York: Wiley, 1982).
Grinder, R. Dale 'The Battle for Clean Air: The Smoke Problem in Post-Civil War America' in Martin V. Melosi (ed), *Pollution and Reform in American Cities, 1870–1930* (Austin, TX: University of Texas Press, 1980).
Hahn, Robert W. and Stavins, Robert N. 'Incentive-Based Environmental Regulation: A New Era from an Old Idea', *Ecology Law Quarterly* (1991), 18:1–42.
Hall, Richard L. 'Participation and Purpose in Committee Decision-Making', *American Political Science Review* (1987), 81:105–28.
—— *Participation in Congress* (New Haven, CN: Yale University Press, 1996).
Hargrove, Erwin C. *The Power of the Modern Presidency* (New York: Knopf, 1974).
Hays, Samuel P. *Beauty, Health and Permanence: Environmental Politics in the United States, 1955–1985* (Cambridge: Cambridge University Press, 1987).
—— 'Three Decades of Environmental Politics: The Historical Context' in Michael J. Lacey (ed), *Government and Environmental Politics* (Washington, DC: Woodrow Wilson Center Press, 1989).
Heclo, Hugh 'Issue Networks and the Executive Establishment' in Anthony King (ed), *The New American Political System* (Washington, DC: American Enterprise Institute, 1978).
Heidenheimer, Arnold J., Heclo, Hugh and Teich Adams, Carolyn *Comparative Public Policy* 3rd edition (New York: St Martin's Press, 1990).
Heinz, John P., Laumann, Edward O., Nelson, Robert L. and Salisbury, Robert H. *The Hollow Core* (Cambridge, MA: Harvard University Press, 1993).
Henderson, James A. and Pearson, Richard N. 'Implementing Federal Environmental Policies: The Limits of Aspirational Commands', *Columbia Law Review* (1978), 78:1429–70.

Hibbing, John R. *Congressional Careers* (Chapel Hill, NC: University of North Carolina Press, 1991).

—— and Theiss-Morse, Elizabeth *Congress as Public Enemy* (Cambridge: Cambridge University Press, 1995).

Hood, Christopher *The Tools of Government* (London: Macmillan, 1984).

Horn, Murray J. *The Political Economy of Public Administration* (Cambridge: Cambridge University Press, 1995).

Ingham, Alan 'The Market for Sulphur Dioxide Permits in the USA and UK', *Environmental Politics* (1993), 2:98–122.

Inglehart, Ronald *Culture Shift in Advanced Industrial Society* (Princeton, NJ: Princeton University Press, 1990).

Ingraham, Patricia W. 'Toward More Systematic Consideration of Policy Design', *Policy Studies Journal* (1987), 15:611–28.

Ingram, Helen M. 'The Political Rationality of Innovation: The Clean Air Act Amendments of 1970' in Ann F. Friedlander (ed), *Approaches to Controlling Air Pollution* (Cambridge, MA: MIT Press, 1978).

Ingram, Helen M., Colnic, David H. and Mann, Dean E. 'Interest Groups and Environmental Policy' in James P. Lester (ed), *Environmental Politics and Policy* 2nd edition (Durham, NC: Duke University Press, 1995).

Johnson, Lyndon B. *Public Papers*.

Jones, Bryan D., Baumgartner, Frank R. and Talber, Jeffrey C. 'The Destruction of Issue Monopolies in Congress', *American Political Science Review* (1993), 87:657–72.

Jones, Charles O. 'Air Pollution and Contemporary Environmental Politics', *Growth and Change* (1973), 4:22–7.

—— 'Speculative-Augmentation in Federal Air Pollution Policy Making', *Journal of Politics* (1974), 36:438–64.

—— *Clean Air* (Pittsburgh: University of Pittsburgh Press, 1975).

—— 'A Way of Life and Law', *American Political Science Review* (1995), 89:1–9.

—— and Strahan, Randall 'The Effects of Energy Politics on Congressional and Executive Organization in the 1970s', *Legislative Studies Quarterly* (1985), 10:151–80.

Kelman, Steven J. *What Price Incentives? Economists and the Environment* (Boston: Auburn House, 1981).

Kempton, Willett, Boster, James S. and Hartley, Jennifer A. *Environmental Values in American Culture* (Cambridge: MA: MIT Press, 1995).

Kennedy, John F. *Public Papers*.

Kenski, Henry and Ingram, Helen 'The Reagan Administration and Environmental Regulation: The Constraint of the Political Market' in Sheldon Kamieniecki, Robert O'Brien and Michael Clarke (eds), *Controversies in Environmental Policy* (Albany, NY: State University of New York Press, 1986).

King, David C. 'The Nature of Congressional Committee Jurisdictions', *American Political Science Review* (1994), 88:48–62.

Kingdon, John W. *Agendas, Alternatives, and Public Policies* (Boston: Little, Brown, 1984).

—— *Congressmen's Voting Decisions* 3rd edition (Ann Arbor, MI: University of Michigan Press, 1989).

Kirzner, Israel M. *Discovery and the Capitalist Process* (Chicago: University of Chicago Press, 1985).

Kneese, Allen V. and Schultze, Charles L. *Pollution, Prices, and Public Policy* (Washington, DC: Brookings, 1975).

Koford, Kenneth 'Different Preferences, Different Politics: A Demand and Structure Explanation', *Western Political Quarterly* (1989), 42:9–32.

Kraft, Michael E. 'Congress and Environmental Policy' in James P. Lester (ed), *Environmental Politics and Policy* (Durham, NC: Duke University Press, 1989).

—— 'Environmental Gridlock: Searching for Consensus in Congress' in Norman J. Vig and Michael E. Kraft (eds), *Environmental Policy in the 1990s* (Washington, DC: Congressional Quarterly Press, 1990).

Krehbiel, Keith *Information and Legislative Organization* (Ann Arbor, MI: University of Michigan Press, 1991).

Krier, James E. 'The Irrational National Air Quality Standards: Macro and Micro Mistakes', *UCLA Law Review* (1974), 22:323.

—— and Ursin, Edmund *Pollution and Policy* (Berkeley, CA: University of California Press, 1977).

Kuchel, Thomas H. 'Public Interest Demands Clean Air' in US Department of Health, Education, and Welfare, Public Health Service, *National Conference on Air Pollution: Proceedings* (Washington, DC: GPO, 1958.

Lacey, Michael J. 'The Environmental Revolution and the Growth of the State: Overview and Introduction' in Michael J. Lacey (ed), *Government and Environmental Politics* (Washington, DC: Woodrow Wilson Center Press, 1989).

Ladd, Carl Everett 'Clearing the Air: Public Opinion and Public Policy on the Environment', *Public Opinion* (1982), 5:16–20.

Landy, Marc K., Roberts, Marc J. and Thomas, Stephen S. *The Environmental Protection Agency* expanded edition (New York: Oxford University Press, 1994).

Latham, Earl 'The Group Basis of Politics: Notes for a Theory', *American Political Science Review* (1952), 46:376–97.

Lave, Lester B. *The Strategy of Social Regulation* (Washington, DC: Brookings, 1981).

Laver, Michael 'Political Solutions to the Collective Action Problem', *Political Studies* (1980), 28:195–209.

Linder, Stephen H. and Peters, B. Guy 'The Logic of Public Policy Design: Linking Policy Actors and Plausible Instruments', *Knowledge and Power* (1991), 4:125–51.

Lippman, Theo and Hansen, Donald C. *Muskie* (New York: Norton, 1971).

Liroff, Richard A. *Reforming Air Pollution Regulations: The Toil and Trouble of EPA's Bubble* (Washington, DC: Conservation Foundation, 1986).

Loomis, Burdette *The New American Politician* (New York: Basic Books, 1988).

Lowi, Theodore 'Decision Making vs Policy Making: Toward an Antidote for Technocracy', *Public Administration Review* (1970), 30:314–25.

——— 'Four Systems of Policy, Politics, and Choice', *Public Administration Review* (1972), 32:299–310.

Lowry, William R. *The Dimensions of Federalism: State Governments and Pollution Control Policies* (Durham, NC: Duke University Press, 1992).

Lundqvist, Lennart J. *The Hare and the Tortoise: Clean Air Policies in the United States and Sweden* (Ann Arbor, MI: University of Michigan Press, 1980).

MacAvoy, Paul *The Regulated Industries and the Economy* (New York: Norton, 1979).

McCubbins, Matthew D. and Page, T. 'A Theory of Congressional Delegation' in Matthew D. McCubbins and Thomas Sullivan (eds), *Congress: Structure and Policy* (Cambridge: Cambridge University Press, 1987).

Malbin, Michael J. 'Delegation, Deliberation, and the New Role of Congressional Staff' in Thomas E. Mann and Norman J. Ornstein (eds), *The New Congress* (Washington, DC: American Enterprise Institute, 1981).

Marcus, Alfred A. *Controversial Issues in Energy Policy* (Newbury Park, CA: Sage, 1992).

Mayhew, David R. *Congress: The Electoral Connection* (New Haven, CN: Yale University Press, 1974).

Melnick, R. Shep *Regulation and the Courts: The Case of the Clean Air Act* (Washington, DC: Brookings, 1983).

Melosi, Martin V. 'Lyndon Johnson and Environmental Policy' in Robert A. Divine (ed), *The Johnson Years, Volume Two* (Lawrence, KS: University Press of Kansas, 1987).

Milward, Brinton H. and Walmsley, Gary 'Policy Subsystems, Networks, and the Tools of Public Management' in Robert Eyestone (ed), *Public Policy Formation and Implementation* (New York: JAI Press, 1984).

Mitchell, Robert Cameron 'Public Opinion and the Green Lobby: Poised for the 1990s?' in Norman J. Vig and Michael E. Kraft (eds), *Environmental Policy in the 1990s* (Washington, DC: Congressional Quarterly Press, 1990).

——— 'From Conservation to Environmental Movement: The Development of Modern Environmental Lobbies' in Michael J. Lacey (ed), *Government and Environmental Politics* (Washington, DC: Woodrow Wilson Center Press, 1991).

Muskie, Edmund S. 'The Clean Air Act: A Commitment to Public Health', *Environmental Forum* (1990), 12:2–16.

National Commission on Air Quality *To Breathe Clean Air* (Washington, DC: Government Printing Office, 1981).

de Nevers, Noel 'Air Pollution Control Philosophies', *Journal of Air Pollution Control Association* (1977), 27:190–204.

Nixon, Richard M. *Public Papers.*

Norvelle, G. Todd and Alexander W. Bell 'Air Pollution Control in Texas' *Environmental Law Review* (1970), 1:239–81.

O'Fallon, James E. 'Deficiencies in the Air Quality Act of 1967' *Law and Contemporary Problems* (1968), 33:275–96.

Organization of Economic Co-operation and Development *Environmental Policy and Technological Change* (Paris: OECD, 1985).

—— *Economic Instruments for Environmental Protection* (Paris: OECD, 1989).

—— *Environmental Policy Benefits: Monetary Valuation* (Paris: OECD, 1989).

Paehlke, Robert C. *Environmentalism and the Future of Progressive Politics* (New Haven, CN: Yale University Press, 1989).

Parker, Glenn R. *Institutional Change, Discretion, and the Making of the Modern Congress* (Ann Arbor, MI: University of Michigan Press, 1992).

Pechman, Joseph A. *Federal Tax Policy* (Washington, DC: Brookings, 1966).

Peltzman, Sam 'Toward a More General Theory of Regulation' *Journal of Law and Economics* (1976), 19:211–40.

Peters, B. Guy and Brian Hogwood 'In Search of the Issue-Attention Cycle', *Journal of Politics* (1985), 47:239–53.

Peterson, Mark A. 'How Health Policy Information is Used in Congress' in Thomas E. Mann and Norman J. Ornstein (eds), *Intensive Care* (Washington, DC: Congressional Quarterly Press, 1995).

Pollack, Lawrence W. 'Legal Boundaries of Air Pollution Control – State and Local Legislative Purpose and Techniques', *Law and Contemporary Problems* (1968), 33:331–57.

Polsby, Nelson W. *Political Innovation in America* (New Haven, CN: Yale University Press, 1984).

Portney, Kent E. *Controversial Issues in Environmental Policy* (Newbury Park, CA: Sage, 1992).

Portney, Paul R. 'Air Pollution Policy' in Paul R. Portney (ed), *Public Policies for Environmental Protection* (Washington, DC: Resources for the Future, 1990).

—— 'EPA and the Evolution of Federal Regulation' in Paul R. Portney (ed), *Public Policies for Environmental Protection* (Washington, DC: Resources for the Future, 1990).

────── 'Economics and the Clean Air Act', *Journal of Economic Perspectives* (1990), 4:173–81.

Posner, Richard A. 'Theories of Economic Regulation' *Bell Journal of Economics* (1974), 5:335–58.

────── 'Economics, Politics, and the Reading of Statutes and the Constitution', *University of Chicago Law Review* (1982), 59:335–58.

────── *Economic Analysis of Law* 3rd edition (Boston: Little, Brown, 1986).

Price, David E. 'Professionals and "Entrepreneurs": Staff Orientations and Policymaking on Three Senate Committees' *Journal of Politics* (1971), 33:316–36.

Rajan, Sudhir Chella *The Enigma of Automotibility* (Pittsburgh: University of Pittsburgh Press, 1996).

Reagan, Ronald *Public Papers*.

Riker, William H. *The Art of Political Manipulation* (New Haven, CN: Yale University Press, 1986).

Ringquist, Evan J. *Environmental Protection at the State Level* (Armonk, NY: Sharpe, 1993).

────── 'Evaluating Environmental Policy Outcomes' in James P. Lester (ed), *Environmental Politics and Policy* (Durham, NC: Duke University Press, 1995).

Ripley, Randall B. 'Congress and Clean Air: The Issue of Enforcement, 1963' in Frederic N. Cleaveland and associates (eds), *Congress and Urban Problems* (Washington, DC: Brookings, 1969).

Roberts, Marc J. and Farrell, Susan O. 'The Political Economy of Implementation: The Clean Air Act and Stationary Sources' in Ann F. Friedlaender (ed), *Approaches to Controlling Air Pollution* (Cambridge, MA: MIT Press, 1978).

Robinson, William H. and Wellborn, Clay H.(eds), *Knowledge, Power and the Congress* (Washington, DC: Congressional Quarterly Press, 1991).

Rochefort, David A. and Cobb, Roger W. 'Problem Definition, Agenda Access, and Policy Choice', *Policy Studies Journal* (1993), 21:56–71.

Rogers, Peter *America's Water* (Cambridge, MA: MIT Press, 1993).

Rose-Ackerman, Susan 'Does Federalism Matter? Political Choice in a Federal Republic', *Journal of Political Economy* (1981), 89:152–65.

────── *Controlling Environmental Policy* (New Haven, CN: Yale University Press, 1995).

Rowland, C. K. and Marz, Roger 'Gresham's Law: The Regulatory Analogy', *Policy Studies Review* (1982), 1:572–80.

Rowland, Frank S. and Molina, Mario J. 'Stratospheric Sink for Chlorofluromethanes: Chlorine Atomic-atalysed Destruction of Ozone', *Nature*, 28 June 1974, pp.810–12.

Sabatier, Paul 'An Advocacy Coalition Framework of Policy Change and the Role of Policy-Oriented Learning Therein', *Policy Science* (1988), 21:141–2.

—— 'Political Science and Public Policy', *PS: Political Science and Politics* (1991), 24:144–56.

Sabatier, Paul and Whiteman, David 'Legislative Decisionmaking and Substantive Policy Formation: Models of Information Flow', *Legislative Studies Quarterly* (1985), 10:395–421.

Sagoff, Mark 'Economic Theory and Environmental Law' *Michigan Law Review* (1980–81), 79:1393–1419.

Salisbury, Robert and Shepsle, Kenneth 'US Congressman as Enterprise', *Legislative Studies Quarterly* (1981), 6:559–76.

Schattschneider, E. E. *The Semi-Sovereign People* (Hinsdale, IL: Dryden Press, 1960).

Schneider, Anne and Ingram, Helen 'Behavioral Assumptions of Policy Tools', *Journal of Politics* (1990), 52:510–29.

Schneider, Mark and Teske, Teske 'Toward A Theory of the Political Entrepreneur: Evidence from Local Government', *American Political Science Review* (1992), 86:737–47.

Schrenk, H. H., Heinman, H., Clayton, G. D. Gafafer, W. M. and Wexler, H. 'Air Pollution in Donora, Pa. Epidemiology of the Unusual Smog Episode of October 1948', *Public Health Bulletin* (Washington, DC: Public Health Service, 1949).

Schuck, Peter H. 'The Politics of Regulation', *Yale Law Review* (1981), 90:702–25.

Shanley, Robert A. *Presidential Influence and Environmental Policy* (Westport, CN: Greenwood Press, 1992).

Shepsle, Kenneth A. *The Giant Jigsaw Puzzle: Democratic Committee Assignments in the Modern House* (Chicago: University of Chicago Press, 1978).

Sinclair, Barbara *Unorthodox Lawmaking* (Washington, DC: Congressional Quarterly Press, 1997).

Sinclair, Upton *The Jungle* (New York: Signet, 1990, first published 1906).

Skocpol, Theda *Protecting Mothers and Soldiers* (Cambridge, MA: Harvard University Press, 1992).

Smith, Hendrick *The Power Game* (London: Fontana, 1988).

Smith, Zachary A. *The Environmental Policy Paradox* (Englewood Cliffs, NJ: Prentice-Hall, 1992).

Stavins, Robert N. (ed), *Project 88: Harnessing Market Forces to Protect Our Environment – Initiatives for the New President*. A Public Policy Study sponsored by Senator Timothy E. Wirth and Senator John Heinz (Washington, DC: December 1988).

Stein, Robert M. and Bickers, Kenneth N. *Perpetuating the Pork Barrel:*

Policy Subsystems and American Democracy (Cambridge: Cambridge University Press, 1995).

Stern, Arthur C. 'Prevention of Significant Deterioration – A Critical Review', *Journal of Air Pollution Control Association* (1977), 27:440.

—— 'History of Air Pollution Legislation in the United States', *Journal of Air Pollution Control Association* (1982), 32:44–61.

Stern, Philip M. *The Best Congress Money Can Buy* (New York: Pantheon, 1988).

Stigler, George J. 'The Theory of Economic Regulation', *Bell Journal of Economics and Management Science* (1971), 2:3–21.

Stockman, David *The Triumph of Politics* (London: Coronet, 1986).

Stoker, Gerry 'Introduction' in David Marsh and Gerry Stoker (eds), *Theory and Methods in Political Science* (Basingstoke: Macmillans, 1995).

Stone, Deborah 'Causal Stories and the Formation of Policy Agendas', *Political Science Quarterly* (1989), 104:281–300.

Sundquist, James L. *Politics and Policy* (Washington, DC: Brookings, 1968).

Tarr, Joel and Bill Lamperes 'Changing Fuel Use Behavior and Energy Transitions: The Pittsburgh Smoke Control Movement, 1940–1950', *Journal of Social History* (1981), 14:561–88.

Tobin, Richard J. 'Revising the Clean Air Act: Legislative Failure and Administrative Success' in Norman J. Vig and Michael E. Kraft (eds), *Environmental Policy in the 1980s* (Washington, DC: Congressional Quarterly Press, 1984).

Toffler, Alvin 'Congress in the Year 2000', *GAO Review* (1980), Fall, pp.38–48.

Truman, David *The Governmental Process* (New York: Knopf, 1951).

US Department of Health, Education, and Welfare, Public Health Service, *Automotive Air Pollution* (Washington, DC: GPO, January 1965).

—— *Proceedings, The Third National Conference on Air Pollution* (12–14 December 1966).

US Environmental Protection Agency, *National Accomplishments in Pollution Control: 1970–1980* (Washington, DC: EPA, 1980).

—— *Environmental Progress and Challenges: EPA's Update* (Washington, DC: EPA, 1988).

—— *National Air Pollutant Emissions Estimates 1940–1987)* (Washington, DC, EPA, 1989).

—— *Environmental Investments: The Cost of a Clean Environment* (Washington, DC: EPA, 1990).

—— *National Air Pollutant Emissions Estimates 1940–1990)* (Washington, DC, EPA, 1991).

Uslaner, Eric 'Policy Entrepeneurs and Amateur Democrats in the House of

Representatives: Toward a More Party-Oriented Congress?' in Leroy N. Rieselbach (ed), *Legislative Reform* (Lexington, MA: Lexington Books, 1978).

Van Dyke, Brennan, 'Emissions Trading to Reduce Acid Deposition', *Yale Law Review* (1991), 100:2707–26.

Vig, Norman J. 'Presidential Leadership: From the Reagan to the Bush Administration' in Norman J. Vig and Michael E. Kraft (eds), *Environmental Policy in the 1990s* (Washington, DC: Congressional Quarterly Press, 1990).

Vogel, David *National Styles of Regulation* (Ithaca, NY: Cornell University Press, 1987).

Walker, Jack L. 'Setting the Agenda in the US Senate' *British Journal of Political Science* (1977), 7:423–45.

Weber, E. *Air Pollution: Assessment Methodology and Modelling* vol. 2 (New York: Plenum, 1982).

Weissert, Carol S. 'Policy Entrepeneurs, Policy Opportunists, and Legislative Effectiveness', *American Politics Quarterly* (1991), 19:262–74.

Welborn, David M. 'Conjoint Federalism and Environmental Regulation in the United States', *Publius* (1988), 18:27–43.

Wenner, Lotte M. *One Environment Under Law* (Pacific Palisades, CA: Goodyear, 1976).

Wilson, James Q. 'The Politics of Regulation' in James W. McKie (ed), *Social Responsibility and the Business Predicament* (Washington, DC: Brookings, 1974).

Wilson, Woodrow *Congressional Government* (Baltimore: Johns Hopkins University Press, 1981, original edition published in 1885).

Yeager, Peter C. *The Limits of the Law* (Cambridge: Cambridge University Press, 1991).

Zimmerman, Joseph F. *Contemporary American Federalism* (Leicester: Leicester University Press, 1992).

Zwier, Robert 'The Search for Information: Specialists and Non-Specialists in the US House of Representatives', *Legislative Studies Quarterly* (1979), 4:31–42.

Index